Managing Global Alliances

Key Steps for Successful Collaboration

The EIU Series

This innovative series of books is the result of a publishing collaboration between Addison-Wesley and the Economist Intelligence Unit. Our authors draw on the results of original research by the EIU's skilled research and editorial staff to provide a range of topical, information-rich and incisive business titles. They are specifically tailored to the needs of international executives and business education worldwide.

Titles in the Series

Managing Global Alliances

Key Steps for Successful Collaboration

M. Cauley de la Sierra

E·I·U

The Economist
Intelligence Unit

ADDISON-WESLEY PUBLISHING COMPANY

Wokingham, England • Reading, Massachusetts • Menlo Park, California • New York
Don Mills, Ontario • Amsterdam • Bonn • Sydney • Singapore
Tokyo • Madrid • San Juan • Milan • Paris • Mexico City • Seoul • Taipei

© 1995 Addison-Wesley Publishers Ltd, Addison-Wesley Publishing Co. Inc. and the
Economist Intelligence Unit

This book uses material drawn from the Report, *Managing a Successful Global Alliance*,
first published by Economist Intelligence Unit.

Cover designed by Viva Design Ltd, Henley-on-Thames
incorporating photograph by Kerry Lawrence
and printed by The Riverside Printing Co. (Reading) Ltd.
Text designed by Valerie O'Donnell.
Typeset by Meridian Phototypesetting Limited, Pangbourne.
Printed in Great Britain at the University Press, Cambridge.

First printed 1994.

ISBN 0-201-42771-0

British Library Cataloguing in Publication Data
A catalogue record for this book is available from the British Library.

Library of Congress Cataloging in Publication Data applied for.

Preface

Few companies believe that they alone can develop, manufacture and market the products their global businesses require. Increasingly, firms seek partnerships to stay ahead of the competition – even survive – in today's global economy. In fact, a company cannot rely only on its internal strengths; it must reach out to partners for the complementary resources it lacks. For better or worse, global markets may soon be dominated by extended corporate families with multiple links and partners. Given the rush to alliances, it is wholly possible that companies must get into the venture game soon or they will be frozen out. Yet for most companies, managing competitive alliances is a relatively new art and developing alliance management skills represents one of the biggest challenges to companies.

For instance, how many companies are prepared to embrace head-on the alliance challenge? Why have alliances become so popular? Why do so many ventures fail? How do companies make alliances work? How do partners share power? How do companies manage conflict? How much conflict is healthy? How do firms learn from their partners? How are new ideas and technology transferred to parent operations?

Managing Global Alliances is an effort to address these and many other issues. Research into the alliance phenomenon for this book began in 1984 with a series of articles for a Business International (Economist Intelligence Unit) weekly newsletter. These articles later provided the foundation for a 1987 report, *Competitive Alliances: How To Succeed at Cross-Regional Collaboration*.

This book refers to the still-valid 1987 guidelines but breaks new ground in discussing the management complexities of making an alliance work. It provides an analytical framework on how to structure and manage ventures. It serves as a tool to assist companies in assessing the risks and strategic importance of alliances. The material is divided into two main sections.

Part One – Getting organized for alliances – identifies seven basic steps companies can use to construct a workable alliance:

- Justify an alliance strategy against other alternatives,
- Seek and select potential partners,
- Analyse the range of alliance structures,
- Set up the logistics of cooperation,
- Craft a negotiating strategy,
- Structure the agreement, and
- Address specific structuring considerations for joint ventures.

Part Two – Making cooperation work: the critical tools for management – explores how companies manage alliances, what makes them work and how to solve problems. Based on interviews with over 50 companies, the material gives firsthand accounts of how companies juggle the daily challenges of managing a partnership in a bilingual or multilingual, cross-cultural environment. Companies frequently make the mistake of thinking the contract is an end in itself. When alliances fail, they tend to blame it on faulty structure, not on poor management. Yet this book offers new insights into how different companies are honing their alliance management skills.

Part Two begins by suggesting three guiding principles that can assist alliance practitioners in laying the foundation for a solid partnership. Subsequent chapters deal with some of the daily headaches and challenges of alliance life. For instance, how do alliances cope with conflict and change? Corporate case studies illustrate how maintaining a steady, smooth relationship is not necessarily the primary goal in an alliance. Instead, companies can profit from competitive tensions.

The management section also offers a number of practical techniques on how to design a solid management and human resource base, foster close communication links and manage the risks of competitive cooperation. How different partners cope with the challenges of collaborating in different operating functions – R&D, product development, production and marketing – are analysed. A key chapter highlights how learning from alliance partners is one of the greatest challenges and benefits of partnering. Corporate case studies illustrate how companies overcome internal obstacles in order to assimilate new skills and knowledge from alliances. Finally, since as many valuable lessons can be learned from analysing why some partnerships fail as can be gleaned from studying the alliance success stories, the final chapter in the management section analyses why many alliances dissolve.

The conclusion to the book outlines the long-term challenges facing alliance strategists. The material emphasizes how partnerships are hardly a corporate fad for the 1990s but a reality of doing business in today's global markets.

The cases presented throughout this book offer many different, and often opposing, views on how to structure and manage alliances. This illustrates that there is no single recipe for success. Instead, management needs to be open to a variety of ideas and practices when managing a partnership.

In using this book, executives should bear in mind that companies view and speak of intercorporate partnerships in two distinct ways. In one regard, companies really do think of them as *alliances*, with all the macroeconomic, strategic and tactical implications of the word. At the same time, executives continually characterize these arrangements as *marriages*, which implies intimacy, an ongoing relationship and a give-and-take attitude. Both approaches are accurate, and executives must apply strategic and tactical skills as well as relationship skills if their competitive alliances are to succeed.

Margaret Cauley de la Sierra
Mexico City, October 1994

Contents

PART ONE

Getting organized for alliances

Alliances can entail a potential minefield of trouble, yet many problems can be eliminated with careful planning up front. According to Howard Hill, a Detroit-based lawyer, 'It is easier to walk away from the negotiating table than from an already established business venture. In the latter case, everybody loses except the lawyers called upon to handle the divorce. Alliances are very much like marriages. At the beginning, the partners are enamored with each other. Multinational companies should take advantage of the positive atmosphere to identify and settle as many substantive issues as possible.'

Most executives concur that building an alliance can be much easier if management uses a step-by-step building process. In Part One the experiences and internal guidelines of many companies are used to outline seven critical steps on the path to constructing a viable alliance:

(1) Justify an alliance strategy against other alternatives;
(2) Seek and select potential partners;
(3) Analyse the range of alliance structures;
(4) Prepare for cooperation;
(5) Craft a negotiating strategy;
(6) Structure the agreement;
(7) Address specific structuring considerations for alliance joint ventures.

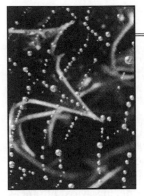

1

Understanding the alliance phenomenon

In growing numbers, multinational corporations are embracing a new strategic option – the global competitive alliance. These proliferating co-operative arrangements among multinationals from different countries and/or regions are transforming the global business environment. In many industries such as automotive, aerospace, chemicals, computers, telecommunications, and robotics, the dynamics of the world economy are forcing companies to cooperate in order to compete.

Because international competition is almost unavoidable (even in the domestic market), companies also need a presence in foreign markets to expand operations and monitor competitors' activities. Few firms have the human, financial and technical resources to 'go-it-alone' in every market and with every product.

For this reason, EniChem SpA (Italy) has argued that the factors dictating success in the future will be less associated with independence and self-reliance than with cooperation. According to EniChem, 'Companies that cling to a "go-it-alone" mentality are in danger of going the way of the dinosaur as we move toward the 21st century.' Olivetti's chairman has said that the traditional loner stance of multinational corporations (MNCs) has already had its day: 'We have entered the age of alliances [because] only through alliances can companies find the resources required in the global marketplace.'

Yet, for starters, what is a useful definition for today's alliances and how are they different from traditional joint ventures? What can management accomplish with global partnerships? This chapter offers insights into what competitive alliances really are and why most MNCs inevitably rely on ventures to accomplish important strategic objectives.

What are alliances?

Commonly called competitive alliances or global strategic partnerships, these arrangements are ventures between strong international companies that generally remain competitors outside the relationship. Because the partners usually are also competitors, the term 'competitive alliances' can better illustrate the challenges and risks of partnering. Most alliances have well-defined – often limited – strategic objectives and are designed to serve global or at least regional markets. Alliances are based on reciprocity; partners pool, exchange or integrate specified business resources for mutual gain. Partnerships cover a broad spectrum or hierarchy of different sorts of cooperative ventures. Whatever the structure, all alliances entail some degree of intercorporate integration among partners – less integration than an outright merger but more than a simple buy/sell relationship. Low on the alliance hierarchy are partnerships such as cross-distribution agreements or licensing pacts. At the other end of the alliance spectrum are partnerships such as joint ventures (JVs) or cross-equity shareholdings. These partnerships involve a substantial meshing or integration of business resources. Unless used as an exit strategy, most alliances are related to the core business of the partners.

Cross-border relationships between large companies are not an entirely new phenomenon – Westinghouse and Mitsubishi have a 70-year-old relationship, as do Philips NV and Matsushita. MNCs have been involved in various kinds of joint ventures, cross-licensing and cross-marketing arrangements for years. What is new is the scope of the competitive alliances, their accelerating numbers and the fact that they have become key elements in MNCs' global strategies.

Global alliances place a fresh set of demands on companies. Management must learn how to share power – and share it with equals coming from other national and corporate cultures, speaking different languages and often with dissimilar underlying corporate objectives. Special care must be taken to structure these alliances and new techniques must be developed to manage them.

How alliances differ from traditional joint ventures

Alliances are distinguished from the traditional MNC-host JV and the strong–weak relationships inherent in such ventures by the fact that they are partnerships among equals. Another novel aspect is that many companies are forming not only single ventures, but entire networks of alliances. These partnerships are also more flexible; their form and duration suit the needs of the project or programme and the relative contributions of the partners. Today's competitive alliances are often quite dynamic – an alliance that begins as a licensing agreement may later blossom into a variety of technology-sharing agreements, joint venture companies and cross-equity shareholdings. Or, as in the IBM–Apple case, the partners simultaneously may start out with several different cooperative vehicles. Although a number of partnerships examined in this book involve equity holdings, several do not.

Moreover, there is no set time-limit for alliances. Their duration is a function of the objectives and structure of the partnership, the prevailing business conditions and the management capabilities of the partners. Some alliances may be short-lived, but others are long term. For instance, the alliance between International Computers Limited (ICL) of the UK and Japan's Fujitsu commenced as a collaborative technology pact in 1981. Over the decade of its existence this alliance has grown to include a majority equity holding by Fujitsu in ICL as well as two mainframe computer projects, product swap arrangements, joint technology development projects and technical exchange programs.

Another long-standing global alliance is Fuji Xerox. This 50–50 joint venture between Fuji Photo Film and the Xerox Corporation of the US is now approaching its 35th anniversary. William Glavin, former vice-chairman of Xerox and current president of Babson College of Massachusetts, remarks that 'The longevity of the Fuji–Xerox venture may be an exception to the rule. However, I do not think that Fuji Xerox is an exception to the rule that MNCs need some alliances to compete in today's global environment. Without a doubt, a company is much better off when it tries to grow a business in another culture with a partner that has the local capabilities, knowledge and talent.'

Why companies seek partnerships to compete in a global economy

An alliance is just one of several strategic options available to companies. Management must weigh the benefits, costs and risks of a partnership against other possibilities, such as acquisitions or the go-it-alone approach. Many multinationals would still prefer going it alone since it enables them to retain management control over all elements of the business system – technology, design, products, manufacturing, marketing, distribution and service. However, the approach is also the most demanding in terms of resources required.

Simply put, most firms enter into alliances out of need. According to Corning, 'There is no big secret why Corning – which receives approximately 37% of its revenues from alliances – often relies on 50–50 ventures. With alliances, we can do more for less. Firms are always limited in their resources. In many Corning activities we may have the technology but lack an important piece of the puzzle, such as market access. Alliances allow Corning to get a running start on tapping new business opportunities or overcoming obstacles.'

Whatever the need or driving force behind forming an alliance, however, it is critically important that management take the time to analyse why an alliance is the best strategy. The president of ITT Automotive has said, 'Understanding why you need a partnership is the most critical step. Sorting out the whys in the equation will in turn dictate the answers to key issues such as with whom you want to collaborate, how the partners will combine their strengths in an alliance and how the venture will be structured and managed.' Based on interviews with over 50 companies, the whys in most alliance equations can be pinned down to ten main strategic targets.

Ten reasons for tapping the alliance advantage

As the following ten reasons suggest, alliances offer the ability to share risks and capabilities, thereby minimizing the time and resources necessary to develop or introduce a new technology or product into the market. Leading in product introductions and innovations in turn enhances a company's global prowess:

(1)   Build global market capabilities

The Ford Motor Company estimates that 60% of the automotive growth over the next 20 years will be in markets where Ford now has little or no presence. Many of these markets are in Asia. Ford's alliance with Mazda Motor Corp. of Japan is a key element in its efforts to tap the opportunities in these emerging Asian markets.

(2)   Cope with escalating technology and R&D costs

High financial stakes and a cutthroat global market have fuelled a spate of competitive alliances in a number of industries. According to Jean Bilien, president of CFM International, which is a 50–50 joint venture between US-based General Electric and Snecma of France, 'The design, development and production of a new aircraft engine require more than ten years of R&D efforts at a cost close to $2 billion. Given such risks, neither GE or Snecma wanted to tackle this market alone.'

(3)   Pre-empt competitive threats

In industries where markets are increasingly dominated by a few large players, some companies resort to an 'If you can't beat them, join them' approach. Clark Equipment and Volvo merged their earth moving equipment businesses in the mid-1980s; alone neither could generate enough volume in their traditional home markets (US and Europe, respectively) to fight for survival against such global industry leaders as Caterpillar and Komatsu.

According to Don Dancer, senior vice-president at GE Fanuc Automation Corp., General Electric (GE)'s factory automation business was facing virtually insurmountable odds in overcoming FANUC in the market for computer numerical control (CNC) products. And both GE and FANUC faced formidable competition in the market for programmable logic controllers (PLCs) from Allen Bradley and other rivals. 'The logical choice', observes Dancer, 'was to pool our resources and tackle the global markets for CNCs and PLCs together.'

(4)   Speed innovation and product introduction

The narrowing of the development-to-market lead time has been a crucial feature of the past decade. In many sectors, the first company to introduce a new product enjoys a dominant market position and stands the best chance of recouping costs before the competition arrives to drive prices down – or before patent protection expires. According to a former Siemens executive, cooperative agreements between Siemens and its partners illustrate the need to be among the first to the marketplace. Take for instance, Siemens' alliance with Toshiba Corp. and IBM to develop the 256-megabit dymanic random access memory (DRAM) chip. There is really no doubt or question as to whether Siemens, Toshiba or IBM could develop the chip on its own, but it would take longer to reach the marketplace. Nor does one company alone want to shoulder the $1 billion-plus burden in costs for developing new generations of chip technology. Adds one former Siemens executive, 'The losers in the chip industry are the companies that arrive late to the market.'

(5)   Cope with the integration of technologies and markets

The integration of various branches of technology, such as developments in the 'information highway', calls for an ever-wider range of expertise. Given the complexities and costs of the various branches of technology, it becomes almost impossible for a company to operate alone.

Customer demands in many markets are also changing. In office automation, customers now prefer a 'systems solution' and want to be able to rely on a single company to service all equipment. According to a director for business development at Xerox Corp., 'Since Xerox was not equipped with the resources or technical staff to develop, market and service a complete system on its own for its globe-spanning markets, we sought collaborative ventures with other companies. With this strategy, we have solidified our customer relationships and transformed our image in the market from a "box company" to a "document processing company".'

(6)   Build world class capabilities

Companies that are leaders in their fields can maintain that position by using alliances to capture new ideas and developments. The Big Three US auto manufacturers – General Motors, Ford and Chrysler – have used their alliances with Toyota, Mazda and Mitsubishi Motors, respectively, to assimilate new skills and boost competitiveness. According to a Ford executive, 'Many Western firms take a narrow view of alliances. Management tends to focus on the operating objective only – for instance, to jointly manufacture X product. Yet what companies often fail to realize is that collaborative projects offer a unique opportunity to observe and learn about a competitor's tactics. Venture employees need to keep their eyes and ears open to learn as much as possible, and whatever new knowledge and skills an employee may acquire, bring the know-how back to parent headquarters and spread it around.'

(7)   Establish global standards

The need to develop a uniform computer-operating system was a major motivation behind the $1 billion-plus IBM–Apple link to produce software, hardware and network systems for a new generation of personal computer (PC) technology. Long considered arch-enemies with incompatible computer systems, these rivals' coalition is expected to transform dramatically the competitive dynamics of the more than $90 billion PC industry. As former Apple president John Sculley remarked in a *Business Week* article, 'It's hard to imagine what high-tech company will even try and get by in the 1990s without an alliance.' A classic case is how Philips and Sony used favourable licensing terms for their jointly held compact disc technology to establish their product as the world standard (both companies having learned a bitter lesson in the failure of their independent VCR standard).

(8)   Jump market barriers in emerging markets and regional trading blocs

Many alliance strategists seek local partners to secure an insider's position in regional trading blocs or key markets, such as the European Union, the North American bloc formed by NAFTA (North American Free Trade Agreement) or Japan. Many MNCs, particularly Japanese industrial giants with little or no direct presence in Europe, have moved aggressively to establish partnerships with their European counterparts. And alliances are rapidly changing the competitive climate in post-NAFTA Mexico. During 1992 and 1993, several highly publicized ventures were formed between US and Mexican retail giants, including: Wal-Mart and Cifra, Fleming and Gigante, Radio Shack and Gigante, Price Club and Commercial Mexicana, and K-Mart and El Puerto de Liverpool.

Monumental changes in Eastern Europe and the Confederation of Independent States (CIS) have also paved the way for potentially enormous new opportunities for MNCs, but cultivating these markets can be a daunting task, even though the difficulties can pay off handsomely. Most firms, such as Tambrands, say that an alliance is often the only practical means to prise open these virgin markets. Tambrands launched joint venture operations in 1989 in the Ukraine to manufacture and distribute disposable Tampax and sanitary napkins. From its inception, developing a market was hardly a problem. Since Tambrands' products were the only such disposable items on the market, the venture could command as much market share as it could produce.

(9)   Cut exit costs

Alliances can be used to cut the costs of leaving a business. Exiting an industry via a joint venture permits management to withdraw with the flags flying. General Motors formed a joint venture with Chrysler to produce manual transmissions at a plant in Indiana. GM had a plant in Indiana that barely reached 30% capacity. Meanwhile, capacity at Chrysler's neighbouring facility was over 150%. When Chrysler approached GM to purchase its underutilized operation, GM suggested first beginning with a joint venture to minimize any negative repercussions in its markets and the local community.

(10)   Tap opportunities from the greening of global businesses

Environmental control and management represent a key industry for the future. To date, environmental regulations differ from country to country. Thus, firms vary in their pollution-control technologies and capabilities. Many MNCs are now seeking to combine their technological abilities and expand together into different regions and markets. A good example is the alliance between Corning Inc., Mitsubishi Heavy Industries and Mitsubishi Petrochemicals.

In 1990, the US added regulations concerning stationary emissions to its 1975 regulations covering mobile emissions. A 1978 clean air act in Japan already covered both stationary and mobile emissions. When the 1990 US law presented an opportunity for Corning to expand its emission-control business, its technology was limited to mobile or auto emissions. Hence, it sought a partnership with Mitsubishi, which holds worldwide patents on technology for such stationary emissions as nitrogen dioxide.

Alliances versus other strategies

Many companies, such as Fujitsu, believe that alliances better suit the goals of globalization than do acquisitions or the go-it-alone route. Michio Naruto, senior vice-president and director of the global marketing group at Fujitsu says, 'When building a global presence, some companies prefer having a parent company with satellite subsidiaries. In my view, subsidiaries are usually treated as one rank below the parent company. There is an inherent superiority/inferiority bias. Alliances do not have this superior/subordinate structure. In fact, it is essential that partners meet each other on a level playing ground, with each party offering a powerful contribution. MNCs need strong partners to win in today's global marketplace, not weak subsidiaries.'

On alliances versus acquisitions, Naruto adds, 'In many high technology sectors, a company's prowess and the engine for growth is its brainpower, its human resources. Hence, the company is its people. In an acquisition, management wants these people. But it is a risky strategy. There is nothing that really binds the people to the company. They may not like you and seek new jobs.'

Siemens has also cited the risk of losing vital brainpower as a reason why acquisitions can be riskier than alliances. According to Siemens' Communications Systems Group, 'An acquisition does not make sense unless you can guarantee control over the assets you are purchasing. For Siemens, in most cases, the value of the acquisition is the people who do the R&D, marketing, etc. We are therefore very careful during and after an acquisition to try to preserve a company's culture while integrating it into the Siemens' family.' Otherwise, the record shows how the talented people and engineers leave.

Case 1.1   Why Xerox is down on acquisitions

In an effort to diversify beyond copiers into the document processing business, Xerox first tried going it alone, then turned to acquisitions and finally became a proponent of alliance building. Efforts to develop new office products in-house failed when the new offerings arrived late and encountered a poor reception in the market. Management then focused on acquisitions. While the acquisitions initially did well, according to Xerox's director for business development, 'Most of the talented people in the firms had no interest in being acquired and eventually left. Their departure created considerable problems for Xerox.' Said the director, 'We painfully learned that in many acquisitions, one is really after the people; once they depart, one is left with an empty shell.'

In the end, added the head of Xerox's business development, 'We decided that alliances are a safer bet. First, it is a lot easier to withdraw from an alliance; if they leave, you leave. If you acquire a company, you are stuck with it. Second, alliances are likely to be more successful than acquisitions because they represent the interests of both parties. In many acquisitions, only the interests of the predator are represented. Third, acquisitions are driven by a need or desire to internalize and own the desired assets of the targeted company. Experience has shown us that one does not need to acquire or internalize a given capability in order to achieve a particular goal.'

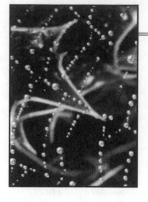

2

Choosing a partner: the three Cs

Once a company has decided to form an alliance, its management will probably want to analyse a host of factors and criteria for selecting a partner. Though some MNCs draw up lengthy lists of criteria against which they can measure a prospective partner, what companies look for can be captured by the three Cs: compatibility, capability and commitment.

In doing research during 1984–86 for the author's previously published 1987 study of competitive alliances, common themes emerged on what companies seek when looking for partners. Based on interviews with executives, it was clear that the three Cs were the crucial criteria when selecting a partner (Business International, 1987). And since first creating the three Cs for the 1987 report, many executives have remarked how useful the concept can be in analysing potential partners. If the three Cs are present, the partners will have a good chance of working successfully together. This chapter explains what the three Cs are, how companies can use the strategy and includes case examples of how some alliances apply the three Cs.

The first C: compatibility

Executives rank compatibility as one of the most important ingredients for a successful alliance. No matter how elegant the strategic business concept behind a cooperative deal or how capable the participants, the partners have to be able to work together. Otherwise, there are slim chances the venture will stand the test of time and be able to cope with changing market and environmental conditions.

Many MNCs talk of alliances in terms of 'marriages'. This does not mean that they view alliances as romantic. On the contrary. It simply means that – as in marriages – compatibility and the ability to resolve problems and differences are key ingredients of a prosperous relationship. Nor does compatibility mean without friction. However, if there is some 'chemistry' and the partners respect each other, they will be able to manage their differences. Virtually all alliance practitioners cite the value and importance of compatibility in corporate partnerships. Perhaps more than those of any culture, Japanese companies emphasize the particular importance of compatibility (see Case 2.1). But how do companies cope with the challenging task of finding a compatible partner?

Case 2.1   How a UK–Japan alliance placed a premium on compatibility

Most executives agree that personal friendships and close ties are of crucial importance in alliances. Good chemistry between the parents' management, but especially among the executives charged with running the alliance, is the cement in a venture's foundation.

For David Dace, recently retired director of collaboration for ICL, his first encounters with Fujitsu crystallized the importance of personal relationships and of getting along with one other. 'We were putting the final touches on several issues in our negotiations with Fujitsu. Robb Wilmot, then ICL chairman, wanted to conclude with the final details. Suddenly, the Fujitsu executive vice-president leading the negotiations stood up and said, 'Now we go to dinner.' Wilmot fought and argued about finishing the contract. But the Fujitsu executive vice-president persisted, finally saying, 'Mr Wilmot, we know we can work with your company from a business perspective. Now we want to see whether we want to.' Everyone likes to think alliances are based on business rationale. At the end of the day, however, partnerships are determined by whether you can work with someone or not.

Michio Naruto, director of global markets, has agreed wholeheartedly. He also recalls the early days of the alliance and how first impressions can shape a relationship. Wilmot had just been appointed to the helm of ICL by former prime minister Margaret Thatcher. Since his ICL appointment was unexpected, his arrival in London from Cambridge

continues

continued

was similarly rushed. Naruto noted, 'Our first meeting was at Wilmot's house outside London. There was no furniture except a sofa. The ICL group surrounded me as I sat on the sofa, offering me plenty of whisky with no ice cubes. I thought to myself, who are these crazy Englishmen? The ICL team was lobbying me to agree to a cooperative arrangement with ICL. Certainly, many business details and issues needed to be analysed. Yet I knew instinctively we could work well with this group.'

Several executives, including Peter Bonfield, made a strong impression on Fujitsu; Bonfield later became chairman of ICL and principal liaison with Naruto on the ICL–Fujitsu relationship. In addition to the personal ties among top management, relationships have developed at all levels of the organization. According to Dace, many of the original Fujitsu engineers and managers assigned to the ICL projects have since returned in more senior executive positions to work again with ICL.

Naruto affirms that 'Disagreements in an alliance can always be solved as long as the arguments are business conflicts. But conflicts in a relationship are different. They can almost never be resolved. You really need to know you can work with a partner. Otherwise, making an alliance is not worth it.' In fact, it is no secret that the Japanese will likely take a long time to determine whether they are compatible with and can work with a particular partner. Many experienced US and European alliance practitioners advise firms to use the time to their advantage. One executive explains, 'No matter how much you kick and scream, you are not going to speed up the process. Why not use the time to determine whether you can also get along and work with your prospective Japanese partner?'

Start with current allies

A good first step when looking for a compatible partner is to examine existing relationships. Forging an alliance with a company with which you have already done business has a number of advantages:

- The history of the relationship provides proof of how well the two companies can work together.
- Personal ties will already be established. It is often easier to strengthen a relationship with a known entity than to start anew.
- Each company has a fair idea of the capabilities, business ethics and culture of the other company.
- The partner will be well versed in operating collaborative ventures.

Many of the cases examined in this book have been built on previous ties between partners. The alliance between Mitsubishi Electric and

Westinghouse Corp. proceeded step by step. Ties between the two companies date back to the 1920s. Previous relationships also were behind the partner selection process when LOF Glass and Nippon Sheet Glass (NSG) each spotted an opportunity in the nascent Korean auto industry. Their 40-year relationship (highlighted by LOF–NSG ventures in the US and in Mexico) was proof that they could work together. Similarly, NSG and Hankuk – which became the venture's local Korean partner – had had technical and capital tie-ins for 15 years.

IBM and Siemens also have built on early ties to broaden and strengthen their alliance. Their cooperation dates to a 1989 agreement to develop 16-megabit chips. This project was followed by joint manufacturing pacts in 1991 to launch volume production of 16-megabit chips. Their success in these efforts also encouraged the partners to seal two alliances for the development of 64-megabit and 256-megabit dynamic random access memory (DRAM) chips. The latter alliance, referred to earlier, also includes Toshiba, a long-term ally of Siemens.

Don't put all your eggs in one basket

On a cautious note, some companies warn of the danger of heavy reliance on extending existing relationships. Since it is frequently less risky and more expedient to build on ties with current partners, companies may shy away from the gruelling process of finding new ones. By restricting one's scope to existing partners, one may not find the optimum partner for a given business venture.

This approach could result in a compromise; a firm may not select a new, unknown company, which has the best skills and technology for the alliance, and instead opts for a familiar firm, which has adequate resources but not the best. Further, some MNCs fear they could lose their individuality by becoming either too dependent on or too synonymous with just one company. Such a tight bond can diminish a firm's chances of attracting other partners.

Testing for compatibility: hard factors

Whether a company is extending an existing relationship or entering its first cooperative venture with a firm, management will still have to ascertain whether it is or could be compatible with a particular firm. Most companies base their compatibility test on an evaluation of both hard and soft factors, the tangible and intangible features. If allies possess compatibilities in operating strategies, decision-making styles, corporate philosophies, organizational structures and policies on safety, health and the environment (SHE), and so on, the incidence of conflict in the alliance can be significantly reduced. When sizing up potential candidates, some important hard factors to analyse include the following:

Comparable in size and capabilities

Companies must seek partners similar in size and capabilities. Otherwise, as one computer executive warned, 'Making an alliance with a company stronger than you in a strategic field is like dancing with a bear'. In fact, multinationals, such as IBM, cite equal capabilities and strengths as key criteria when searching for a partner. According to Dr John Kelly, an IBM executive involved in the IBM–Toshiba–Siemens research pact for the 256-megabit DRAM chip, 'companies must find a partner with comparable capabilities. Otherwise, you can find yourself in a severely imbalanced situation.'

Consultants attribute some of AT&T's alliance difficulties in Europe to substantial differences in the size and strengths between AT&T and its European partners. First, AT&T's venture with Olivetti failed and then Philips Electronics decided to withdraw from its Dutch-based telecommunications equipment venture with AT&T in the late 1980s. Negotiations have also collapsed for a potential alliance with Cable & Wireless and in three-way talks with France Telecom and Deutsche Bundespost Telekom. According to consultants, AT&T's most delicate task is reassuring would-be European partners that they won't be devoured by the $67 billion US company. 'Everyone is worried about being skinned alive by AT&T,' says Keith Mallinson, research director at Yankee Group Europe in Watford, England (Edmondson, 1994).

Yet AT&T has cited several arguments on the contrary. According to Ramesh Barasia, vice-president for marketing at AT&T Network Systems, 'First, size is not the only measure of strength and compatibility. Second, most alliances within AT&T are forged by a particular unit. Hence, one does not ally with all $67 billion of AT&T's assets and its 320,000 employees. Further, the strength and size of AT&T within the US often has little impact or power over winning deals in, say, France where decisions can be highly political. In sum, I consider consultants' arguments in Europe over AT&T's size as akin to the bogeyman theory.'

Existing alliance network

Companies need to consider some of the following questions:

- Is your ally working closely or likely to work closely with any of your stiffest competitors?
- If so, is it in an area in which you are vulnerable?
- Can you live with the situation?
- Does the company have the mechanisms in place to prevent proprietary data shared by the two of you from spilling over to competitors?
- At the very least, do your partner's other alliance connections prevent you from expanding the relationship into desirable areas?
- At worst, will your ally become a permeable membrane through which trade secrets will leak to the competitors?

Alliance track record

No news can be good news; just because a company has not entered alliances before does not mean it cannot succeed. The danger sign is a bad alliance record.

Strategy

The most competent partner in the world will not make a good alliance for you if there are contradictory strategies within the alliance.

- What are the motives and goals of a potential partner for a venture?
- What is a partner's key resource contribution to an alliance?
- What are the strengths and weaknesses of a potential mate's strategy?

Corporate culture

Every company has its own unique corporate culture. Yet companies need to ascertain how manageable are the differences. Management needs to weigh the pros and cons of any differences and how they will impact the alliance.

Management practices and organization

Step by step, a company needs to take a close look for compatibility in organizational and management practices with a potential partner.

- For instance, are both companies centralized or decentralized? If not, are both managements flexible enough and committed enough to overcome potential conflicts?
- Do prospective partners use line or matrix organizations, international departments or global product groups?
- How compatible are customer service policies and philosophies?

Manufacturing

- What are your strategies for sourcing products, components, and so on?
- If you are co-producing, are both partners' facilities up to task?
- Do you have the same attitude toward – and skills in – quality management?
- If the alliance is to be a separate joint venture company, what are your respective compensation programmes, hiring strategies, and so on?
- How do practices for labour relations compare?
- Are the partners union or nonunion? Are relations smooth or strike-prone?
- How does management view its employees?

Marketing and distribution

- What do analyses of market share and sales growth of a potential partner reveal?
- How close are your customer service policies and philosophies?
- What image does a potential partner project in different regional markets?
- What are the market perceptions of a potential partner's products?
- How do the products rank in quality, image and pricing?

Finance

- How do you and your prospective partner compare regarding financial strength, risk orientation, dividend policies, reinvestment, debt/equity ratios, currency management, and so on?
- Based on analyses of sales and profitability trends, how well could a potential partner weather unforeseen financial pressures?
- Who are the key shareholders in a partner?
- Are the partners publicly held, privately held, state-owned?

Safety, health and environmental (SHE) policies

Many MNCs demand that partners share comparable philosophies and policies for ethics and SHE factors. In the event of a problem, they are likely to be held accountable (in terms of public image, if not legally and financially) as if they hold 100% ownership. A company would not want its reputation with customers or its public image damaged because of a partner's actions. Firms in sensitive industries, such as pharmaceuticals and chemicals, need to be particularly careful. For a company that has incorporated rigid standards and practices into its own management procedures, it is not only preferable but necessary that it find a partner with matching philosophies and standards on SHE issues. For one US firm, if a company's standards and practices are not acceptable, it will identify alternative partners rather than risk a compromise. In fact, the firm severed year-long negotiations with a company because of lax SHE standards.

Understanding the soft factors... 'Our kind of people'

Soft factors are equally important. Even when hard factors fit well, the alliance can fail miserably if the people involved cannot get along. Chemistry – between corporate cultures or, more importantly, between both senior managements and the executives who will be charged with managing the venture – can make or break an alliance. The search for the right chemistry is not limited to any single regional or national group of executives. Managers from Asia, Latin America and Europe share the judgement of one US executive, who stated, 'First and foremost, companies are people. They are not business or financial machines. Consequently, the strength and success of a venture rest on the interactions of its people.' Thus when meeting with a potential partner, many executives admit to explicitly asking themselves, 'Are they our kind of people?'

Clearly, however, there is no hard-and-fast rule for determining whether there is any 'chemistry' between a given set of partners. In fact, each alliance is different, and the 'chemistry' can be based on virtually anything. It can be created by factors totally unrelated to the core business of the venture.

For instance, in one Italian–US venture, one executive attributed much of the venture's success to the compatibility factor and a close friendship between the two companies' chairmen. According to the executive, at the root of the close bonds is the fact that the US chairman is of Italian origin. When the US MNC first sought a European partner, the chairman zeroed in on the Italian company because of his desire to maintain strong ties with the country of his ancestors. As a result of the connection, the chairman has taken an active role in the venture, and an amiable and trusting atmosphere between the partners has developed and contributed tremendously to its success.

The intangible value of trust

Perhaps one of the most important soft factors to seek is 'mutual trust'. According to William Glavin, mutual trust was the single most important factor that former Xerox presidents Peter McCullough and Joe Wilson advocated. As Glavin explains, 'Outside of the US, every Xerox entity commenced as a joint venture; whether you look at Rank Xerox or Fuji Xerox or any other operation within Europe, Asia or Latin America. When I started with Xerox in 1970, I worked primarily with Rank Xerox and Fuji Xerox. At the time, McCullough explained to me, "Bill, you have to trust them in all endeavors. If you lose trust, the alliance crumbles." Initially, I wondered how the success of a joint venture could weigh so heavily on simple trust. Yet, through the years, it proved accurate. Mutual trust at senior management levels has carried Xerox's ventures through some turbulent times.'

As Glavin says, 'There will always be a certain amount of quibbling and mistrust among lower management levels in alliances. In fact, there were periods during the 1970s and 1980s where 60 to 70% of Xerox employees dealing with Fuji Xerox did not trust them. Plenty of times, bitter complaints and grievances reached top management about Fuji Xerox. However, the senior management never doubted the relationship; we trusted each other's judgment and integrity.' In fact, most complaints and problems in alliances hatch from jealousies or misunderstandings. If the partners trust each other, they can rise above pettiness and iron out the problems.

Perhaps the greatest testimonial for the importance of trust in a partnership occurred as a result of the relationship between Westinghouse and Mitsubishi. These two companies have been linked through a variety of cooperative ties for more than 70 years. Yet difficult market conditions and new competitive pressures forced the breakup of one of their 50–50 joint ventures, in high-voltage circuit-breakers. As Jon Elmendorf, former president of Westinghouse Energy Systems in Japan and current director for Westinghouse's environmental compliance operations, says, 'The collapse of the circuit-breaker venture was a true test of the relationship. There was a great deal of unhappiness and frustration. But the long-standing trust and commitment between the partners enabled us to deal with the immediate problems and focus on the future. In fact, the breakup of the circuit-breaker venture potentially could have destroyed the entire alliance. Yet this mutual trust and respect prevented any ill will or resentment from boiling over and ruining our other collaborative activities in nuclear energy and gas and steam turbines.'

The second C: capability

The capabilities of the potential candidates are obviously of prime importance. When evaluating the capabilities of candidates, companies may want to compile a dossier on each and evaluate their strengths and weaknesses.

- Who is active in widgets?
- What is their market strength?
- What is the state of their technology, manufacturing capabilities, distribution networks?
- Is the company a leader – or is it foundering?

In general, what most companies look for in a partner is the ability to contribute complementary strengths and resources to the alliance. Alliance makers seek a partner that can help a company overcome any weaknesses that prevent or inhibit the ability to achieve its business objectives. Complementary strengths were a major driving force behind the formation of Clark Equipment and Volvo's 50–50 venture to jointly operate and compete worldwide in the construction equipment business. Individually, neither partner had sufficient respective geographic presence and distribution capabilities to compete with the market leaders, Komatsu and Caterpillar. But Volvo had roughly 70% of its sales in Europe and the Middle East, where Clark was very weak; Clark had 70% of its sales in North America, where Volvo had virtually no presence. Pooling their marketing resources resulted in a much broader geographic scope.

Is the candidate ready, willing and able?

Before seriously approaching any prospective ally, the capabilities of the targeted candidates should be subjected to a rigorous test. Many alliance practitioners recommend establishing a team of experts to undertake a feasibility study of each candidate. The team's composition and the delineation of its investigation, of course, will depend on the nature and scope of the venture. However, in general, it should be a multifunctional team that includes the operating managers plus functional experts from finance, legal, tax, and so on.

All companies try to present themselves in the best possible light. Your partner may tell you that it has exciting technology, marvellous managers and sales staff, penetrating distribution networks, and so on – you probably would say the same. The danger sign is when your own investigations reveal that what the company says about the hard figures and what the balance sheet/independent analysts say are not the same.

The team should be prepared to undertake a tough, critical examination of a potential partner. A former ICI executive said companies should not make the mistake of letting apparent compatibility interfere with a thorough analysis of a partner's capabilities and resources. According to him, 'Alliances are analogous to marriages. You should not be too starry-eyed or in love with your partner. A company has to take a hard look at its potential mate to ascertain whether it has the capabilities and resources to combat adverse market conditions.'

He recalled the company's experience with a Spanish joint venture in basic chemicals: 'Although we had an excellent working relationship with our Spanish partner, the venture still collapsed. We had overestimated the market potential for the venture's products and the speed of reaching plant capacity, and we underestimated the JV's capital requirements. When both firms were required to contribute additional capital, our Spanish partner could not meet its financial obligations because it had run into serious financial problems. Despite our "compatibility", we had to withdraw from the venture.'

The third C: commitment

Executives concur that finding a partner with an equal sense of commitment to the alliance is the third keystone to success. Even if partners appear capable and compatible, unless they are willing to invest the time, energy and resources to make the alliance a success, the chances of the venture weathering changing market conditions are slim. Several companies have suggested two important tips on how MNCs can test whether their potential partners share a sufficient degree of commitment to the alliance:

Does the alliance fall within a core business or product line of the partner?

There are several dangers if the proposed alliance is in a business area that is only peripheral to the partner's mainstream activities. First, the company will probably not be willing to devote the time and resources necessary to making the venture succeed. Second, the partner could easily withdraw from the alliance and leave you in the dust. An alliance that is central to your partner's business or to its growth strategies reduces both of these dangers.

This unfortunate mishap occurred in a venture between TRW and Fujitsu. Fujitsu and TRW were optimistic that their venture would benefit both firms. TRW was to market Fujitsu-made point-of-sale terminals, automated teller machines and small business computers in the US. Fujitsu would thus gain access to US markets, and TRW's products would become a player in new business markets. But less than three years after the venture was formed in the early 1980s, TRW wanted out. According to Sidney Webb, who was president of TRW-Fujitsu, 'It became apparent after two or three years that to penetrate the US market with Fujitsu products was going to take a lot longer than expected...TRW came to the conclusion that, whereas in Fujitsu's case this joint venture was at the heart of their computer business and they must do it no matter what it takes and how long it takes, in TRW's case, it was very peripheral to the main core businesses.' (Alster, 1986).

Siemens ran into similar difficulties in the early days of developing computers in its alliance with RCA Corp. According to Siemens executives, the German MNC attached a high priority to developing its computer business. Siemens formed an alliance with RCA, trusting that its partner shared the same business priorities. But when IBM proved to be a more formidable competitor than either partner had anticipated, RCA quickly decided to abandon the mainframe market and the venture. This presented a serious dilemma for Siemens: it was left empty-handed by the withdrawal of RCA's technology and was forced into a demanding programme of self-sufficiency.

Determine how difficult it would be for a potential partner to withdraw from the alliance

As the Siemens case illustrates, one of the dangers of the alliance option is that one partner will incorporate the objectives into its global strategy, pour in considerable efforts and resources, and suddenly be left high and dry. Following the RCA mishap, Siemens refined its partnering techniques. One of its most reliable tools is a test by which Siemens can examine how easy it would be for its potential partner to either withdraw from the venture or neglect the interests of the German MNC.

Case 2.2   The three Cs in action: CFM International

This case illustrates how the three Cs laid the foundation for success in CFM International – a joint venture between General Electric and Snecma. CFM International has defied the odds against cooperation between potential competitors. Initially launched in 1969 to develop commercial jet engines, CFM did not garner its first order until eight years later. Yet despite start-up struggles, 1991 annual revenues exceeded $3 billion, with an order book worth over $6.5 billion. As Jean Bilien, CFM's president, observed: 'Results do not lie. While ventures can be difficult to manage, the payoff can be tremendous.' Much of CFM International's success can be attributed to the clear presence of the three Cs in its makeup.

Compatibility

Executives frequently rank compatibility among the individuals working for a venture as a critical foundation stone in any alliance. No matter how elegant the business strategy, the venture will fail without the right chemistry between the people involved in the alliance. As Bilien emphasized, 'Personal relationships make things work in alliances.' Certainly this principle is well exemplified by CFM International. A personal friendship had been built up based on shared experiences in World War II between the two MNCs' senior executives: Snecma's René Ravaud, a one-armed French Resistance hero, and Gerhard Neumann, a legendary US Air Force pilot. This personal bond laid the groundwork for the venture.

Yet the personal ties were not restricted to the levels of top management. The two firms of GE and Snecma had previously worked together on a number of subcontracting projects, nurturing direct contact between individuals of the two companies.

These business ties also offered an opportunity to test for the compatibility of such critical 'hard factors' as similarities in operating strategies and styles; corporate philosophies; employee and labour policies; organizational, operating and management structures; and environ-

continues

continued

mental policies. These and other such factors, combined with different managers' ability simply to get along, are fundamental in creating a climate in which a venture can grow and prosper. CFM also encourages personal ties among its employees by organizing a variety of informal social activities and events, such as a student exchange programme for employees' children. Above all, CFM International places a high priority on compatibility when screening new employees. As Bilien said, 'If management gets any indication that an individual cannot work in a cross-cultural environment, we immediately disregard the candidate.'

Capability

As commonly occurs in most alliances, GE and Snecma each sought a partner with an ability to contribute complementary strengths and resources. Each partner enjoys advantages in separate yet complementary technologies and skills. GE's expertise is in the core or heart of the jet engine and its high-pressure turbines, compressors and chambers, while Snecma excels in technology for low-pressure turbines, compressors and chambers. The two partners also had their own unique marketing strengths – GE in the US and Snecma in Europe – that together offered a broad sales base for CFM International.

These complementary capabilities have enriched CFM with certain specific competitive advantages in having powerful products. In technological advances, CFM International initially targeted the jet engines' thrust levels as being between 22,000 and 24,000 pounds. The new CFM models significantly surpass these original expectations, however, in having thrust levels that range between 18,500 pounds and 34,000 pounds. The existing models also have more than 17 different applications, well above the number initially planned. Bilien remarked that 'We have combined our strengths to produce a powerful competitive weapon – outstanding products.'

Commitment

This third keystone to success gave the alliance the strength to weather its first eight years without a single sale. Both partners' realization that it would take a long time to develop products and market acceptance helped the alliance survive.

Furthermore, both parties recognized the high stakes required to compete in today's global aerospace market. With development costs for new generations of commercial jet engines being in excess of $1 billion, these firms' cooperation offers each an opportunity to compete in this high-stakes market. Hence, need is a powerful driving force behind the individual companies' commitment to make CFM International a success.

Checklist

Choosing a partner: critical questions to ask

In sum, the following checklist of key issues may assist companies in finding a partner that satisfies the three Cs:

- What are you looking for – technology, market access, manufacturing capabilities, distribution channels?
- Can an existing relationship be extended?
- Have you examined a number of potential candidates?
- How will you go about determining compatibility? Focus on compatibility, not similarity.
- Is there any 'chemistry' between your senior and middle management?
- Are your corporate cultures compatible? If cultures are significantly different, could you successfully blend the two cultures? How?
- Does your partner have previous experience in collaborative ventures? How does its track record stack up?
- Are there any conflicts of interest? Does your partner have any alliances with some of your competitors? Can they affect you? How will you cope with that situation?
- Do you and your partner have complementary capabilities in technology, market access, manufacturing, distribution, and so on?
- Does the candidate have strengths that might benefit more than one division?
- Have you thoroughly researched your partner's capabilities? Some companies have been burned when a partner's technology or market prowess proved considerably weaker than originally expected.
- How committed will each partner be to the venture? Does the partner appear willing to contribute the resources and skills that are necessary to make the alliance a success?
- Is the activity central to your businesses? If not, what are the chances the venture will be relegated to the sidelines by one of you?
- Are you trying to forge too many alliances at the same time and consequently overlooking critical issues and problems that may disrupt the relationships? Is your emphasis on the quality, not the quantity of alliances?

- How difficult will it be for your partner to withdraw from the venture?
- What benefits will the partner derive from the venture? Are they greater than yours? How can you keep them equal?
- What are the partner's direct costs?
- How much can you learn from your partners? How do you plan to transfer any new knowledge, technology and/or skills acquired from partners and the venture to the parent company?
- How much does the partner need the alliance to meet its tactical or strategic objectives?
- Is the venture in a business segment that the partner must have for growth or survival purposes?
- How willing and able will the partner be to devote additional resources – capital, human, technologies, time – to the venture?
- What are the alternate strategies available to your company, and to the potential partners?
- What are the internal and external barriers to the partner's participation?
- What is the price of failure?

References

Alster N. (1986). Dealbusters: why partnerships fail. *Electronic Business*, 1 April, p. 70

Business International (1987). *Competitive Alliances: How to Succeed at Cross-regional Collaboration.* July, p. 9

Edmondson G. (1994). AT&T is no smooth operator in Europe. *Business Week*, 11 April, p. 48

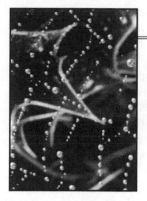

3

The range of alliance structures

Companies contemplating alliances need to consider how different alliance structures can satisfy their individual alliance strategies. Of course, none of the alliance structures considered below necessarily brings an alliance to fruition; they are a means to an end. The structure simply provides the foundation for an alliance, the partners make a partnership. Depending on the goals and objectives of the participating companies, management can choose from a broad range of structures. This chapter analyses and compares some of the most popular structures, including a separate joint venture company, equity investments, functional agreements for collaboration in a specific area such as joint manufacturing or research projects and broad-framework pacts.

Alliance joint ventures

Many firms seek to establish separate legal entities – joint ventures – for their partnerships. The essential feature of the joint venture is that an entirely new entity is created with its own identity and management structure, and with the operating and strategic problems inevitably posed by creating a new company. There is no end to the creativity in which alliance partners can structure these ventures. The equity breakdown may vary, but most companies seek to create a 50–50 joint venture.

Classics of the 50–50 genre are the Toyota–GM Nummi auto venture, the GE–Snecma aircraft engine global venture, and a Corning–Mitsubishi venture to manufacture and market pollution-control equipment for stationary emissions in the US market.

In some instances the partners limit their cooperation to certain functions. For example, in many of the vehicle and component joint ventures within the auto industry, the parents cooperate only in product development and/or manufacturing. Responsibility for marketing and distribution remains with the parent organizations. Other ventures opt to merge the entire spectrum of functions, such as the 50–50 joint venture between General Electric and FANUC in factory automation. In an effort to ward off formidable global competition, the partners agreed to jointly develop, manufacture, market and service their factory automation equipment.

A common feature in today's joint ventures is that the partners tend to cooperate for one specific product or in one region while operating as competitors in other markets. Hence, the ventures have a narrow focus. Partners leave no ambiguities as to when, how, where, and in what areas they agree to collaborate. Otherwise the deal can invite problems.

Some alliances create two or more separate entities that allow each partner to preserve an extra modicum of control in its home or key markets. When structuring GE Fanuc Automation Corp., the parents created a 50–50 holding company at the parent level, with three regional operating units below it: GE Fanuc Automation North America, 90% owned by the holding company and 10% directly by GE; Fanuc GE Automation Asia, 90% owned by the holding entity and 10% by FANUC, and GE Fanuc Europe, owned entirely by the holding company.

Case 3.1   Unwieldy JV structure derails Corning–Vitro

On a cautious note, organizing two or more separate joint venture entities can become cumbersome, particularly when partners are battling formidable competition in the marketplace. Consider the problems in a venture between Corning of the US and Mexico-based Vitro. When launching the alliance in 1992, the partners first merged their consumer housewares divisions – including research, manufacturing, marketing, distribution, and so on – into two separate entities, one based in Mexico and the other in the US.

continues

continued

Equity in the US-based venture – Corning Vitro Corp. – was split 51–49, with Corning assuming majority ownership. In the Mexican-based entity – Vitro Corning SA – Vitro owned 51%, with the remaining 49% held by Corning. The partners primarily selected the 51–49 arrangement to comply with existing Mexican restrictions on foreign ownership. However, the partners also thought that they could give the alliance greater agility by conferring primary management responsibility and control for daily operations to the local partner. At the helm of each venture to address major issues and design strategy was the same executive committee, comprised of equal Vitro and Corning members.

Despite Vitro and Corning's willingness to work together, heightened competition offered the partners little time to pull the alliance through the difficult start-up period. Neither Corning nor Vitro sufficiently gauged the threat and impact of less expensive Asian imports into Mexico. Nor did the partners anticipate the impact of a slowing US economy on their business. Lower tariff barriers combined with the Mexican peso's value *vis-à-vis* Asian currencies made the Asian imports very price-competitive. While market pressures mandated swift decision-making, the complex organizational and ownership structure worked against them. There were too many layers and structures in which decisions needed to travel.

Consequently, plummeting revenues forced Corning and Vitro to abandon plans to jointly own and manage a global housewares business in favour of a more narrow cross-distribution agreement. While the US-based venture – which became a 100%-owned Corning entity on 1 January 1994 – managed to break even on weak sales in 1993, profits had still decreased substantially from the venture's first year. Moreover, the Mexican venture lost money. Corning's share of the loss from Vitro Corning SA – now owned 100% by Vitro – approximated $12 million. This amount – combined with a $9.5 million writedown – translates into a $21.5 million loss on Corning's 1993 profits. According to Stephen Albertalli, recently retired director of investor relations for Corning, 'When you're losing over $21 million from a venture, there was no time to continue working together to iron out problems. It was a crisis and both companies needed to take control of their own operations to turn-around the situation.'

In response, Corning and Vitro restructured the alliance to concentrate on where the two companies had concrete synergies: cross-distribution. In fact, there was little reason to have a broad joint venture combining all operations, particularly the manufacturing and administrative functions where each faced internal problems. Instead, they now are focusing on what is mutually beneficial in the relationship, namely the cross-supply of products. Although sales from cross-distribution were modest, they had met the partners' initial goals for the start-up phase – a target of approximately 5% of total sales for each joint venture company. For example, Corning sales in Mexico went from less than $1 million to approximately 5% of Vitro Corning SA's $260 million sales for

continues

continued

houseware products in Mexico in 1992. Similarly, Vitro products accounted for 5% of the US-based Corning Vitro Corp.'s $700 million in sales for 1992. Moreover, a narrower arrangement can offer the time and energy to concentrate on building sales.

Unfortunately for Corning and Vitro, having common equity ownership in a joint venture structure – and the creation of separate legal entities in Mexico and the US – worked against the partners' interests and plans. While joint equity holdings in an alliance can demonstrate greater commitment to the alliance, equity can also be a hindrance. In the Corning–Vitro case, having cross-ownership did not add any value to the relationship. In fact, it hampered the agility of the alliance. From the inception of the Corning–Vitro alliance, both companies separately needed to restructure their housewares business to boost competitiveness. However, the dynamics of both markets offered little opportunity or time for the partners to solve their individual problems. Yet having joint equity holdings in the two JVs only aggravated the situation since they had to jointly agree on how to solve each other's problems.

By abandoning the JVs, each company is now able to address its problems. Without cross-equity ownership via the JVs, each firm can take unilateral decisions on how to revitalize their operations. For instance, says a Vitro spokesman, the company is moving quickly to reduce the number of moulds used for manufacturing its glassware from 2500 to 500. Adds Albertalli, 'Imagine us within Corning trying to decide which of the 2500 moulds needs to be eliminated. Yet, technically, when we had the equity ties via the JVs, that was precisely what we had to do.'

Vitro also is replacing the use of the more expensive raw material opal boro-silicate – which is used to make the glassware heat resistant – with the less expensive soda lime glass. Most Asian imports, adds the Vitro spokesman, use soda lime glass. While the soda lime glassware is not heat resistant, its competitive price was luring customers away from Vitro. Vitro has also consolidated its four separate companies within the glassware division into one entity, eliminating overlap and excess administrative costs. The Mexican company will also prune its workforce in the consumer housewares division by approximately 30% to around 1300 individuals. Corning aims to focus on administrative and sales costs where the company estimates that it needs to trim its costs by 30%. Some restructuring of factories as well as a consolidation of shipping and distribution warehouses is also needed.

Functional agreements: a garden variety

Many companies building alliances – even strategically central alliances – do not see the need for either equity stakes or the creation of a joint venture. Instead, they opt for functional agreements. These alliances are projects in which two or more companies decide to cooperate in one or more specific functions such as R&D, manufacturing, marketing, technology sharing or licensing, distribution and the like. With functional agreements, no new entity is created and the cooperation tends to be limited. As the above Corning–Vitro case illustrated, functional agreements are inherently more flexible than alliances built around JVs or equity holdings – they can be the best responses in the ever-changing global market. Further, easily rewritable functional pacts allow 'continual refocusing' of an alliance. Some alliances – such as the R&D pact between IBM, Siemens and Toshiba to develop the 256-megabit DRAM chip – include provisions to allow the partners to extend cooperation to manufacturing. Successful functional alliances also can easily be transformed into equity- or JV-based partnerships. Some common functional alliances and their features are outlined below:

Joint manufacturing

Benefits of manufacturing agreements include scale economies and sopping up excess capacity or reducing capacity in market downturns. For example, IBM and Siemens announced plans in 1992 to jointly manufacture 16-megabit chips by sharing the reported $800 million costs of expanding an existing IBM factory in France. The cooperation is to be limited to manufacturing, as each party will separately sell the chips or use them for in-house products.

Technical assistance

Nippon Sheet Glass (NSG) and Pilkington have technical-assistance pacts in quality and manufacturing. This collaboration is aimed at improving Pilkington's ability to win business from Japanese auto transplants in the UK and other European countries. Yet the cooperation is clearly limited to technical assistance. In fact, both partners must be very careful to avoid collaborating in marketing, because of monopoly regulations.

Joint marketing

In 1992, Westinghouse and Mitsubishi Heavy Industries embarked on a series of marketing agreements for cooperation in building and marketing nuclear plants in third-country markets. Jon Elmendorf, former president of Westinghouse Energy Systems Japan and current Westinghouse director for environmental compliance, has said that the two partners recently signed a pact in Indonesia and plan to conclude similar deals for China and Taiwan. Yet the two firms operate as competitors in the Japanese market for nuclear plants.

Cross-distribution

This rather traditional alliance form permits firms to broaden their product offerings by arranging to market the products of another company in their home territory or a specified region. In line with changing customer demands, distribution agreements are quite common among office systems suppliers. For example, some of Xerox's product offerings are sourced from other manufacturers. Similarly, given Xerox's strength in reprographic products, the US MNC has a number of alliances under which it supplies products to other office system suppliers.

Distribution agreements frequently complement other alliances. For example, in exchange for sharing their technology in an R&D venture or licensing arrangement, the licensee will offer its partner the right to distribute the finished product in its home region. For instance, Harris employed this technique when it forged an alliance in the mid-1980s with Matsushita, Philips and AT&T in the market for private satellite data communications. Harris enhanced its joint development programme with Matsushita with cross-distribution agreements under which the Japanese MNC obtained nonexclusive rights to distribute PACTs and related equipment in the Far East.

On a cautious note, there are dangers in alliances where the payment for technology is distribution. Usually, the technology can be transferred quickly, the distribution benefits achieved only slowly. There is a sore temptation for one partner to take the technology and run.

Cross-licensing

Like distribution agreements, licensing is not new; the difference is primarily one of scope and strategic fit. For instance, Himont, a Montedison Group company, is a world leader in polypropylene process technology, with numerous patents worldwide on its catalyst and polymerization technologies. Its Spheripol process technology was developed in 1983 and has been agressively licensed throughout the world. Catalyst technology was developed under a cooperative research and development alliance with Mitsui Petrochemicals. To date, 87 licences have been granted for the use of the Himont and Mitsui catalyst and propylene polymerization technologies. Approximately 60% of the world's existing polypropylene capacity and announced expansions are under one or more licences from Himont.

As another strategy, licensing deals are often used to promote global standards for a particular technology. For instance, in the compact disc (CD) market, Philips NV's strategy of actively licensing its CD player technology for a low fee has fostered the worldwide growth and acceptance of the Dutch company's CD system.

Research pooling

R&D ventures are an attractive option in industries where the cost of innovation is enormous and where shortened product life cycles create undue pressure to be first with a new product to the market. A general easing of antitrust activity in the US and Europe has also nurtured the growth of multicompany R&D ventures. The scope of cooperation is clearly limited to research – the partners individually manufacture and market the resulting products. Depending on partner preferences and the nature of the project, the partners may or may not work side by side in the laboratory. For instance, in the IBM, Siemens and Toshiba alliance for the development of the 256-megabit DRAM chip, the 150 engineers from the three partners work side by side at an IBM facility in New York.

Consortia

These are common in research and development in advanced technology industries. Companies find consortia most useful in precompetitive research. In many instances, the projects are partially or completely funded by government agencies such as Japan's MITI, various US-government entities or European Union institutions.

Although consortia have a mixed reputation, a number of them have proven successful. Sematech, created with US government funding to help semiconductor manufacturers compete with Japan by improving manufacturing technology and supplier infrastructure, has won general praise. In 1992, the US recaptured leadership in worldwide semiconductor market share.

Many observers claim credit should go to Sematech, which brought arch-rivals such as Texas Instruments, Motorola and IBM together. None the less, the conflicting demands of participants make careful monitoring and management in consortia doubly important. Companies continually must juggle the delicate balance between offering assistance and technical input to the consortia pool while receiving equal know-how and technology in return.

Equity investments

Buying a piece of your prospective partner is another type of alliance strategy. Unlike a straight portfolio investment, in an equity-stake alliance, the partners usually draw up a number of functional specific agreements to exploit complementary strengths. Equity ownership is no guarantee of success in a partnership. In fact, the Ford–Mazda and AT&T–Olivetti cases illustrate sharp contrasts of the potential successes and failures of an equity alliance (see Cases 3.2 and 3.3). Most executives differ sharply on the benefits – and propriety – of an equity-stake alliance.

Proponents maintain that the equity commitment solidifies the relationship and increases the chances for success of functional agreements. Equity holdings can create personal understanding between senior officers of potential partners; they can lay a firm basis for alliances to which a company may not yet be ready to commit itself.

An executive with a telecommunications company takes up the marriage theme and calls the equity commitment 'the ring on the finger'. According to him, the equity provides two important ingredients. First, the equity highlights a partner's commitment to the alliance. In other words, it is not just a 'one-night stand'. Second, the equity sends an important message to the market that you have joined hands.

A Mitsubishi Motors executive involved in various collaborative arrangements between Chrysler and Mitsubishi believes Chrysler's former 10% ownership of Mitsubishi established a solid foundation for the long-term relationship between the two companies. 'Because of the equity tie, we were able to explore our complementary strengths and launch a number of agreements.' According to a Xerox executive, 'Buying a piece of a company enables you to really get inside the doors of the company and see what is going on. It significantly widens the opportunities of exploring a broad range of options in which the two partners could collaborate.'

The strategy of inviting a partner to purchase a minority stake can also be used as an added defence against hostile corporate raiders. For instance, Pilkington Glass of the UK sold 20% of LOF Glass – its US operation – to its long-standing Japanese partner, Nippon Sheet Glass, to add an extra degree of protection against an unfriendly acquisition. The deal included a put transaction in which any hostile bidder for Pilkington would be required to buy back NSG's shares.

Similarly, Fujitsu's purchase of a majority stake in ICL was a defensive move. According to Michio Naruto, director of global markets for Fujitsu, when Canada-based Northern Telecom purchased ICL's parent company, the British telecommunications giant STC, in 1989, Northern Telecom was interested only in the telecommunications division and was ready to sell off the computer businesses of ICL. The choice for the Japanese company thus came down to either buying a large part of ICL or else seeing its UK partner wind up in the hands of an acquiring European or US competitor.

The downside of equity stakes

Some executives find that buying an equity stake is a very expensive and risky way to try to know a company. According to a former Siemens executive, 'I find that most of the time, equity stakes and other types of alliances are not as synergistic as is usually assumed. I do not believe that having an equity stake in a company automatically increases the opportunity to forge deeper ties or gain better access to the partners' operating units. In no case will an equity stake substitute for well-positioned and well-formulated functional agreements at the operating level. Companies starry-eyed over the prospects of an equity stake's strengthening an imperfect functional alliance could be deeply disappointed.'

Glenn Gardner, head of the LH programme for Chrysler, also cautions against the dangers of overreliance on equity or of unrealistic expectations. According to Gardner, 'Holding equity stakes is like going into business with your brother'. Added Lino Piedra, senior executive at Chrysler and key coordinator in many Mitsubishi–Chrysler ties, 'An equity stake is convenient, yet it sometimes can artificially bind two companies together. It can force firms to try to collaborate in areas where it does not make sense. In some respects, this is the reason why Chrysler and Mitsubishi often acted like an old married couple.'

Fujitsu's Naruto has suggested another pitfall: 'Equity stakes can compromise the independence of the company. It is extremely important to have a partner that operates with an autonomous spirit. An equity hold on the company can reduce its independent spirit and create a weak partnership.'

Case 3.2   Ford–Mazda build a solid foundation

Why do some equity links work and others fail? There is no easy answer yet a review of the key pillars supporting the Ford–Mazda alliance may offer some pointers for success.

The Ford–Mazda relationship originated in the early 1970s with a pact in which Ford purchased small pickup trucks from Mazda. When Mazda encountered financial difficulties in the late 1970s, Sumitomo Bank, Mazda's principal financial institution, invited Ford to take a 25% equity stake in Mazda in exchange for cash. Ford agreed, in part because it already knew a strong potential for building a powerful business relationship with Mazda existed. The purchase of the equity stake was an expression of the recognition by top management that the relationship between the two companies had grown in a special way beyond the normal buyer/seller relationship.

Paul Drenkow, a Ford executive involved with the Ford–Mazda relationship, has commented, 'At the time of Ford's purchase of an equity stake in Mazda, Ford sought three major objectives from the equity link. First, it had been supplying its Asian markets with Ford cars

continues

continued

manufactured in Europe. Management wanted to develop sources inside Asia to supply key markets in New Zealand, Australia and Taiwan. Second, management wanted to tap Mazda as a supplier for key components such as transmissions. Third, Ford was eager to increase its presence and market share in Asia.' Drenkow added that 'These were the goals of the relationship 12 years ago. In many respects, the objectives still apply. Yet, I do not think anyone in management envisioned how the relationship would blossom to include over 40 collaborative projects, including major car and truck projects in North America and Europe.'

Said another Ford executive, 'The equity link makes good judgement prevail and gets quick reactions to what appear to be problems; it also prevents overreactions. People take time to make sure they understand what's going on.' Both companies strive to ensure that each company maintains its own identity and distinct competitive advantages. Senior management at Ford and Mazda met regularly to demonstrate their commitment to the alliance. Having the visible support of top management sends a strong signal to the employees that both companies are determined to make the relationship work.

He added, 'The equity is not used as a lever with individual Mazda managers. The individual programs stand on their own merit, and the two companies do not do anything together unless there are benefits for both companies.' The executive emphasized that Ford goes to great lengths to avoid any implication that Ford is trying to run or control Mazda's business at all. This allows Mazda to continue to 'keep its own self-respect and the respect of its employees, customers, and the Japanese public' as an independent, bona fide Japanese automaker. This is essential to Mazda's long-term survival; it needs the help of its suppliers, the ability to recruit good people in Japan and consistently high morale among its employees. 'Without its independence,' said the executive, 'that would be difficult to do.'

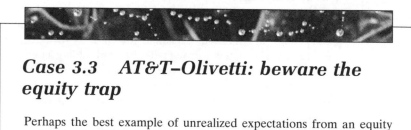

Case 3.3   AT&T–Olivetti: beware the equity trap

Perhaps the best example of unrealized expectations from an equity stake was the highly publicized Olivetti–AT&T link. Jacques Meyer, international market planning director at AT&T, has traced the rocky relationship between the US telecommunications giant and Olivetti.

continues

---

continued

AT&T's business alliance with Olivetti began in 1983 with the former assuming a 22% equity position in Olivetti. After a series of mishaps, AT&T liquidated its Olivetti stake in 1989. As Meyer says, 'Equity stakes can pose a unique dilemma. On the one hand, if the partners do not have some equity links, I think it is too easy for them to walk away from each other when troubles begin. On the other hand, however, the equity tie is not going to make the relationship happen. Instead, what makes an alliance work [is] common objectives, complementary capabilities and mutual expectations on what exactly the alliance can and cannot do. In the AT&T–Olivetti case, we believed we could sell their computers in the US and they in turn would help us market PBXs in Europe. At the end of the day, however, neither party was successful.

'There have been lengthy discussions on the convergence of computers and telecommunications. From an academic perspective, this confluence is all well and good. But when you get down to the basics of having a computer and telecommunications company work together, it is a different story. The AT&T–Olivetti divorce was not a case of bad will. AT&T simply was neither ready nor able to sell the Olivetti computers in the US. Plus, both partners had a significant overlap in their computer product lines which exacerbated the problems. And in Europe, Olivetti did not have the technical capabilities and support to sell our telecommunications equipment.'

Broad-framework pacts

A number of alliances proceed by first outlining a broad agreement to work together, then supplementing that with contracts concerning products, technology or certain function-specific areas. The IBM–Apple alliance illustrates how some alliances may involve an intricate web of links and agreements in several areas. IBM and Apple's commitment to collaborate on the development of new generations of computer technology offers some of the best proof of how powerful the alliance advantage can be. Even traditional go-it-alone companies such as IBM as well as arch-rivals – such as IBM and Apple – find it difficult to compete in the 1990s without competitive alliances. When forging their alliance in late 1991, Apple and IBM simultaneously committed themselves to collaboration in a number of critical technology areas:

- *Software* Joint development of new software to allow customers to integrate Apple Macintosh computers into IBM's personal computer networks. Collaborative efforts also aim to combine both partners' versions of AT&T's UNIX system. The companies plan to create a new UNIX version that can be used with the machines and networks of both IBM and Apple. A separate joint venture plans to develop a novel systems software that will offer new functions and simplify programming.

- *Microprocessors*   Joint development, in conjunction with Motorola, of a new microprocessor chip – the Power PC – based on IBM's RISC design. In early 1994, Apple introduced a new line of Macintosh computers based on the new Power PC microprocessor chip. With the Power PC, the three partners aim to end the hegemony of Intel, the world's largest chip maker. Apple, IBM and Motorola also have created an industry organization to build support for the Power PC among computer manufacturers and to establish the technology as a new industry standard.
- *Multimedia*   A unique joint venture to create industry standards for 'multimedia', the simultaneous processing of video, graphics, voice and text.

Beware the dangers of broad-framework pacts

On a cautious note, broad-framework pacts can be unwieldy. It can be diffcult to find one partner in which a company can find comparable strengths and needs in a number of business and technical areas. The intricate links between the different projects in broad-framework pacts can also jeopardize success. Problems in one project can spill over into other activities.

Consider the problems in the AT&T–Italtel pact. When AT&T was selected in 1989 as foreign partner to Italtel to implement an ambitious five-year $30-billion government modernization programme in telecommunications, the two partners forged a series of collaborative projects. Among the deals were cross-equity shareholdings in which AT&T assumed a 20% stake in Italtel, in exchange for extending a comparable shareholding in AT&T's Dutch-based European joint venture operation, AT&T Network Systems International (NSI); a joint project to market and distribute a catalogue of telecommunications products in countries throughout Europe; agreements to explore cooperation in third-country markets, particularly in Asia, Africa and Eastern Europe; and technology cooperation for transmission equipment. Poor results from a limited domestic telecommunications market – Italtel's annual profits fell to L40.2 billion in 1993 from L133.2 billion for 1992 – plus complex government privatizations and restructurings in the Italian telecommunications sector prompted Italtel's holding company STET to form a new partnership with Siemens. In the opinion of one source close to AT&T, STET's new alliance with Siemens – in which the two companies will form a 50–50 joint venture to develop, manufacture and market telecommunications equipment in Italy and abroad – will lead to the end of the broad AT&T–Italtel relationship. He adds, 'One of the pillars of the AT&T–Italtel alliance was the sale of AT&T equipment to STET via Italtel. Now that Siemens is STET's partner, there is no way that STET will continue to buy AT&T's products.' The new STET–Siemens marriage also makes it difficult for Italtel and AT&T to continue any cooperation, since the former's parent company is now linked with a key AT&T competitor. Already STET has sold Italtel's 20% stake in the Dutch-based NSI to AT&T. In turn, AT&T is likely to sell its 20% stake in Italtel to STET. But for AT&T, the jury is still out as to whether the new Italtel–Siemens pact will prevent any future cooperative endeavours between the US telecommunications giant and Italtel. According to Ramesh Barasia, vice-president for marketing at AT&T Network Systems, 'Italtel and AT&T are still continuing their joint research and development of new transmission equipment. In the future, the two companies could collaborate in the sale and marketing of these new transmission offerings. It will depend on market opportunities and business conditions.' Moreover, he adds, 'Does the sale of the cross-equity shareholdings in Italtel and NSI and the new Italtel–Siemens alliance make the situation more complex? Yes. But complexity is the name of the game. Companies need to separate emotions from business. Cross-equity shareholdings are not the only driving forces behind an alliance. Markets, namely business opportunities and customer needs, also bring companies together. The fact that Italtel and AT&T will no longer be linked via equity stakes does not mean that they cannot have a collaborative relationship in the future.' Concludes Barasia, 'Alliances are a very integral part of AT&T's global strategy. Ventures can be difficult but we cannot shy away from them. Some will work and some may not.'

Checklist

Depending on the goals and strategies of the partners, management can choose from a broad range of alliance structures: a separate venture company, equity investments, functional agreements (such as joint manufacturing or joint R&D) or broad-framework pacts. The structure selected for the alliance is crucial both in defining the objectives and in allowing them to be accomplished. Some issues to consider when deciding on the appropriate venture structure include:

- Will a separate joint venture entity best serve the partners' interests and needs?

- What is the equity breakdown for the JV?
- Will cooperation in the JV be limited to one function or cover a broad range of activities?
- What are the pros and cons of creating two or more separate JV entities that allow each partner to preserve an extra dose of control in its home or principal markets?
- Rather than create a new JV entity, have you considered creating a more focused – and flexible – functional agreement?
- In what specific functions – in R&D, joint manufacturing, cross-marketing, distribution, licensing, technical assistance, and so on – do the partners plan to cooperate?
- Have you analysed the different options for structuring, organizing and managing the different functional agreements?
- What is the value of taking an equity stake in your prospective partner?
- Will cross-equity shareholdings deepen the prospects for collaboration and how?
- What other agreements – joint ventures, functional agreements – will accompany the equity stake alliance?
- Do you need a broad-framework pact and why?
- Have you adequately assessed the challenges of managing multiple links with the same partner under a broad-framework pact?

4

Planning for cooperation

Planning for an alliance can be a complex process. Most executives agree that building an alliance is much easier when management develops a comprehensive game-plan in advance. Several MNCs involved in multiple relationships have developed a basic set of internal ground rules to help guide their managers through the myriad of issues and factors to consider when negotiating an alliance. For example, whenever ICL's managers were interested in a new project with ICL's long-standing ally Fujitsu or with other partners, they increasingly sought advice from David Dace, recently retired ICL director of collaboration, because of his more than 10 years of negotiating experience and his relationship with Fujitsu. 'Consequently,' Dace has explained, 'I decided to write up 12 important tips to assist divisions in their alliance pursuits.' (See Box 4.1.) Given the importance of exchanging business cards in Japan and other Asian societies, Dace had these 12 points printed on the plastic name-card holders of ICL managers and engineers.

Because many other companies have yet to prepare formal guidelines regarding alliances, this chapter offers some pointers on the subject, based on the recommendations and experiences of several alliance practitioners.

Box 4.1 ICL's tactics for successful collaboration

(1) Treat the collaboration as a personal commitment. It is people that make partnerships work.

(2) Anticipate that it will take up management time. If you cannot spare the time, do not start it.

(3) Mutual respect and trust are essential. If you do not trust the people you are negotiating with, forget it.

(4) Remember that both partners must get something out of it (money, eventually). Mutual benefit is vital. This will probably mean you have got to give something up. Recognize this from the outset.

(5) Make sure you tie up a tight contract. Do not put off resolving unpleasant or contentious issues. However, once signed, the contract should be put away. If you find yourself referring to it, something is wrong with the relationship.

(6) Recognize that during the course of a collaboration circumstances and markets will change. Recognize your partner's problems and be flexible.

(7) Make sure you and your partner have mutual expectations of the collaboration and its time-scale. One happy and one unhappy partner is a formula for failure.

(8) Get to know your opposite numbers at all levels socially. Friends take longer to fall out.

(9) Appreciate that cultures – both geographic and corporate – are different. Do not expect a partner to act or respond identically to you. Find out the true reason for a particular response.

(10) Recognize your partner's interest and independence.

(11) Even if the arrangement is tactical in your eyes, make sure you have corporate approval. Your tactical activity may be a key piece in an overall strategic jigsaw puzzle. With corporate commitment to the partnership, you can act with the positive authority needed in these relationships.

(12) Celebrate achievement together. It is a shared elation, and you will have earned it!

And, finally, two further things to remember:

- If you are negotiating a product deal with an original equipment manufacturer, look for a *quid pro quo*. Remember that another product may offer more in return.

- Joint development agreements must include joint marketing arrangements. You need the largest market possible to recover development costs and to get volume and margin benefits.

Getting ready for cooperation

Many companies find that setting up the internal logistics of cooperation is an excellent exercise in the run-up to negotiations. The process includes the following elements:

- Culling a multifunctional team to analyse alliance issues;
- Testing the viability of the proposed alliance in terms of needs, structures and personalities within its own organization. This includes building support for the alliance and spotting potential 'deal-killers'.
- Spelling out what a company needs, expects and wants from the alliance;
- Ironing out structural and procedural issues;
- Expecting the unexpected – hoping for the best but planning for the worst;
- Sketching a preliminary plan on how to manage the venture;
- Assessing the risks of collaboration;
- Analysing human resource needs for the alliance;
- Factoring competitors/government reactions into the alliance equation.

The exercise can streamline the negotiations process and help identify and resolve potential problem areas, rather than waiting for the issues to explode at the negotiating table. Results from the analyses can reveal whether cooperation is feasible and can save companies from signing an ill-conceived letter of intent.

Who are the planners?

How two MNCs arranged housekeeping

Many firms will assign responsibility for delineating the logistics of cooperation to the group that conducted the feasibility studies for partner selection, since these experts are already familiar with the potential partner and deal. Although most teams concentrate on internal issues and work separately, when ICI and EniChem set up their joint venture – European Vinyls Corp. – in the late 1980s, the partners had their teams work together before negotiations started.

Deteriorating competitive conditions in the maturing polyvinyl chloride (PVC) market spawned a unique marriage between UK-based ICI and Italy's Enichem. As a front-runner to the negotiations, each partner organized teams – which included marketing, finance, legal, research, manufacturing and technical experts – to undertake an analysis of the pros and cons of creating an alliance to manufacture, market and sell PVC. The groups worked together for a year to sort through a number of complex issues. The teams tackled such delicate issues as assessing the value of the partners' various assets; coordinating different depreciation schedules; devising a systematic schedule for transferring assets to the JV entity; and agreeing on additional rational measures to eliminate surplus capacity from the older, more costly plants.

According to the president of ICI Italia, 'The work of these teams was vital. It laid the groundwork for smooth, timely negotiations.' In fact, by having the teams jointly resolve some delicate issues at the onset, the partners were able to reach a final agreement in a comparatively short period of two to three months. The team strategy also built camaraderie. Said the ICI Italia president, 'We were able to make significant progress on the problem of meshing two very different corporate cultures.' For the alliance, it was generally agreed the venture would adopt a management style similar to ICI's, a structure that embodied the concept of teamwork and players. However, Enichem – which was an outgrowth of the reorganization of the Italian petrochemicals industry – was only three years old at the time of creating the alliance. Since it was a much younger company, it had not had the time to foster team management and was not used to the approach. Conducting the joint feasibility studies gave both sides an excellent training ground for working well together and smoothed the implementation of a team management strategy in the joint venture.

Testing for internal support

When planning for cooperation, alliance strategists first need to steer the alliance idea through internal channels to test for support and/or opposition to the project. Prior to launching any formal discussions with a potential partner, managers may want to look inside the company – not only to identify the executives who wield the power to propel the venture forward but also to find those 'deal killers' who will try to sabotage the partnership. In many cases, this turns out to be a difficult task. But a McKinsey consultant offers some advice: try to force a decision relating to the forthcoming venture through the same channels that the ultimate decision will travel. This can involve a preliminary partnering decision, such as putting out a development contract or putting up some 'earnest' money. The people who feel threatened will typically rise to the surface.

Sending the wrong or mixed signals to potential alliance partners is another good reason to steer the alliance proposal first through internal channels. Managers often prematurely approach a prospective partner without first testing for support for the project idea internally. This can be a particularly acute problem when a company has wide-ranging links with the same partner, such as in the Ford–Mazda alliance.

How Ford measures internal support for an alliance

Paul Drenkow, a Ford executive closely involved in the Ford–Mazda alliance, has said that a chief goal of Ford's Asia-Pacific group is to ensure that different divisions steer their alliance ideas through all appropriate internal channels before contacting Mazda or other Ford partners in Asia.

Drenkow observed that 'It is very easy for a Ford manager to get an idea for collaboration and then jump on a plane to brainstorm with Mazda. Yet, Japanese companies, such as Mazda, would never approach an outside firm before its management has fully endorsed the project. Not only were we really confusing Mazda, [but] it was putting a real strain on the Ford–Mazda relationship. Consequently, we outlined a six-step business development process on how to build an alliance.' The first three steps of this process are devoted entirely to tips on how Ford managers can get their act together internally. Important questions asked are:

- Does the project have the support of top management?
- Does it need the support of other divisions or organizations? Have they given their commitment?
- Have you thoroughly analysed the pros and cons of the project? There is nothing worse than starting the negotiation process and then deciding that your own firm can handle it alone.
- What, if any, are the corporate implications of a particular division's project?
- How does the alliance fit into the company's global strategy and ambitions?
- Who within the company is opposed to the deal, and why?
- How powerful are the opponents within the decision-making hierarchy? How serious are the risks of any deal killers sabotaging the project now or later?
- Are the benefits of the deal restricted to only one division, or could other areas profit?
- Finally, have you adequately analysed the risks and costs of collaboration?

A noose or nuisance: early letters of intent

Once senior management has given the green light on a new collaborative project, alliance strategists need to sketch a comprehensive plan in advance that outlines the venture's short- and long-term objectives, organization and management structure. As a start, MNCs should consider running through a prenegotiations checklist (see Box 4.2). By rigorously determining what the company wants and must absolutely have in the venture, management is better able to critically determine whether cooperation is really feasible. Too often, companies decide they want to collaborate and rashly sign a letter of intent (LOI) before proper evaluation.

By signing an LOI too early, companies can really back themselves into a corner. Suppose, after signing an LOI, two firms then try to iron out how the competitive alliance should work. At this point, they discover complications that make cooperation questionable. Rationally speaking, the companies woud probably abandon the idea of collaboration. However, in many cases, MNCs do not bow out gracefully *because* of the LOI. Usually – and especially if the LOI has received significant press coverage – executives feel an obligation to forge some arrangement in order to save face. But the chances of designing a successful alliance under these circumstances are pretty slim, and companies can wake up to a very unsavoury marriage.

The ill-fated GTE–Siemens alliance in the late 1980s suffered from this mishap. Both partners were eager to collaborate and signed an LOI stating their intentions to merge their public switching businesses in a 50–50 JV. However, neither party could agree on how to do so. In the end, the partners were forced to retreat from a full-scale amalgamation and launched a face-saving alternative – an 80–20 venture in which majority owner Siemens absorbed the domestic and international operations of GTE in transmission equipment.

Box 4.2   Prenegotiation checklist: map out musts and wants

In preparation for the negotiations, a number of companies may find it beneficial to list all the important issues that may be raised with the partner. On each issue, companies should map out what they *want* to achieve from the venture, what is necessary for the success of the venture and what makes the most *business sense* in terms of their own corporation's long-term strategy. In particular, MNCs should consider running through a prenegotiation checklist prior to signing any LOIs. By rigorously determining what the company wants and must absolutely have in the venture, management is better able to critically determine whether cooperation is really feasible. The following list culled from numerous alliance makers should provide a comprehensive guide:

continues

continued

- What is the structure (legal, organizational, and so on) best suited to accomplish your goals?
- Is it necessary to establish a JV, or could you reach your objectives with a functional alliance? If setting up a JV, what is the equity breakdown that you are looking for? Is that legally possible in the country of incorporation? When outlining the equity positions of each partner in a JV, have you valued both the hard and soft inputs? (Don't forget to ascertain the market value of soft inputs, such as name and reputation, because they add significant weight.)
- Is the option of taking an equity stake in your partner available? Would an equity position lead to greater cooperation?
- How does the venture relate to the activities of your parent corporation and its global strategy?
- How will the alliance be managed? How are responsibilities divided for operations and functions such as R&D, design, engineering, manufacturing, sales and marketing, customer relations, accounting, legal, finance, and so on?
- For what functions would you want to assume responsibility? How can you justify your position or argument that your company should control, for instance, marketing? How can you effectively convey to the partner that you are in the best position to take responsibility for certain functions?
- What techniques will the partners employ to resolve conflicts?
- What kinds of standards (safety and environment) should be set for the venture? How will they be implemented?
- In the case of a JV, how will the board of directors or the executive management committee be structured? How will you select and compensate officers?
- What are the venture's needs for skilled, technically trained personnel? Where will you obtain these people? Do you want the executives for the venture to come from the parent corporations, subsidiaries or outside sources? For what period should the executives be assigned to the JV? Will the US penchant for job rotation pose a problem to your partners, particularly Asian allies? How will you handle labour relations?
- What contributions will your company make for training and technical support to ensure that the venture will run smoothly?
- What is the scope of the operations of the venture? From where will it operate? How will you coordinate the activities of all partners?
- Will the venture's products be exported? Which firm will be responsible for the export strategy? How will the venture's export strategy mesh with your own activities?
- How will you handle budget and financing responsibilities?
- What accounting systems and methods will the partners adopt? How compatible are these accounting approaches with parent procedures?

continues

---

continued

- What level of debt/equity is appropriate?
- Have you determined an earnings formula for the alliance? What assumptions are you making for earnings projections? What are your market projections?
- Will any products or raw materials be supplied by either partner? How will these contributions be priced? Transfer pricing is one of the biggest minefields for ventures.
- How does the alliance gain access to new technology? Should or will new technology be transferred to the venture?
- Are you providing technology to the alliance? How will you be compensated for the technology? Are you going to get paid up front or receive a running royalty? Does your method of compensation incorporate the tax effects of the transactions?
- Have you set up dividend policies? What percentage of earnings should and can be paid out?
- How will the partners acquire and/or dispose of assets? What methods and accounting procedures are suitable?
- What are some of the possible scenarios that may force a change in the powers and direction of the alliance?
- Have you mapped out the divorce clauses? On what grounds do the partners separate?
- Have you analysed the responses of your competitors to the pro-. posed link? What has been the government reaction? Do their actions and opinions change your views on the alliance?

Expect the unexpected: do your homework

Signing an LOI prematurely is not the only reason why companies need to devote considerable time and energy in planning for cooperation. If nothing else, the other partners, particularly if Japanese, will be well prepared once they reach the negotiating table. Companies do not want their negotiators at a disadvantage because of poor planning and preparation.

In fact, it is common knowledge that Japanese firms are scrupulous about preparing for a new business endeavour. Many US and European executives have cited the disadvantages of not being able to meet the Japanese on level ground in grasping the implications and complexities of all issues related to a venture. For instance, Robert Ecklin, senior vice-president and general manager of the industrial products division at Corning, recalls the time and effort it took to convince Mitsubishi Heavy Industries, Corning's partner in a new US-based pollution-control alliance, to use variable-compensation packages in the venture, with Mitsubishi arguing that Japanese firms were accustomed to using only fixed-compensation packages. However, Ecklin later learned that Japanese firms traditionally pay out semi-annual bonuses to all employees, based on corporate performance. 'Technically,' he says, 'these bonuses are a form of variable compensation. Had I known about them I would have been in a better position to illustrate how the Japanese also use some form of flexible compensation.'

Similarly, Howard Hill, who was a principal legal adviser for Chrysler in its negotiations with Mitsubishi for the Diamond Star Motors venture, recalled the detailed planning tactics of the Japanese team. Mitsubishi had charts covering all the walls of an entire conference room that traced the movements of the yen/dollar exchange rate since the switch to a flexible exchange rate system in 1973. They also had the average amount of snow and rainfall for each county in all the states under consideration as potential plant sites.

Insufficient planning can also affect a venture's profit and revenue expectations. For instance, the Mexican partner at Citra, a US–Mexican–Japanese alliance to produce and sell chicken *yakitori* in Japan and other Asian markets, was initially caught off guard by a custom known as 'the Japanese 2%'. Profit and revenue expectations had to be scaled back once the Mexicans became aware that the Japanese require food suppliers to include an extra 2% in weight at no additional cost. The Japanese argue that this 2% is needed to ensure that the customer is not cheated. Yet this extra small percentage, when applied to millions of chickens, adds up.

Protect corporate jewels in links with competitors

Prior to signing any LOI, many experienced companies also conduct a thorough analysis of the risks of cooperation. The benefits of partnering can evaporate unless management successfully maintains a critical balance between cooperating with competitors and protecting the company's most treasured assets and its contribution to the venture, whether that be technology, capital or marketing expertise. In fact, research for the author's 1987 report – *Competitive Alliances: How to Succeed at Cross-Regional Collaboration* – highlighted an important reason to define ventures as 'competitive alliances': companies should never forget that their allies are often also their competitors (Business International, 1987).

Alliance planners should consider some of the following questions to identify trouble spots, assess whether the benefits of cooperation outweigh the costs and map out strategies to minimize the risks:

- Is the partner a direct competitor, and if so in what markets?
- How critical is the venture to the partner's long-term business strategy, and how much does it need the venture to meet strategic and tactical objectives?

- What are the bargaining chips that can inhibit an ally from extracting valuable contributions from the venture?
- What is the partner's track record on cooperation?
- What measures have been taken to protect a contribution, whether it be technology, capital or marketing expertise?
- How will management govern information flows?
- How much protection is provided for the technology under patents?
- What other protection mechanisms are in place besides broad-scope patents, which are not an effective deterrent under many countries' intellectual property laws?
- Has the company considered a strategy of filing a patent but then regularly supplementing the application with additional information, so that it never actually gets published and reaches the public domain?
- What measures are available to protect know-how, which is perhaps the most valuable yet most difficult contribution to safeguard?

Analyse human resources' needs

As part of the planning process, alliance partners need to seriously study the human resource needs and requirements of the alliance. As a general rule, companies spend 90% of their time structuring the alliance and only 10% on human resources and management issues. Yet according to alliance executives, failure to adequately plan for human resources can doom a venture before it starts. A Coopers & Lybrand/Yankelovich, Skelly and White Inc. (1985) study of some 38 ventures confirms the common wisdom: of the 100–5000 hours involved in the creation of an alliance, only 8% of the time was spent on setting up management systems and a scant 4% on resolving human resource issues.

With the benefit of hindsight, many executives said serious consideration needs to be devoted to these questions:

- How will alliance managers be chosen? Should the alliance rely on internal resources or use outside personnel?
- How will the partners divide senior management responsibilities?
- How will contact points be set up within each partner?
- How will JV–parent relations be handled?
- What guidelines for management and staffing have been set?
- How can management dispel staff resistance to JV transfers? What happens to seniority, benefits and pension rights?
- Should the parents provide job and re-entry guarantees to venture employees in the event the alliance fails?

Integrate reaction from governments or competition

On a final note, planners need to consider how the responses of governments and/or competitors will impact the alliance strategy and structure. Alliances can often alter the competitive landscape of a company or industry, thus triggering a strong reaction from either competitors or governments. This response can affect the goals, strategy and structure of the alliance. For instance, French Prime Minister Edith Cresson made no secret of her fears and criticisms of the Japanese. In fact, her sentiments played a prominent role in negotiations reported in July 1991 for an equity swap between French-government-owned computer manufacturer, Bull, and NEC of Japan. The partners in this venture wanted to transfer NEC's 15% stake in Bull HN, a US unit formed by Bull, Honeywell and NEC in 1987, into a direct minority equity holding in Groupe Bull, but the French government was apparently wary of the deal. Madame Cresson wanted to restrict the link, emphasizing that such an agreement should not restrict Bull's chances of attracting other partners, particularly other European firms. In the end the deal went through, with NEC's share limited to 4.7%. The government also added a last-minute clause that gives it the right to buy NEC's shares.

Similarly, GE and FANUC had to renegotiate their joint-venture contract because of a change in government policies. As Don Dancer, senior vice-president at GE Fanuc Automation Inc., has explained, 'Originally, we planned to manufacture one of the venture's principal offerings – the computerized numerical control (CNC) products – in Japan. However, after we reached our agreement, the US government concluded a deal with Japan's MITI outlining a voluntary restraint agreement (VRA) on all Japanese machine tools entering the US. Since the CNC is classified as a machine tool, the VRA threw a wrench into our manufacturing strategy. We reconvened and renegotiated a new manufacturing plan which relies more heavily on manufacturing the products in the US.'

Checklist

Creating an alliance is much easier when management develops a comprehensive game plan in advance. Crafting a clear plan of action in advance can streamline the negotiations process and help to identify and resolve potential problem areas. Companies should consider the following elements when getting ready for cooperation:

- Identify who are the planners;
- Test for internal support for the venture;
- Uncover who is opposed to the deal and why;
- Do not make premature promises with early letters of intent;
- Map out a list of musts and wants for the venture;
- Plan, plan and plan some more. You can never finish your homework.
- Iron out structural and procedural issues;
- Identify potential trouble spots to minimize the risks of collaborating with competitors;
- Assess human resource needs for the alliance;
- Factor competitors' and/or government reactions into the alliance equation.

References

Business International (1987). *Competitive Alliances: How to Succeed at Cross-Regional Collaboration.* July, p. 114

Coopers & Lybrand/Yankelovich, Skelly and White Inc. (1985). *Collaborative Ventures: A Pragmatic Approach to Business Expansion in the Eighties.* p. 5

5

Negotiating strategies for alliance partners

Negotiating an alliance can be a real quagmire. Selecting the right negotiating team is one of the most important elements in creating a workable alliance – and one of the most controversial. Qualified negotiators must be able to effectively convey what their companies expect to achieve from the alliance, the plans for structuring and managing the alliance, the value of the contributions each partner brings to the table and useful solutions to potential problem areas. Good negotiators also need to be aware of the culturally rooted negotiating styles of the parties. This is equally true for long-standing multiproject alliances and for first-time partners. Negotiations are never easy, but they become much less so when the discussions involve partners from diverse cultures and backgrounds.

The executives interviewed for this book had radically different views regarding who makes the best negotiator and what roles senior management, functional experts and the future alliance managers should play in the negotiations. Many companies say that senior management involvement – at the CEO or chairman level – is critical to successful alliance building and to the long-term health of the venture. CEO participation not only highlights a company's commitment to the venture, it also can break deadlocks that arise during the discussions.

Dr John Kelly, an IBM executive responsible for managing the IBM–Siemens–Toshiba chip alliance, emphasizes the importance of top management involvement. According to Kelly, 'One or more senior executives, usually the division president, is involved in the discussions.'

In fact, senior management support continues throughout the entire negotiating process. Adds Kelly, 'During the negotiations, lots of reasons for not doing the deal crop up. There has to be someone involved from senior management with the vision and long-term strategic focus to keep the discussions going.'

Assembling the negotiating team

The perils of a top-down strategy

None the less, many alliance practitioners caution against relying too heavily on top-management involvement, which is frequently referred to as the 'top-down' approach. When relations among the CEOs are quite amiable, for example, rather than ruin the congenial atmosphere, some CEOs will avoid discussing any potential conflicts and presume that the alliance managers will resolve them.

Of course, this is a dangerous assumption; the conflicts may prove insoluble, in which case the partners should never have entered the arrangement. Senior officials may fail to make a sufficiently detailed analysis of the basic technologies, markets and/or services under discussion. According to an executive with a US manufacturer of heavy machinery, alliances are sometimes created by cool handshake deals among chief executives and other powerful people in the corporations. In some instances, these deals turn out to be great successes. Obviously, however, the approach is terribly risky.

A former Siemens executive and Munich-based consultant recalled a broad-based cooperative agreement that was concluded between the top management of Siemens and US-based Texas Instruments: 'One of the problems of such broad-based, "top-down" agreements stems from the department manager who is charged with the day-to-day execution of the agreements. In a broad agreement, such a manager is not always the one who receives all the benefits of the arrangement. Moreover, in US companies, where a division manager is under pressure to satisfy quarterly profit obligations, he may be reluctant to spend time and resources on a venture in which the immediate and tangible results for his own bottom line are not obvious. Consequently, he does not devote enough effort to the venture, which can seriously hamper the success of the alliance.'

Two-track negotiating

One successful strategy for most MNCs is to have two levels of negotiations. On one level, senior executives meet to define the general goals, levels and form of cooperation. The negotiations concern broad strategy and whether the partners not only want to but *can* work together. At the second tier, operational managers and functional experts gather to thrash out the details of the contract – its structure, partner contributions, management, and so on. Some companies feel that at the second level it is a good idea to include executives who are experienced with negotiating and managing partnerships. Both groups continue their separate discussions to the conclusion; senior officers direct working groups, working groups feed information to senior officers, senior officers provide continued strategic direction.

Within the second group, having the divisional or department managers involved in the negotiations is one way to avoid problems with the 'not-invented-here' syndrome. Department managers can be unenthusiastic about partnerships, but they are particularly resentful when the responsibility is simply foisted on them. However, when executives give operational managers a role in the decision-making process, they feel that management values not only their judgement but also the work of their division.

One US manufacturer of heavy equipment typically follows a double-track strategy. At the senior management level, the CEOs meet and informally discuss the proposed collaboration venture. The actual details of the alliance are worked out by a Company A team of about six legal, financial and technical experts at a separate meeting. After each meeting, the Company A team will provide the CEO with a status report. This is particularly useful when the negotiations reach a deadlock. The CEO can frequently broach the subject when he next meets with his counterpart.

Siemens, Toshiba and IBM followed a similar strategy when they negotiated an R&D alliance to develop the 256-megabit DRAM chip. First, senior executives at the three companies met and agreed on the principal objectives of the alliance contract. The three partners then organized a team to address many structural and managerial issues. Engineers and lower-level managers from each partner formed a single team to iron out the specifics of the development project, such as how to organize the engineers into different teams, map out the work schedule and set milestones and interim goals for the project.

For six months, the team held 'working meetings' in Japan, Germany and the US to develop the business plan. According to Dr John Kelly, an

IBM executive responsible for managing the 256-megabit project, 'While a company alone does not use six months for upfront planning, the time is not wasted. These "working meetings" are extremely productive. The team designs exactly how they want to organize and manage the project. And since the ideas and strategy are their own, they "go like hell" to make the project work. Consequently, you quickly recoup those six months.'

One US executive added a bitter caveat – 'Be sure that the negotiations are not run by "fast-track yuppies". A young executive on the fast track will only be interested in the glory of signing the deal. He is not too concerned with the humdrum of figuring out how the venture will be managed and operated since once the contract is signed, he may be off looking for some new reward or job.'

Other executives caution against overdependence on culturally astute negotiators. Based on experience acquired while negotiating a US–Mexican–UK partnership, an executive with the US firm cautions against overrelying on so-called cultural experts. He explained that 'as a Mexican national, I was asked by senior management at the US firm to participate in the tripartite negotiations. The experience revealed to me the potentially powerful position of the cultural negotiator. Many members of the negotiating team look to you for advice, and it is easy for that power to go to your head. Yet you have to remember that ultimately the other members of the negotiating team will have to manage and live with the deal. You will not be around to interpret different cultural or language nuances. They need to start building a relationship immediately with their counterparts. They have to learn how to interpret different language and cultural signals. Hence, while I think a cultural adviser is useful, it is important for this person to try to step back as soon as possible.'

Should alliance managers be negotiators?

Companies differ over whether future alliance managers should also be alliance negotiators. In the alliance activities of ICL, Fujitsu, Westinghouse, Glaxo, Tanabe, Philips, Montedison and Hercules, the companies usually bring their alliance executives to the negotiating table. In a US–Italian venture, many of the seven executives responsible for strategic planning and management were placed at the helm specifically *because* of the role they played in creating the venture.

Some companies believe the alliance managers' participation helps to lay the groundwork for success for several reasons:

- It provides the executives with an opportunity to see whether they are compatible with their potential partners. If they do not like each other, the deal can easily sour.
- It provides continuity. A venture manager involved in structuring the deal will be aware of its objectives, its limitations, and the partner's strengths and weaknesses.

- The expertise of the individuals who will manage the venture can be valuable to the structuring of a workable contract.
- A venture manager who takes part in creating the alliance is more apt to be committed to its success (and feel more assured of it) than one who has had the responsibility thrust upon him.
- Of all potential negotiators, the executive who has to produce results is least likely to forget operational realities and managerial necessities in the excitement of dealmaking.

Other firms take a different view. Several companies prefer to exclude alliance managers from the negotiations entirely, citing the following risks:

- A good alliance manager is not necessarily a skilled negotiator.
- The future venture managers may be put in an ambiguous position since they are forced to wear two hats. On the one hand, they ardently negotiate and haggle over the contract to secure an advantageous agreement for the company. On the other hand, the alliance executives want to establish a rapport with their future colleagues. Some MNCs fear that the venture's managers may inadvertently compromise the company's interests in order to establish a good working relationship with the partner.
- Negotiations can be heated and highly politicized. The future alliance manager could become biased against individuals on the other side or resent some of the compromises reached, which could jeopardize the smooth functioning of the alliance.

A few MNCs opt for the middle road. These companies have alliance managers enter the negotiations at a later stage, after most sensitive issues and problems have been ironed out. According to one US executive, 'We agree that having venture managers on the team can help to ensure a smooth transition from negotiations to executing the contract and operating the venture. However, venture managers should be brought in toward the end of negotiations, after all key issues have been hammered out.' The only problem, however, is that negotiations rarely follow as planned, and it is difficult to find the most opportune moment for alliance executives to join the negotiating table.

Making sure all the key players are at the table

In addition to weighing the pros and cons of including alliance managers, several companies offered the following suggestions to help firms boost the bargaining strengths and capabilities of their core negotiating team. Companies may also want to run through some basic but critical questions (see Box 5.1).

Box 5.1 Choosing a negotiating team: crucial questions

When deciding the controversial questions of who to bring to the negotiating table, and who leads the negotiations, companies should ask themselves the following questions:

- Who will serve as the chief negotiators? Why did you select these individuals?
- Will the executives who will eventually manage the alliance participate in the negotiations? Should you bring them in from the start or wait until the most critical and sensitive issues have been resolved? When is the best time to introduce the alliance managers to the negotiating table? If you are excluding the alliance managers from the discussions, are the negotiators carefully briefing them on all issues and seeking their input?
- What is the best role for top management in negotiations? Do you have the support and commitment of top-level executives to the alliance? Has this been demonstrated to your partner and also to the chief architects/negotiators of the deal within your company?
- How sensitive are the negotiators to the national and corporate cultures of your partners? How extensive are the experiences and knowledge of the negotiators regarding the partner and the region?
- Have you included line managers in the negotiations? What about the functional and technical experts? If not, have you made some provisions to incorporate their inputs?
- If you are excluding alliance and line managers, what early steps can you take to avoid antagonisms that could endanger the alliance?

First, management needs to cull a multifunctional team. While each alliance has its own unique needs in terms of negotiators, companies must at least start with a multifunctional team to cover all of the basics. Executives identified the following individuals when organizing a negotiating team:

- A business or divisional head
- A member of the future management team for the venture
- A technical adviser
- A marketing expert
- A legal expert

- A regional or country liaison/translator
- A financial analyst
- An environmental compliance/control expert
- A human resources adviser
- A manufacturing expert
- An engineer.

Second, management needs to check whether both local and corporate headquarters input is needed. When and if necessary, bring in negotiators from corporate headquarters. Many companies, such as Ford, rely on their different regional operations to handle negotiations directly. As Paul Drenkow, a Ford executive closely involved in the Ford–Mazda alliance explains, 'Since the local operations will have to live with the deal, it is best that they negotiate the contract.' There are exceptions. For example, Ford's Asia-Pacific operation primarily handles negotiations and relationships with such Asian partners as Mazda. However, when a particular project with a partner such as Mazda has implications beyond Asia, a North American corporate headquarters team often will manage the negotiations, receiving input from all appropriate divisions.

Setting the ground rules for table tactics

Once companies have identified the suitable negotiators for a deal, the executives should be well prepared to sit down and flesh out an agreement. Every alliance is a challenge, and that is never more apparent than at the negotiating stage, where personalities can be more important than business categories. Nevertheless, interviews with companies suggest guidelines for alliance negotiators. The following points suggest a judicious blend of trust and scepticism that alliance negotiators have to bring to the table:

Enter negotiations with strategy in place

Has the company established what strategic need the alliance is supposed to satisfy? What business assets does it seek to capture from the alliance? During the discussions, negotiators need to undertake a constant review of the venture's viability. Is the company truly convinced that the alliance makes business sense?

Know your bargaining strengths – and your partner's

Companies must clearly understand the bargaining strengths that each party brings to the table and what is important to each. This helps negotiators know where and when they can push for concessions and where they are likely to have to compromise. A firm's bargaining power is determined by its strengths and weaknesses; its need for the alliance and its partner's resources; any alternative strategies available to the firm; the benefits it expects to derive from the venture; the costs of cooperation; and the internal and external barriers to collaboration. If the company has done a thorough preparation, its negotiators will be well informed about their potential partners.

Don't be too ambitious in disclosing information

Negotiations release information, about products, markets, and strategy, and it may be that this is all your negotiating partner wants. Companies should always be aware that negotiating may be as far as the 'partner' wants to go in this relationship.

When negotiating with a potential partner, do not lay all of your cards on the table immediately, since you are not sure if the negotiations will be successful. You do not want to risk disclosing too much information, particularly if you are dealing with a competitor. This is particularly true when proprietary technology, skills and/or know-how is involved. (See Box 5.2 on protection pointers.)

According to one European executive, 'Generally speaking, for the first meeting, we put together a corporate profile and present reasons on where and how there might be synergies between the companies. Typically, the information for these first presentations is rather generic, such as product and company brochures that are already in the public domain. Thereafter, if continued interest in collaboration is ascertained, the negotiators will provide additional data at each subsequent meeting.'

Write a press statement together

Midway through the negotiations, partners should jointly write a press release on what the alliance aims to accomplish and how. Even though the partners will not release this press statement until all negotiations are finalized, this simple exercise can reveal whether all the partners in fact do agree on the basic goals and objectives of the partnership. Many companies fail to take this elementary precaution of having all prospective partners repeat to each other – in their own words – their understanding of the proposed alliance. Yet this simple task can save a lot of time and trouble.

Don't make commitments you cannot keep

A negotiator for a Canadian institution offers the following advice: 'Pay attention to the political realities of living up to commitments. Any alliance involves a balance of mutual concessions. Therefore, each side is relying on the ability and willingness of the other side to deliver on its part of the deal. Do not ask for more and do not offer more than you can realistically deliver.'

Take a hard look at your partner at every step

After each meeting one needs to ask, 'Based on what I learned today, do I want to continue the negotiations? Am I interested enough to provide additional data? Do I want to work with this company? Can I work with this company? Do I want to marry them?' Depending on the responses to these questions, one decides whether to continue or sever the negotiations.

Be ready and willing to walk away

Most executives agree that if trouble already starts brewing in the negotiations, companies should quit while they are ahead. For instance, analysts point to the troubles that beleaguered an alliance between Swedish–Swiss Asea Brown Boveri (ABB) and Finmeccanica of Italy. One year after a 1989 news report alluded to difficulties in negotiating and structuring a contract, the partners had locked horns over whether to dissolve their joint venture. Court battles and bitterness surrounded the relationship. In a June 1990 news article, Fabiano Fabiani, Finmeccanica's president, remarked, 'How can you have a marriage when one partner has to go to court to make the other honour its commitments?' Another Finmeccanica executive bitterly added of ABB that 'they have treated Italy like a banana republic'.

As one Canadian expert concludes, 'Above all, never place too much faith in a dispute settlement process to resolve future hurdles. One must always be ready to walk away from the negotiating table if the deal is not working out. Do not go in with preconceived notions that an agreement is essential. Parent companies would rather see no agreement than one that contains provisions that are unacceptable to headquarters.'

Box 5.2 Protection pointers for negotiators

The benefits of a competitive alliance can evaporate unless negotiators ensure that the company's most treasured technology and know-how are not dangerously compromised. Consider the following tips on how negotiators can fine-tune their skills on protecting assets:

continues

continued

Detect early warning signals

From the start, having a forthright discussion of each partner's strategic objectives, plus why and how the venture should help each company achieve these long-term goals, is a useful strategy for exposing high-risk deals. Joel Marcus, partner at Los Angeles-based Brobeck, Phleger and Harrison, has said that such discussions usually help uncover any hidden agendas and enable the company to promptly sever negotiations before losing valuable technology and corporate assets to an ill-conceived alliance. Marcus reckoned that approximately 25% to 30% of all alliances have hidden agendas.

Marcus has highlighted how certain actions during the early stages of negotiation can serve as red-flag indicators of high-risk relationships. He has advised clients to seriously reconsider going the cooperative route if a potential partner employs such tactics as making upfront demands for proprietary data, maintaining a guarded posture, being eager to outline spending plans and commitments, showing the absence of any good faith gestures, exhibiting undue pressure to close the deal quickly, and having inadequate senior management involvement up front.

Pick a partner that wants to build a long-term alliance

That is, check the track record. Having a partner with a history of fair dealings with other allies can signal that the company is likely to be an honourable ally.

Steer clear of OEM agreements

A computer manufacturer suggests companies shun straight OEM (original equipment manufacturer) agreements. This helps to alleviate a problem that has plagued other companies – when OEM suppliers turn around and compete directly with you for your customer base.

Analyse how easily skills/technology can be assimilated

Firms must select carefully what skills and technologies they plan to pass on to their venture partners. Depending on a company's contribution, the risks can vary:

'The potential for transfer is greatest when a partner's contribution is easily transported (in engineering drawings, on computer tapes, or in the heads of a few technical experts); easily intepreted (it can be reduced to commonly understood equations or symbols); and easily absorbed (the skill or competence is independent of any particular cultural context.)... There is an important distinction between technology and competence. A discrete, standalone technology (for example, the design of a semiconductor chip) is more easily transferred than a process competence, which is entwined in the social fabric of a company.' (Hamel *et al.*, 1989).

In fact, criticisms that the Japanese reap greater benefits in ventures than Western partners is often because the latter are trying to adopt new

continues

> *continued*
>
> process technologies. Adds Dr C. K. Pralahad, professor of business at
> the University of Michigan, 'Absorbing a Japanese partner's quality and
> inventory strategies mandates tremendous dedication and commitment
> from management. It also requires a willingness to change among
> employees, which unfortunately many US firms find difficult to do.'
>
> ### Investigate senior management support
>
> From the onset of discussions, negotiators need to verify senior
> management commitment and support for the deal. Marcus recalls
> mishaps in a recent US–Japanese venture. Project teams from both
> partners had worked diligently together to prepare the business plan
> and iron out the details of the contract, the procedures for technology
> transfer and various management/organizational issues. Then senior
> management at the Japanese firm refused to approve the deal. The US
> team later discovered that this rejection had been part of their agenda
> all along. By the time the working groups had finished, substantial infor-
> mation had already been traded. After a significant loss of valuable
> know-how, the US partner had already invested substantial time and
> money in the proposed venture. The firm believed it had no other choice
> than to proceed, but its bargaining strength and position had eroded. In
> hindsight, Marcus has advised other potential alliance seekers to ensure
> that this critical top management commitment is there in advance.
>
> MNCs should pursue several communication avenues to their
> potential partner's top management echelon, to verify their support for
> the deal. For instance, in another US–Japanese alliance Marcus said the
> US firm acquired the names of all the board members of the Japanese
> entity. The US company then developed relations and communications
> with various of those members, to test the viability of the venture.

Who takes the bull by the horns?

Finally, companies face a critical issue: determining how much decision-
making power to give negotiators. The degree of latitude given the team
varies widely, depending on the company's culture and structure and the
makeup of the negotiating group. It is very possible that the negotiating
powers given the different partners' teams will not be equal; all sides need
to be aware of this, particularly in a cross-cultural negotiation.

Some MNCs restrict the decision-making power of the negotiators to
reduce the risk that the discussion leaders may inadvertently compromise
the company's position. Other companies have two different teams
involved in the alliance structuring process. For example, one MNC has
an executive committee that appoints the negotiating team and also
wields the final decision-making power over any agreements. Said one
senior executive, 'We do not believe that our company can get what it

wants if the negotiators can agree on the spot to partners' requests.' The negotiating team may feel pressured to break any deadlock in the discussions by relaxing or compromising their position and, as the executive remarked, 'We do not want them to have this power.'

Checklist

Interpersonal dynamics among alliance negotiators can have an important influence over the future management of the venture. How firms handle the negotiations; who leads the discussions and what bargaining tactics are used can shape the future relationships and interactions among partners and alliance executives. When designing an alliance negotiating strategy, companies should consider the following issues:

- Appoint a chief negotiator. Agree in advance on how much decision-making power the chief negotiator wields.
- Map out a negotiating strategy in advance. Does your approach reflect your alliance needs and goals?
- Make sure all interested parties are represented on the negotiating team. Having a broad-based group – including all appropriate functional and technical experts – builds strength and boosts confidence.
- Include regional and cultural experts in the discussions. Their ability to interpret signals from partners is valuable. Otherwise, you may not be sure whether you are agreeing or disagreeing with your potential partners over key issues.
- Weigh the pros and cons of including the executives who will eventually manage the alliance in the negotiations.
- Seek the involvement of top management in the discussions. While senior executives may not necessarily get involved in the fine details of the contract, their visible support and commitment to the negotiations sends a strong message to your potential partners.
- At each stage in the discussions, adequately assess you and your partners' bargaining strengths and weaknesses. In what areas can you push for concessions and why?
- Review what information you are willing to disclose.
- Understand the maximum and minimum levels of commitments – in capital, resources, technology, and so on – you have the power to make.

- Remember to take a hard look at your partner at every step of the negotiations.
- Always be ready and willing to walk away if negotiations do not go as planned.

Reference

Hamel G., Doz Y.L. and Pralahad C.K. (1989). Collaborate with your competitors – and win. *Harvard Business Review*, Jan.–Feb. 1989. Copyright 1988 by the President and Fellows of Harvard College, p. 136

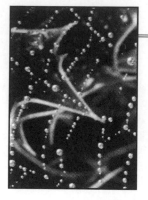

6

Structure the agreement

Once a company has defined its own goals, adequately evaluated its partners and mapped out a basic negotiating strategy, management is ready to sit at the table and create a profitable accord. One executive advised, 'Identify and address as many tough and sensitive issues as possible when structuring the contract. It is an illusion to think you can shove the unpleasant issues under the rug or that with time the potential problems will work themselves out. The issues can swell into insurmountable problems that eventually force a messy divorce.' This chapter offers alliance strategists some ideas and approaches on how to craft a workable alliance. The concluding section provides companies with a technique for making one final but vital evaluation – the acid test – before sealing the deal.

The ten commandments for structuring an agreement

There is no single recipe for a successful alliance. However, interviews with many companies revealed a remarkably consistent set of ten basic commandments for negotiators to consider when structuring an alliance accord.

(1)   Outline a tight focus for the alliance

Executives agree that a well-defined, well-focused agreement is essential
to the success of the alliance and will serve to safeguard the interests of
the parents. Problems and failures in alliances can often be traced to
poorly designed arrangements that do not clearly delineate the objectives
and scope of cooperation nor spell out how the venture will exploit
the partners' complementary strengths. A tightly focused contract can
also add a measure of protection since it can reduce the risk that trade
secrets and technology will migrate to your partner/competitor (see
Box 6.1).

Jean Bilien, president of CFM International, a 50–50 joint venture
between General Electric of the US and French-based Snecma, has said
that you must clearly spell out the objectives and scope of the operation.
As he noted, 'The easiest way to get into mischief is to draft loose ambitions. If the two partners are competitors, the venture may start moving
into areas that compete with either partner's separate operations, creating havoc and tension.'

In retrospect, it appears that a loosely structured agreement was one
of the reasons for the failure of one US–European JV in consumer goods.
The companies had planned to combine their European outlets into a
single network that could jointly market their products. Company A was
eager to have Company B's sophisticated and popular products to complement its own more basic line. Company B was interested in tapping its
partner's significant retail market presence. Despite their complementary
objectives and product lines, the venture swiftly collapsed. The partners
failed to address key operating details of the venture – namely how their
respective distribution and marketing outlets would cooperate and how
pricing, promotion and compensation decisions would be made.
Consequently, the two marketing chains continued to compete head-on
in the market.

(2)   Set up a specific structure for a specific alliance

At a minimum, negotiators need to cover all the basics regarding the
legal and management structure of the partnership. The contract should
address key issues such as:

- What legal structure best suits the partners' goals and strategy?
- Will the partners use a joint venture, cross-equity shareholdings or
  functional agreements?
- What are the tax consequences of the legal and financial structure
  selected for the alliance?
- What types of decisions need unanimous approval from all partners?
- What decisions can the alliance managers take independently?
- How will deadlocks be handled?
- How will the officers of the alliance be selected?

- How frequently will the executives rotate?
- What types of benefits and compensation plans have been arranged?
- How will management resolve conflicts?
- What is the common language among the employees in the alliance?
- Have you outlined a structure to manage any exchanges of information?
- How will you record information flows?

(3)   Address financing and tax considerations

Financing and tax concerns can exacerbate the already complex issue of trying to structure an alliance. For example, how should partners establish reasonable debt/equity ratios, cope with currency fluctuations, assess government incentives, and so on? The venture's capital needs and sources of funds (partner contributions, debt, equity, government incentives) must be carefully outlined. With all financing issues, management also needs to weigh the effects of national tax regimes. Regarding debt-to-equity ratios, companies generally like to keep the ratio around the 50:50 mark. However, in countries that offer attractive incentives such as zero interest loans, some companies do allow the ratio to reach 70:30. Partners also need to investigate different government incentives (tax holidays, grants, training stipends, and so on)

Based on experience, a treasurer at a US company noted, 'Mapping out the venture's financing strategy can be tricky: each partner is usually required to raise his proportionate share of capital. But if one company can normally raise money more cheaply than its partner, it can lead to funding inefficiencies.' Negotiators must closely evaluate the availability and liquidity of the foreign currencies needed to finance the venture. If, for instance, a desired currency is in undersupply, it may thwart the partners' ability to proceed with the alliance.

A vice-president for finance at a US auto parts supplier says that financing was one serious short-term difficulty in his company's Korean-based JV with a Japanese partner and a local Korean company in the mid-1980s. Each partner had to line up a proportionate share of local currency for financing the debt portion of the $43 million of initial capital. Given a serious shortage of Korean won at the time, obtaining the US firm's share 'required some creative financing'.

Yet another strain on the venture can develop because of different priorities in exposure management. Volatility in the markets forced one capital goods manufacturer to buy out all of its alliance partners because it needed to centralize control over its exposure management. 'Prior to that, we let the operations' managers manage their own exposures', said the firm's assistant treasurer. 'We wanted to maximize dollar income; our partner wanted to maximize French franc income. How could we impose our will on them?'

Finally, alliance partners from different business cultures also can disagree on the basic substances of financial management – accounting practices, budgeting and financial reporting. How will partners reconcile differences between the accounting methods and procedures of the alliance and those of the parent corporations? From the interviews conducted, it is clearly necessary for alliance-makers to ensure that the agreement includes specific provisions that outline the venture's financial and accounting structures and designate the partner responsible for controlling the system.

(4)   Provide a scorecard for dividends and intercompany transactions

Determining equitable transfer pricing and earnings formulas is critical. As Howard Hill, a Detroit-based lawyer, advised, 'Keep a close scorecard on all transactions. There are at least 50 different ways to get money out of a venture, with dividends often the last option. By the time some partners slap on all the intercompany transactions for goods and services, there is no money left for dividends.' For instance, he recalled how Mitsubishi Motors Corp. wanted to use a Japanese-based construction firm to build the Diamond Star Motors plant, even though there were several US construction firms within close proximity that were familiar with US regulations.

Therefore, step-by-step a firm needs to identify all potential cash leaks – who is getting reimbursed for services such as legal, accounting, financial and insurance; who are the building and engineering contractors for a new facility; what raw materials and components are being supplied to the venture from other partner-owned or related operations; who are the shippers and freight forwarders, the distributors and suppliers of marketing support and other services, and so on. Thereafter, earnings formulas need to incorporate a number of factors: Does either partner have a specific minimum rate of return in mind? Is that acceptable or similar to what the other partner expects? How is it measured – before or after taxes? On gross or net assets? What percentage of earnings should be distributed and how will it be distributed?

(5)   Putting a price tag on asset contributions

A quantitative and qualitative evaluation of asset contributions is a number-one priority. The value of each partner's input has a decided influence on how the venture is structured and managed. In the case of a separate joint venture entity, each company's contribution to the venture is a key determinant behind structuring the equity-ownership split. This includes an accurate valuation of a partner's hard and soft inputs. Some have made the mistake of neglecting the importance of sizing up soft inputs – name, reputation and expertise in managing global operations.

However, these factors can significantly boost the venture and potentially reduce the amount of additional capital a company must contribute to the venture.

One of the most important yet difficult assets for alliance makers to price is intellectual property – technology, trademarks, copyrights and know-how. For example, Japan-based Fujitsu frequently provides a unique technology and/or know-how to its different alliance partners. In negotiating the contracts, Fujitsu faces the arduous task of determining the value of its technologies. The job is often further complicated by the fact that some of the know-how is yet to be developed. According to Michio Naruto, director of global markets at Fujitsu, 'Calculating the price of intellectual property is almost impossible. I essentially base the price of our technology on opportunity costs. For instance, in one of Fujitsu's projects with ICL in the mid-1980s, I made the assumption that about 200 Fujitsu engineers were involved in the three-year computer project with ICL. I then calculated what the profit potential would be. I used this figure as a benchmark for setting the price of our technology to ICL.'

Equations for pricing intellectual property should also consider local and foreign tax costs of transferring know-how and technology. What are the tax consequences of different strategies? For instance, should the intangible(s) be licensed to the foreign venture or transferred outright by way of a sale or contribution to capital? Is it preferable or required by local laws to have any intellectual property included as part of a partner's equity contribution to the venture?

(6)   Reciprocity reigns: tally contributions and benefits

After all the cards are laid on the table – assets, technology, know-how, and so on – negotiators then need to ensure that the deal is fair. For the health of the alliance, both the resources each partner contributes and the benefits each receives should be balanced. If one partner feels cheated, the venture is on very shaky ground. Consequently, in drawing up the contract, have you carefully evaluated your contributions *vis-à-vis* your partner's? Are they fairly equal? If not, what concessions are you seeking? Have you weighed the benefits against the costs of cooperation? Is the arrangement fair and equitable?

David Dace, recently retired director for collaboration at ICL, insists that 'Mutual benefit is fundamental. Partners must recognize that they have to give something to get something. It is not a one-way street. Too many firms enter alliances with preconceived notions that they can gain access to their partner's technology, products, engineering, and so on yet give nothing in return.'

A major ingredient in a Japanese–US alliance is an acknowledged principle that the two companies do not do anything together that does not result in clearly mutual benefits. Both parties must realize economic and other advantages or, says a senior US executive, 'You're going to have trouble maintaining interest and commitment to the venture on both sides.'

When Siemens and Intel set up their microprocessor alliance, they used a 'device-by-device' negotiating strategy to ensure that the deal would be balanced. Siemens used Intel as a second source for three Siemens peripheral chips. According to the corporate vice-president formerly in charge of the Intel relationship, 'Every time you exchange something, you look at it and say, "What do you give me?" and "What do I give you?", then you put them on a scale to see if they are equivalent.'

(7) Include provisions for substantial changes

Hill suggested that contracts include a 'substantial changes' provision. This would require partners to renegotiate the deal when unforeseen developments in the business environment occur that severely affect the venture. For instance, the Chrysler and Mitsubishi negotiators for Diamond Star Motors (DSM) were worried about fluctuations in the yen/dollar exchange rate. (DSM was first established in 1986 as a 50–50 JV. In November 1991, Mitsubishi assumed 100% equity control of DSM but retained important marketing and supplier pacts with Chrysler.) In the original discussions, DSM negotiators planned to source engines and transmissions for the venture's vehicles from Japan. However, plans backfired when the yen/dollar exchange rate moved from Y250:$1 to Y130:$1. The existence of a 'substantial changes' clause in the DSM contract provided the parties with the means to meet and arrange a different solution. In fact, sourcing of the engines and transmissions was moved from Japan to the US.

(8) Consider an 'until death do us part' clause

Hill suggested that MNCs may want to include a clause in which the partners agree to give the alliance at least five years. This helps give the venture a sense of permanence and mission that can affect how each partner views the venture. As Hill advises, 'The partners should make a firm commitment to each other. Include a condition in which there are no grounds for termination of the venture – short of murder – before five years have passed.'

(9) Structure a deadly divorce clause

According to attorneys, no company should go blindly into an alliance. A firm, along with its legal counsel, would be either naive or stupid if they did not prepare for a divorce. Alternative scenarios and action plans must be ready well in advance. Tim Leuliette, president and CEO of ITT Automotive, agreed, adding that 'Divorce clauses are a good and necessary evil of any contract. Nonetheless, I think firms should make them as painful as possible. You should not make it easy for one or more partners to withdraw from the alliance. By making a divorce as painful as possible, this will force the partners to come to agreement on tough issues once the venture is running. It also helps to actually diminish the number of conflicts, because no one wants to deal with a divorce.'

Companies should try to pinpoint problems or scenarios that could invite divorce proceedings. The exercise can produce unintended benefits. Partners are aware of the risks of separation and strive to avoid them. Other divorce issues to consider include an analysis to assess and determine the valuation of assets – both those that are individually and jointly owned – up front. The values set in the beginning may be more accurate and less emotionally charged than if the partners wait until they split. Yet even when partners must negotiate asset transfers at the time of separation, firms should, Hill urged, handle asset transactions on their own. Relying on a third party to do so invites more trouble and leads to weaker results. As Hill said, 'Outside attorneys tend to value assets on a "fire sale" basis. The figures may not reflect the true value of the assets. Or if attorneys are called in, at least make sure that the partners specify that the venture should be valued as an ongoing concern.'

(10) Do not neglect child support

In the event of a separation or the premature withdrawal of one partner, the contract should spell out how the venture or alliance can continue to operate. Parent companies may need to provide comfort letters or guarantees in the aftermath of a divorce. This step should help ensure that a former joint venture can still stay afloat and gain access to valuable financing, if necessary. In some cases, partners may supply valuable components to a venture. When firms then decide to part ways, management must outline agreements for a continued flow of critical supplies and components. As Howard Hill saw it, 'A company cannot automatically shut off the supply tap because it is unhappy with the relationship. In my experiences, ex-partners pledge to continue the flow of components for transition periods between two and five years.'

When Westinghouse withdrew from its 50–50 venture with Mitsubishi in high-voltage circuit breakers, it offered both financial and nonfinancial support. Roger Barna, president of the new 100% Mitsubishi-owned entity, said that indeed 'Westinghouse's commitment to provide full support made the divorce considerably less painful and more amicable.' One of Mitsubishi's greatest fears had concerned how the US market would react to the new 100% Japanese entity. And the former venture had relied heavily on Westinghouse's extensive network of salesmen, marketing experts and corporate representatives to win sales. Mitsubishi wondered how they would reach the market without the Westinghouse distribution and marketing channels. As part of the divorce, Mitsubishi gradually scaled back its reliance on Westinghouse's marketing resources as the Japanese subsidiary built its own independent network. During the transitional phase, Mitsubishi Power Products established three regional offices – in Los Angeles, Houston and Charlotte – to supplement its activities from the company's Pittsburgh headquarters. In addition, its management acquired an independent sales network of 26 representatives located throughout the US and Canada. Mitsubishi also implemented a novel advertising strategy to ease market reaction to the change in ownership, a unique advertising and marketing campaign that intriguingly tracked its evolution from a Westinghouse–Mitsubishi venture to a Mitsubishi company.

Box 6.1   Four pillars for structuring an airtight deal

Interviews with executives and legal experts identified four key pillars for the contract to alleviate the inherent dangers of cooperating with a competitor:

Pillar 1: Agree on self-policing mechanism

In addition to having a well-defined, narrowly focused agreement, organize a schedule on how partners can routinely monitor progress and developments in the alliance. For instance, the contract should specify periodic checks to ensure that the venture is on target toward meeting its stated objectives.

Pillar 2: Create a separate standalone entity

Use of a separate company for cooperative ventures, particularly joint technology development endeavours, can eliminate a host of protection problems. First, it ensures that the aggregate technology and know-how contributions of each partner are legally and jointly owned by all participants. It also means that any future spinoffs or second-generation products from the cooperative endeavour are jointly owned and controlled by all the partners, via the separate legal entity.

For instance, suppose that Company A and Company B are competitors in a broad range of products but enter into a joint technology development agreement to improve the manufacturing process for product Z. Both partners contribute technology and know-how, but the research is conducted in Company A's R&D centres. Company A identifies innovative ways to use Company B's technology for new

continues

continued

applications and enhancements for many of its other products. However, unaware of this valuable discovery, not only does Company B fail to receive the appropriate licensing and financial rewards, but it inadvertently helps Company A become an even more formidable competitor. This risk may be averted by having all rights to the technology and its applications owned jointly through a separate company.

Pillar 3: Include back-licensing arrangements

Many savvy MNCs insist on having back-licensing arrangements in which the partners must license back any improvements or changes made to the original technology. For instance, Joel Marcus, partner at Los Angeles-based Brobeck, Phleger and Harrison, said that in a recent deal a US firm required back-licensing and stiff confidentiality provisions before beginning contract discussions. The confidentiality specifications stated that the US licensor had exclusive royalty-free licensing privileges on any changes or improvements to the originally licensed technology. This tactic, claimed Marcus, smokes out many fraudulent future partners.

Pillar 4: Establish benchmarks

Most discussions on protection centre on technology or marketing expertise, but partners contributing capital must also develop contingencies to hedge against risks to it. Mapping out well-defined milestones for an alliance is an effective strategy for safeguarding a venture's financial partners. For instance, Marcus represented the Kirin Brewery in a joint venture with Amgen. Amgen's contribution centred on its technology plus $4 million in cash, with Kirin providing $12 million of the $24 million aggregate value. Kirin minimized the risks to its investment by providing the capital in incremental amounts where each new contribution was contingent on Amgen's reaching certain technological milestones. This strategy, noted Marcus, also satisfied Amgen's protection needs. Under such a tight schedule, Amgen could not possibly have the time to provide all the technological details and valuable know-how behind its research to Kirin, thereby preserving Amgen's technological edge. Similarly, in technology for market access deals, have the technology partner incrementally increase its know-how and technology to an alliance only when the marketing partner achieves certain milestones in higher market share and sales.

Making a final check: the acid test

Before sealing an alliance, several executives have recommended making one final analysis of the alliance's ability to fend off adverse or changing conditions. Certainly, history has not been kind to partnerships. Some consultants believe the mortality rate may be as high as two out of three. Misreadings of the marketplace, cost overruns, and unforeseen changes in the environment or government policy are frequently cited as tragic flaws in competitive alliances. A Coopers & Lybrand/Yankelovich, Skelly and White (1985) study on 38 collaborative ventures reported the following:

- Twelve ventures met or exceeded the expectations of the partners.
- Seventeen achieved limited success but fell short of partners' expectations.
- Six either were permanently disbanded or one partner assumed responsibility for the venture.
- Three alliances were too new to categorize.

Given the rather hefty empirical evidence supporting this 'early death syndrome', executives will do well to perform some rigorous tests on a potential venture's seaworthiness. Analysts at Coopers & Lybrand (1984) recommend applying an 'acid test' to help evaluate an alliance's durability. The idea is to gather initial statistics on a venture's profitability and exaggerate the cost and operational bottlenecks according to the following:

- Discount prices by 20%;
- Increase R&D costs by 30% and development time by a year;
- Move revenue projections and related variable costs out by one year;
- Increase advertising and promotion budgets by 50%;
- Increase overheads by 50%;
- If applicable, add a year to the time necessary to secure government approvals or registration.

Now does the venture measure up to the partners' expectations? And are the companies willing to proceed in the face of rough going? Do these figures warrant a re-evaluation of the agreement's foundations?

In addition, running a scenario on the potential responses of the competition can shed some light on the probable strength and viability of your alliance. Certainly a combination of two or more MNCs in a venture can create a formidable new player in the market. Have you answered questions such as:

- How will the competition react?
- What would happen if two or more of your competitors joined forces?
- Does your alliance have the resources to withstand a competitor's counteroffensive?

The Saab-Scania–Fairchild ordeal

The collapse of the 1980 Saab-Scania–Fairchild alliance to develop, manufacture and market a new commuter aircraft is a clear example of the importance of the acid test. In the 1970s, US deregulation spawned the growth of regional airlines and consequently the demand for new commuter aircraft to service their markets. Saab and Fairchild put the 55–45 JV together to share the $100 million cost of developing a new aircraft (the SF 340) and to jointly capitalize on this market opening.

At the onset, all components for success were apparent. The partners had complementary technical skills, manufacturing capacity and market access. Using an integrated design office, they were able to roll out the prototype in October 1982. Production was split equally; Fairchild provided the wings and tail sections, and Saab was responsible for manufacturing the fuselage. Final assembly and flight tests were done in a Saab facility. In June 1984, the partners set up a jointly managed marketing centre in the UK and had regional marketing offices in the US and Sweden; the venture also created a finance company to help customers purchase the $5.6 million aircraft. By October 1984, 11 European aviation authorities as well as the US Federal Aviation Authority (FAA) had accepted the airworthiness of the new aircraft. The first delivery was made in mid-1984. By May 1985, the SF 340 was in service with six airlines in North America, Australia and Europe.

However, despite the sound mechanics of the venture, Fairchild withdrew in November 1985. It took a final $104 million write-off and paid Saab $35 million to assume 100% control of the venture. What went wrong?

- Costs had to be continually adjusted upward, largely as a result of engineering and technical changes required in order to gain FAA certification for the SF 340. Fairchild took an initial write-off of $50 million in the fourth quarter of 1984 and another $85 million in the second quarter of 1985.
- Sales took off more slowly than expected, leaving revenues far below projections. The break-even point for the SF 340 was around the 200th aircraft sold; by mid-1985, the venture had firm orders for approximately 50.
- Expectations regarding European deregulation were overly optimistic at the time.
- Competition proved more intense than anticipated; an analyst with Goldman Sachs said, 'Although the commuter industry is probably the fastest growing segment in the general aviation sector, there is considerable oversupply since there are several companies competing for business. Consequently, no one can be very successful.'
- From the start, Fairchild's commitment to the venture was less than its Swedish partner's. Saab initiated the partnership, taking 55% of the equity, and built a new facility specifically for commercial aircraft.
- Fairchild found itself in a cash crunch. Involved in two costly aircraft development projects, both of which needed further investment, the company could only afford one. It decided to stay with the more familiar (and it thought, more profitable) defence aircraft sector. Unfortunately for Fairchild, the US defence contract was cancelled.

A little 'acid test' goes a long way

Conducting an 'acid test' as described earlier would most likely have given the partners some clues about the dangers that lay ahead. By means of such an analysis, some of these problems could have been anticipated and possibly factored into the venture's strategy in order to avoid a collapse.

Checklist

Structuring an alliance accord can be a complex process. While there is no such thing as a 'standard' alliance agreement, there are a few common steps that companies can follow. The ten commandments – followed by a final check with an acid test – cover important essentials for any venture pact:

(1) Outline a tight focus for the alliance.

(2) Set up a specific structure for a specific alliance.

(3) Address financing and tax considerations.

(4) Provide a scorecard for dividends and intercompany transactions.

(5) Put a price tag on asset contributions.

(6) Reciprocity reigns: tally contributions and benefits.

(7) Include provisions for substantial changes.

(8) Consider an 'until death do us part' clause.

(9) Structure a deadly divorce clause.

(10) Do not neglect child support.

References

Coopers & Lybrand (1984). *Collaborative Ventures: An Emerging Phenomenon in the Information Industry.* p. 5

Coopers & Lybrand/Yankelovich, Skelly and White, Inc. (1985). *Collaborative Ventures: A Pragmatic Approach to Business Expansion in the Eighties.* p. 10

7

Unique challenges of joint venture entities

Equity joint ventures (JVs) remain one of the most popular – and challenging – vehicles for cooperation. There is no end to the list of pros and cons facing partners when creating a JV. Proponents argue that a new identity (achieved through the new JV entity) can be advantageous – even necessary – in new markets. JVs also tend to be more profitable than functional agreements or cross-equity shareholdings. As a separate legal entity, JVs have limited liability, offering greater protection. Plus, JVs can provide the ideal external environment for learning and testing out new skills and techniques from partners.

Opponents complain that JV start-up costs can be heavy. There is also the inevitable tension of when and how to provide the JV with the autonomy it requires. Moreover, when partners have a falling out, JVs can be more difficult to unravel. Nonetheless, despite the structural and managerial obstacles of JVs, many firms find that this type of alliance embodies the true spirit of a partnership. This chapter explores several of the unique dimensions involved in establishing a JV (Phase I), launching operations (Phase II), and building a prosperous long-term business (Phase III).

Phase I: Establishing a JV

Reassessing the equity options

Today's JVs are very different from the traditional joint ventures, which were generally between strong and weak partners. In particular, the proliferation of ties between two very powerful MNCs has forced executives to reassess the value of 50–50 JVs. Since today's alliances tend to be a pairing of equals, it is usually not possible for one powerful MNC to wrest greater control from a partner that is just as mighty. Consequently, the 50–50 form of JV has become the most popular type for many companies. Yet 50–50 deals are not without their headaches.

On the plus side, a 50–50 JV guarantees that both parties' interests are protected and forces partners to sit at the negotiating table as equals and thrash out any problems. It also serves as proof that the partners share an equal commitment to the venture. On the negative side, one US executive thought that 50–50 deals do not mesh with reality. According to him, 'Conceptually, they sound great. But in reality, JVs are playing a very important role in our global strategy. We want to be able to have control of the JV and its destiny in order to coordinate its operations with our other global activities.' Added another sceptical manager, 'Companies cannot run a business – namely a JV's activities – through a committee'.

Working around the obstacles

Nevertheless, these executives realize that they frequently have no choice but to play by the 50–50 rules. Some firms circumvent the disagreeable aspects of a 50–50 equity breakdown by advocating that overall responsibility of the JV be split 50–50, but at the same time, allowing individual partners to retain control over functions of strategic importance to them. Another way to eliminate the dangers of deadlock in decision making is to invite a third party to serve as a tie-breaker. For instance, firms may each take a 45% equity stake and offer the remaining 10% to a neutral party.

Practically speaking, many management consultants frequently recommend this option, but the method is the brunt of sharp criticism among some alliance makers. One UK executive firmly believed that tie-breakers can produce a disastrous situation. 'Suppose you and your partner each have 45% and an outsider holds the remaining 10%. Both partners would then spend their time and effort lobbying the third party – at the expense of attending to the needs of the JV.' None the less, the individual circumstances of each venture will dictate what works best, and tie-breakers should not be disregarded since they can help solve certain problems. In one of its ventures, ICI wanted a 51–49 split, taking the minority stake. However, its partner did not want the 51%, since it would have to classify the JV as a consolidated subsidiary. As a solution, ICI invited a UK financial institution to participate by taking the 2%, and the outside party was given no power to cast a deciding vote.

Checklist

Organizing the JV's structure

In terms of governance and site selection for the JV, there is a host of issues partners need to address. Depending on the location, a variety of tax and corporate formation laws must be assessed. Partners also need to agree on the JV's basic management structure – composition of board, policy-making committees, advisory groups, and so on. In most 50–50 JVs, partners contribute an equal number of directors. However, some MNCs, such as Toshiba and AT&T, have secured a higher number of board seats in some of their JVs because of their contributions to the venture. Nor can partners neglect the delicate but crucial issues of what happens when one partner wants to withdraw from the venture. Consider the following questions:

- Will the joint venture be a separate corporation, a partnership, association, interest grouping?
- Under what jurisdiction(s) will the joint venture operate?
- What is the equity breakdown among partners?
- What percentage of earnings will be distributed from the JV? How will the earnings be distributed?
- What are the laws/restrictions concerning capital and profit repatriations?
- What are the currency and import regulations?
- What intercompany agreements have been arranged?
- Is your intellectual property protected under local laws?
- To what tax authorities must the JV report?
- Are losses going to be deductible?
- Will foreign taxes be creditable?
- Who will sit on the board of directors?
- How many directors are necessary from each partner? Is each partner contributing an equal number of directors? If not, why?

- Will the directors of the venture be elected annually?
- What is the minimum number of board meetings for the JV?
- What kinds of decisions require unanimous consent, majority voting, and so on?
- What dispute resolution procedures apply?
- Under what circumstances can a partner transfer or sell its equity ownership in the JV?
- When one partner wants to sell its equity share, what are the specific terms and conditions for the transaction?

Boost JV autonomy with a neutral country site

For many companies, locating the headquarters of a JV in a third or neutral country gives the alliance the best chance of meeting its objectives and developing into an independent self-sustaining entity. This tactic alleviates problems of control that can surface when the venture is located near one of its parent headquarters. Below are examples of how two JVs utilized a third country location to strengthen the independent yet cooperative spirit of their ventures:

Clark and Volvo believe that an independent 50–50 JV, VME Construction Corp., offered them the best chance for achieving their goal – to become the world's premier supplier of construction equipment. Headquartering the JV in a third country was viewed as a cornerstone of this strategy – with the added tax benefits of choosing the Netherlands as the site.

ICI and EniChem also selected to headquarter their 50–50 JV, European Vinyls Corp. (EVC), in a third country because they 'wanted a location that was in neutral territory to reduce the risk that any one partner would try to dominate the venture.' But the logistics have an interesting twist. Although EVC's legal headquarters is in the Netherlands, allowing it to benefit from the Dutch tax treaty network, the venture's management is in Brussels.

Neutrality is not the only advantage of the Belgian site. Brussels' key responsibilities include strategic planning, marketing and coordinating the JV's multiple marketing and manufacturing operations. For manufacturing and marketing, EVC has local operating companies in Italy, the UK, Germany and Switzerland. EVC purchases the raw materials for polyvinyl chloride production, and the Brussels team is responsible for allocating the materials among the various manufacturing sites. Brussels also oversees all orders. Customer requests are transmitted from local operations to the hub for processing. Brussels then designates the appropriate manufacturing plant to handle the order, which ships the products directly to the customers.

Slashing the start-up costs

Negotiating service agreements with parent organizations is one way to give a JV a running start and keep its initial costs low while maximizing its access to talent and resources. But service agreements do have their pitfalls: some JVs have had to expend considerable management time to make the service agreements yield the intended benefits. The bottom line is that parent senior management has to create the conditions under which such agreements will work. Here are some ideas:

Keep a tight rein on the agreements The inception of a US–European chemicals JV coincided with a market upturn and it became vital to begin operations quickly. Through carefully drafted agreements, the JV was able to rely on its parent companies for administrative and operational functions and move quickly to take advantage of the market's cyclical upswing. Initially, the venture had roughly 200 agreements, each negotiated annually. As the JV matured, the venture management built its own capabilities and cancelled the contracts.

When problems arise, confront the venture board, not parent management A European pharmaceuticals company established a JV with a Japanese firm to market its new drug; the two partners set up an agreement with the Japanese parent organization to have the JV use its sales and marketing staff to distribute the product. Recalled an executive with the European firm, 'When the JV started, like most ventures, it contained nothing more than a board of directors, modest capitalization, and a marketable product. We did not have the necessary sales and marketing staff to launch the operations. Hence, we decided to use our Japanese partner's staff. Unfortunately, we had many problems. We were not getting the sales that we expected. Yet we were in a difficult position. We were not dealing with an outsider, but the marketing staff of our partner.'

He continued, 'When the problem first appeared, we decided to confront the sales staff directly. With hindsight, we realized we should have first addressed the JV board. Even though it was a tricky situation for our Japanese partner's sales and marketing chief, who was on the venture's board, we received a better overall reaction to the problem from the directors. The sales and marketing director was counter-balanced by other Japanese board members; they had the ability to look at the problem from the JV's perspective – not the parent's.'

Treat the contract on an arm's length basis According to the European pharmaceuticals executive, 'Just as a company would cancel any marketing agreements with third parties that were not generating sales, a JV should have the gumption to do the same and should make this clear in the negotiations. This basically means that employees assigned to the alliance must be able to put on their JV hats and view problems and issues from the venture's perspective and not simply as an extension of the businesses and interests of the parent company.

After a few hard lessons, Clark Equipment now insists that divisions negotiate their own terms and conditions with outside ventures. Explained a Clark Equipment official, 'There are several different buy/sell arrangements between Clark divisions and the Clark–Volvo venture, VME Construction Inc. For instance, the Brazilian arm of the venture sources transmissions from the Clark factory in Brazil. The deal is handled directly by the two Brazilian companies. Senior management at Clark has no knowledge or involvement. We learned in the 1980s that the best strategy for intercompany business is to keep the business at arm's length, for pricing and the entire business relationship. We used to force different Clark divisions to source components and materials from each other and ventures at favourable prices. Our competitiveness eroded. Giving a division or a venture a break on pricing or the business helps no one.' On this issue Tim Leuliette, director of ITT Automotive, agreed: 'Mandating special pricing and business terms for divisions or ventures basically means an operation is not competitive. This tactic only serves to transfer the problems around.'

Beware the challenges in emerging markets Intercompany transactions can be particularly sticky in emerging markets where controls and reporting procedures may not be a standard feature of the local operating environment. An executive involved in a US–Mexican agribusiness venture recalls his frustration at trying to unravel the problems in the venture. Several factors complicated the problem. For one, the venture operated within the same site as the Mexican partner's other companies. For another, the venture received valuable raw materials from the Mexican partner. And finally, management's responsibility for the venture rested primarily with the local partner. Said the executive, 'We had successfully transferred the appropriate technology to launch operations. Technically, the plant was running smoothly. Yet we were still not making any money.'

The manager summarized the situation by saying that 'there were no great haemorrhages, just many small leaks here and there. Unfortunately, though, our Mexican partner was only concerned about whether the entire group was profitable, not the individual entities. However, one of those individual entities was not a wholly-owned unit, but our joint venture. Further, data and reports on pricing for raw materials and services were sketchy. The Mexican management relied solely on the prices of key commodities – wheat, corn, sorghum and pork bellies – to determine how well the operations were doing. It has been a slow process to win our partner over to the concept of implementing common procedures for pricing, inventory and revenues rather than using commodity prices to forecast profits and manage the business.'

Phase II: Launching operations

While such activities as selecting the JV site and organizing the board can be laborious, few tasks compare with the challenge of deciding how partners should divide responsibility for daily management control of the JV. There are several schools of thought on how MNCs should divide responsibility and control in alliances. Although strategic and policy decisions are commonly made jointly by all partners at board or other regular meetings, the control of daily operational and tactical issues is another matter. In particular, in JVs, it is the decision that tends to spark the greatest controversy when partners meet to divide operational control.

For example, whether they are one-shot arrangements or one entity in a network of ties under an equity link, partners in functional agreements generally split responsibilities proportionately to the contributions and strengths of each party. However, in a JV, control can represent an entirely different challenge.

Most firms tackle the control issue in two phases: an early start-up period (Phase II), and a later firm-ground stage (Phase III). When launching operations, controversy typically centres on how to divide responsibilities between the two partners, either equally or ceding control to one or the other of the firms. Interviews with key executives have identified two main factions on how to run an alliance in its nascent stage. Within these two main schools – characterized by whether or not to divide responsibility or nominate one partner to lead – there are many different options. The main questions that arise are the criteria for determining leadership and what the role of the other partner is to be.

Four ways of sharing equally

Despite the inherent difficulties of sharing power, many alliance strategists argue strongly for working together and jointly managing operational responsibilities. This section examines how some firms divide operational responsibilities and control:

An equal split, as determined by the partners' strengths, with a built-in overlap Nippon Sheet Glass (NSG) and LOF Glass employ this management approach in their joint venture in Kentucky to manufacture and sell glass to automobile producers. As a manager of the international department at NSG explains, 'The venture has a broad division of power based on the partners' strengths: NSG takes the lead in technology, while LOF handles marketing and labour management issues. The technical responsibility is primarily the domain of 12 NSG engineers assigned to work at the Kentucky venture. LOF has sent in a comparable number of management executives to oversee such areas as marketing and human resources. Two resident directors, one from each partner, act together as joint CEOs. Decisions are made jointly, although each director tends to take the lead in his own particular area.'

'Ideally', suggests the NSG executive, 'the partners could maintain a clear split between their two roles. In reality, there are built-in overlaps.' Both partners can gain from the overlaps, however, because they provide an opportunity for each partner to profit from direct exposure to its partner's operating strengths. Having overlapping areas of responsibility also strengthens the competitiveness of the venture. For instance, NSG is responsible for implementing the necessary process technology to meet all customer manufacturing specifications. Yet NSG cannot fully accomplish its task without understanding the dynamics of labour management relations in the US. 'Consequently', says the NSG executive, 'the partners work together and their decisions overlap in order to design a manufacturing strategy that adapts NSG's technology to a US environment.'

For example, the two firms jointly implemented just-in-time (JIT) and other quality techniques at the Kentucky factory. The venture is a key supplier to such auto transplants as Toyota, Nissan and Subaru. These Japanese car companies expect NSG to maintain the same JIT inventory control and quality services that it offers in Japan. Although NSG is indeed well versed in the mechanics of JIT production in Japan, the system operates differently in the US. Yet in both countries, the rigours of JIT demand punctuality and superior workmanship. 'With such a rigorous schedule,' says the NSG executive, 'we need to have very good inventory control, excellent tracking systems, and strong morale among workers. LOF has played an important role in helping the factory's 600-employee work-force adapt to the pressures of JIT.'

An equal split, based on the partners' contributions, with a rotating CEO Some ventures mirror the strategy at the NSG–LOF alliance, but with the addition of a mandatory rotation of the CEO every few years. Take, for example, Himont, previously a 50–50 venture between Montedison and Hercules to manufacture and distribute polypropylene worldwide. According to Alexander Giacco, former chairman of both Hercules and Himont, since Montedison had the most advanced manufacturing technology, this Italian company took the lead in technical and production matters. Because Hercules had a widespread marketing and distribution network, it assumed the key responsibility for marketing. Yet Montedison and Hercules crafted a role for each other within their respective functional domains by supplementing the basic technology/marketing split with geographic responsibility. For instance, Hercules played a role in all US operations, from manufacturing to marketing, while Montedison had the same involvement for Europe. 'This way', added Giacco, 'both sides gained valuable exposure to each other's main area of expertise.' Finally, both partners shared overall geographic and functional responsibility by rotating the CEO position every five years.

An equal division, with an extra dose of control in the home territory Don Dancer, senior vice-president at GE Fanuc Automation Corp., a 50–50 JV to produce and sell such automation equipment as programmable logic controllers (PLCs) and computerized numerical controls (CNCs), says that both partners attached a high priority to operating and treating each other as equal partners. At the same time, each side faced both internal and external pressures to secure a certain level of greater operational control in its home territory. Thus, the partners created a 50–50 holding company at the parent level, with three regional operating units below it: GE Fanuc Automation America, 90% owned by the holding entity and 10% directly by GE; GE Fanuc Automation Asia, 90% owned by the holding entity and 10% by FANUC; and GE Fanuc, owned entirely by the holding company.

Dancer urges that companies should address the initial anxiety among employees over joint ventures. With the holding company structure, all venture employees in the US still felt part of the larger GE family. For one thing, their salaries, benefits, pensions and insurance all remained the same. And psychologically the 10% had an enormous impact. Companies should not underestimate the fear among employees of being 'sold out to the Japanese', Dancer says.

The slight ownership difference in the US and Asian operations in this venture allows the local partner to take the lead in those areas. At the same time, however, notes Dancer, 'We often work side by side to coordinate marketing strategies for global customers, such as General Motors or Toyota. Customers want the same system solution for their factory automation needs; GE Fanuc America cannot market one strategy to Toyota while GE Fanuc Asia proposes another solution.'

Moreover, FANUC has been instrumental in opening doors at many Japanese transplants in the US for GE Fanuc America. In fact, such Japanese firms are a major marketing target in the US. Competition is fierce in the US, with strong brand loyalty (Allen Bradley commands over 85% of the market). The rest – GE Fanuc, Square D and Texas Instruments – are fighting for the remaining 15%. GE Fanuc aims to boost its presence by leveraging its Japanese connection with the Asian transplants.

An alliance between two of the world's largest glassmakers, Vitro of Mexico and Corning of the US, also opted for this strategy – and their breakup reveals some of the difficulties with this approach. In this complex partnership, the housewares divisions of each firm were combined into separate but linked companies, one based in the US and the other in Mexico. Corning transferred its consumer business to Corning Vitro Corp., a US subsidiary 51% owned by Corning and 49% by Vitro. Vitro shifted its housewares operations to Vitro Corning SA, a Mexican company 51% owned by Vitro and 49% by Corning.

Conceptually speaking, the strategy has merits. Practically speaking, however, its collapse illustrates how unforeseen competition and rapidly changing market conditions can imperil even the best conceived JV. Shortly after launching operations in 1992, a soft US economy and a flood of inexpensive Asian imports into Mexico – which was exacerbated by a strong Mexican peso *vis-à-vis* Asian currencies – offered the partners little time to fend off the competition. Having the two separate companies – with independent management – only complicated the situation and hindered the JV's ability to function and launch a counter-offensive strategy. After suffering substantial losses in 1993, the partners were forced to abandon the JV in early 1994.

Equal but separate control, with a small team to coordinate the venture   According to Jean Bilien, president of CFM International, a 50–50 joint venture between GE and Snecma to develop, manufacture and sell commercial jet engines, 'The foundation of the venture rests on a firm commitment to divide equally all work in design, development, manufacturing, marketing and product support for commercial jet engines.' For each new model and application the partners negotiate an equitable division of responsibility. 'In some instances', says Bilien, 'the negotiations may last for weeks to achieve an equitable split, but in the end both partners leave the table satisfied. The venture has never had to renegotiate a project.' Since its inception in 1969, new projects have involved five new models and more than 17 different airplane applications.

The partners split the work along two main divisions, with GE being responsible for the core or heart of the engine. This part of the aircraft includes the air-pressure compressor, air-pressure turbine and air-pressure chamber. Snecma concentrates on the low-pressure systems, including the compressor, turbine and chamber. In marketing and product support, the partners divide responsibilities geographically, with GE managing the Americas and Asia and Snecma taking Europe, Africa and the Middle East. All operations are conducted separately at the respective parent operations. Bilien observes that 'CFM International virtually has no employees. I, along with a few other executives, work in Ohio as coordinators. We ensure that decisions are properly implemented, prepare presentations for meetings on major policy decisions and keep abreast of new market developments.'

Opting for a single leader

These case studies illustrate why some ventures choose to place control in the hands of one partner. Several MNCs cite strong arguments in favour of having one partner take the lead in managing the day-to-day operational challenges of a venture. Their executives differ, however, as to which partner should be nominated. This section looks at four alliances and how each allocated responsibility:

When technology rules the day   According to Tim Leuliette, director for ITT Automotive, businesses cannot be run on a daily basis as democracies with one man, one vote rule. Instead, firms have to appoint one partner to lead and oversee operations. Who is to be designated the leader depends on what each partner brings to the table. However, said Leuliette, 'In my experiences, there is a logical split – the partner who provides the technology and products has the "larger equal share" and should run the venture. A venture's long-term strategy and success is driven by its technology and products. Certainly, the partner that brings marketing capabilities and a distribution network offers valuable assets. In fact, the two contributions – technology and marketing – are roughly on equal footing at the inception of the venture. But as time goes by, the future success of the business depends on how well the technology advances and creates new product innovations. Hence, I believe the importance and influence of the technology partner increases over time, while that of the marketing partner diminishes.'

When marketing is mightier   Robert Ecklin, senior vice-president for industrial products at Corning, suggested having the marketing partner take the helm in the early stages of a venture. According to him, in the formative years of an alliance, before the venture has all the functional capabilities to operate as a separate independent entity, Corning's strategy is to have the marketing partner take the lead. For example, in the first Asahi–Corning venture on Japanese soil, the alliance combined Corning technology with Asahi marketing skills and Asahi took the management lead.

Ecklin also described a reverse scenario for a Corning–Mitsubishi venture in the US to produce pollution-control equipment. In this 50–50 venture, the partners pooled Japanese technology with US marketing muscle. In this case, Corning took the management lead.

Ecklin suggested that Corning's emphasis on giving the marketing partner the lead may be a key reason why and how the US firm avoids the 'hollowing out' syndrome in ventures where a foreign firm comes in, learns the marketing ropes from the US partner, then dumps the US firm. Moreover, in the three big US Corning ventures – Dow Corning, Owens Corning and Pittsburgh Corning – responsibility for daily operational and management issues rested with the marketing partner. In these ventures, Corning contributed technology and the running of the business on a daily basis was left to the marketing partners. As Ecklin outlined the process, 'The alliances follow a similar course. As a venture develops, the technology is infused into the operations. Then, around the ten-year mark, we at Corning management like to see the venture have the capabilities and resources to go off on its own.'

Taking a back seat to learn   According to Lino Piedra, former chairman of Diamond Star Motors (DSM) – formerly a 50–50 Chrysler–

Mitsubishi JV to produce a new range of mid-sized cars and now a 100% Mitsubishi entity with marketing and supplier links to Chrysler – Chrysler deliberately took a back seat in DSM. A key Chrysler objective for DSM was to gain firsthand knowledge and exposure to Japanese management and manufacturing techniques. Hence, having Mitsubishi take responsibility for daily operations provided the best setting as far as Chrysler was concerned. In the original organizational structure as a 50–50 venture, Mitsubishi appointed the president, who managed operations, and Chrysler nominated the chairman. Reporting to the president was a four-member operating committee made up of two executives from each partner. As Piedra said, 'At the operating committee meetings I could attend as chairman, but I did not have a vote. Of course, just being there did give me some influence.'

Notwithstanding Chrysler's desire to cede control in order to learn from Mitsubishi Motors, Piedra also finds 50–50 JVs 'very difficult animals to run'. In the early days of structuring a venture, Piedra suggests that firms negotiate and agree on which partner will run the daily operations. As he observes, 'The worst scenarios are either when partners have a power struggle in the early stages to see which firm will lead or when partners commit to share responsibility. In the latter case, operational issues are never clear-cut. What happens is that partners start to question, "Well, is this my area or yours, etc." Then chaos can unravel the operation.'

When commingled parent–venture businesses force the choice of a leader   Jacques Meyer, international market-planning director for AT&T, believes that one partner has to be in charge. As he says, 'In our experiences, I have yet to see an alliance where the partners had the same objectives in the beginning. Consequently, unless someone takes the helm, the business never gets off the ground.'

Which partner is to assume responsibility will depend on how much the venture's business is commingled with one or both parent companies' operations. If the venture is closely melded with the operations of only one partner, that firm will obviously take the lead. If the alliance's operations are intertwined with both, the two firms will need to agree on the leadership appropriate for the alliance. Other executives say that it usually requires an advance agreement to single out one firm to run daily operations, with joint decisions being made on major policies and strategies.

Xerox's legendary alliances, Fuji Xerox and Rank Xerox, offer two good examples of how one partner can play a more prominent role because of tight business links. As Robert Meredith, resident director for Xerox at Fuji Xerox, explained, 'The Rank Organization and Fuji Photo had other markets and technologies as their primary business focus. Xerox, though, concentrated on copiers and office equipment, the main product offerings of both ventures. Thus, all the partners jointly agreed that Xerox needed to have a more involved role and say in the venture.' However, stressed Meredith, 'The emphasis [was] on "agree". The decisions were based on business objectives and the respective strengths and weaknesses of each partner. Giving one partner a greater role in operations must always be a practical business decision. It should not be viewed as an emotionally charged showdown or a win/lose situation.'

Yotaro Kobayashi, chairman of Fuji Xerox, added that 'Fuji Photo's willingness to concede a greater role in operational decisions to Xerox demonstrates the deeply rooted trust between the two parents. I also admire Fuji Photo because the original 1962 joint venture agreement explicitly states that Fuji Photo is responsible for running the daily business and held accountable for operational results. Yet Fuji Photo understands well that Fuji Xerox and Xerox must communicate and work closely together because we are in the same business. We have a web of links in all key functions, such as technology, marketing, manufacturing, product development and R&D. Fuji Xerox and Xerox hold many operational meetings in which Fuji Photo does not participate. This simplifies the operational challenges of running the business. However, I must always account for Fuji Photo's interests, particularly since their name is prominently affixed in the venture. Yet, the mutual respect and trust between the parents and with the venture permits this operational structure and is a key factor behind Fuji Xerox's success.'

Phase III: Building a prosperous long-term business

Having seen various views on how to run a venture in its early stages, this section now discusses how companies can move beyond the start-up kinks to develop a long-term business. A JV's long-term viability depends considerably on allowing the JV to operate as an independent company. Interviews revealed many different corporate perspectives on when and if alliance partners should allow ventures to operate autonomously. In particular, executives disagree on whether a venture should be given a clear mandate to develop on its own or should always remain on a parental leash, whether short or long. For some executives, such as H. P. Appleby, vice-president for law and administration at Himont, the issue is straightforward. He suggests that most JVs should be structured to operate independently as soon as possible. Partners should outline a clear road map with well-defined time-limits and schedules on how the venture will achieve operational and financial independence. This outline should also be the goal of the executives charged with running the venture. Its managers should want to run an entrepreneurial, independent business, rather than cling to parental apron strings.

Chrysler's Lino Piedra supported this premise but pointed out how industry factors and constraints can make achieving it difficult. For example, the cost of designing and building a new auto-manufacturing facility such as the Chrysler–Mitsubishi Diamond Star Motors plant was close to $1 billion. Apart from this hefty investment, there was substantial engineering and marketing support needed from the parents to sustain the plant. Given the huge investment needed to build the plant, says Piedra, it would be difficult to imagine how two auto companies would then duplicate engineering and marketing efforts so that the joint enterprise could operate independently.

Similarly, several alliance practitioners believe that a venture can and should be allowed to develop all the capabilities and functions needed to operate as an independent business. However, the venture must often still closely coordinate its strategies and tactics with one or both partners, because of overlapping business interests. At this point they often face each other as equals, not in a parent/child relationship. Below are three examples of how some JVs tackled the independence issue.

The mature venture: how much independence

The 'toe in the water' approach   The president of ICI Italia, described how and why ICI and EniChem used a step-by-step strategy to develop the independence of their 50–50 venture, European Vinyls Corp., to produce and sell polyvinyl chloride (PVC). As he said, 'Both partners shared a long-term objective of having the venture operate independently. However, ICI and EniChem initially limited the scope of the venture, created in 1986, to marketing. The partners outlined several factors behind their decision to use the first four years as a testing ground and refrain from building a completely separate operation with a wholesale transfer of all assets to the venture in the beginning. First, market conditions and prices in the PVC market were depressed. The partners were unsure whether the venture could survive. Second, the production of PVC at both firms was tightly integrated with other manufacturing operations. Third, the life and depreciation schedules of the different facilities and equipment made it difficult to assess their value and devise a systematic accounting schedule. Fourth, employees on both sides were reluctant to lock arms with a competitor. Fifth, the partners had only received partial approval from the EC's antitrust authorities. EVC received final approval to merge all operations in 1990.'

The EC antitrust roadblock notwithstanding, the step-by-step approach paid off. EVC's creation triggered a restructuring in the

European PVC market. Prices rebounded, with EVC's results for the first three years registering significantly higher than either partner had originally envisioned. This provided employees with an important psychological boost and increased their willingness to work together. The extra time also permitted the partners to work out the valuations and mechanics of transferring the assets. At the end of 1990, the partners transferred the responsibility and ownership of their PVC operations in the UK, Italy, Switzerland and Germany to EVC's headquarters in Brussels. Employee contracts were gradually folded into the Brussels company over a longer period.

A clear mandate of independence from the start   Formidable market pressures from competitors such as Komatsu and Caterpillar provided a major impetus for Clark Equipment (US) and Volvo (Sweden) to merge their construction-equipment businesses in a 50–50 joint venture. In establishing the venture, VME Construction Equipment (VME), the partners jointly outlined a management creed for the alliance: if the executives running a venture are left alone, they will take a direct – sometimes even personal – stake in working hard and building a successful business. Thus, from the very start, said a Clark equipment executive, the partners set out to equip the enterprise with all the resources, assets, personnel and marketing networks it needed to operate as an independent entity. Some of the managers transferred directly from both Clark and Volvo, but other VME executives, including the president, were recruited from different industries. Of course, added the Clark official, VME followed the traditional course of having a board with equal representation from both partners. Yet, as the executive emphasized, the four-member board essentially operates as a surveillance committee.

VME's organizational structure encourages an independent management style not only at the helm but also within lower management ranks. Locating VME's headquarters and corporate staff in Brussels, a third-country site, puts them away from both parent companies' headquarters. The venture also has three regional operating centres. The European staff and manufacturing facilities are located in Sweden. North America is managed out of Cleveland, Ohio, the site of VME's major US manufacturing operations. This centre is also a principal liaison with the venture's Canadian manufacturing facilities. The third centre has a small staff in Miami to coordinate marketing strategies for Latin America. Brazil, a principal manufacturing site, also plays a prominent management role in the venture's Latin American operations.

The Clark official pointed out that much of the business of the three regional centres is self-contained. For instance, the bulk of VME's sales, which is small to medium-sized loaders, is manufactured in all three locations. Hence, each major area has a factory close to the heart of its market. This enables regional management to focus on the local market and operations, with minimal interference from the corporate headquarters in Brussels.

In fact, there is very little overlap between the three regions. The exceptions are a few large products that are sourced worldwide from one site to reap greater economies of scale. For instance, all orders for big Euclid mining trucks are produced in Canada. Similarly, VME manufactures all its large loaders in the US, which is also the principal market for this equipment.

Keeping the venture at a distance has paid off – VME's management passed the $2 billion mark in global sales in 1990. Using only its own capital and with neither parent contributing funds for the acquisitions, the venture also acquired two European construction equipment firms, Zeddelmayer of Germany, and Ackermanns in Sweden.

Timing as the determinant for independence   William Glavin of Babson College and formerly Xerox concurs that ventures should be empowered with the capability to operate as a standalone entity but points out that timing is extremely important. As he notes, it was well over eight years before Fuji Xerox became a full-fledged separate company, complete with its own manufacturing, R&D, and so on. Besides allowing a venture to strengthen its internal capabilities, timing is frequently tied to market or parent changes. According to Hideki Kaihatsu, managing director and chief staff officer at Fuji Xerox, any venture or business eventually reaches a level of maturity in which the partners need to address how the venture can develop on its own. Management must answer how a venture can secure the enabling products and strategies to grow and compete. At this crossroads, says Kaihatsu, 'the partners must be ready and willing to equip the venture with a full range of capabilities to operate independently.'

Fuji Xerox was a unique case, a venture initially conceived as a marketing company, which, along with Xerox, commanded a dominant market position because of worldwide Xerox patents and the unique nature of plain-paper copiers. However, as patents lapsed in the late 1960s and early 1970s, market conditions flipped. Many Japanese competitors like Ricoh and Canon entered the game with similar but lower-cost plain-paper copiers. As Kaihatsu recalls, 'Fuji Xerox faced a major hurdle. The venture could not continue simply as a marketer for plain-paper copiers. We needed the capabilities and resources to develop and manufacture new product offerings. While it was a difficult period for both parent companies, management realized that Fuji Xerox's future rested on its ability to stand on its own.' Actually, Kaihatsu believes that a venture is no different from any other business: 'If you want to expand a business, you must be willing to give it the capabilities and mandate to develop.'

As Fuji Xerox blossomed into a fully integrated operation, the bonds between Fuji Xerox and Xerox tightened. The operations and strategies of the two firms in the office equipment business now became closely enmeshed. However, the emergence of Fuji Xerox as an independent entity added a new management challenge for Xerox. Xerox realized that Fuji Xerox, with its focus on Japan and other Asian markets, needed its own Japanese management to call the shots on daily operations. According to Jefferson Kennard, current director of Fuji Xerox relations at Xerox, 'The close relationship between Fuji Xerox and Xerox is fertile ground for conflicts. Here was a venture based in Japan, competing head-on with Japanese competition. It obviously needed Japanese management at the helm to call the shots. Xerox quickly realized that it would be rather foolish to attempt to run a Japanese company out of Stamford.'

Checklist

Tips on dividing responsibility in JVs

In sum, there is no end to the creative options available to companies on how they can divide operational control. What is critical in any structure, however, is that all partners agree and support the approach. Since alliances are joint endeavours, no single company can or should unilaterally impose its will or control over operations. The following checklist outlines some key questions and issues companies may want to consider when devising a strategy on how to manage and control operations:

- What are the pros and cons of dividing responsibility equally among partners or ceding control to one partner?
- Will partners divide control based on their respective functional strengths – in R&D, manufacturing, quality management, marketing, and so on – or on their geographic prowess?
- For what functions or regions does each partner want to assume responsibility? How is each partner planning to justify its position or argue that it should control a particular activity?
- How will companies provide some overlap in geographic and functional responsibilities so that all partners have the opportunity to acquire new skills and also improve the overall coordination of operations?
- What are the pros and cons of using an organizational and management structure that allows for an extra dose of power and control over all activities in each partner's home territory?

- What is the role of the venture's headquarters? Where is the corporate centre located? Have the partners considered the use of a neutral, third-country location for headquarters?

- What are the advantages and disadvantages of rotating the selection of top venture executives among all partners? How frequently should the rotation of top management positions occur – every two years, five years, or some other interval?

- What are the venture's needs for skilled, technically trained personnel at all management levels? Where will the alliance obtain these people? Do you want the middle and senior executives for the venture to come from the parent corporations, subsidiaries or outside sources? How expensive is it to use executives from the parents? Can the alliance justify these expenses? For what period will middle and senior managers be assigned to the venture?

- What are the strengths and weakness of giving one partner total control over operations? Which company should take the lead – the technology or marketing partner – and why?

- What are the main objectives for each partner in the alliance? Do any of the firms plan to use the venture to acquire new skills and knowledge about how its partners/competitors operate? If so, how does management plan to acquire this knowledge and then transfer it back to parent operations? Is there a formal training programme? Do any of the partners object to training sessions and why? How will management ensure that any training programmes will not interfere with regular operational routines and schedules?

- Do all partners agree that the venture should eventually operate as a separate independent unit?

- Is there any need to keep the alliance on some parental leash and why?

- How does the venture relate to the activities of each parent – are they entwined or operating at arm's length?

- What are the short- and long-term plans on how the venture will develop the capabilities and resources to operate completely independent of all parents?

Making co-operation work: the critical tools for management

Part Two focuses on the realities of trying to make an alliance succeed. If alliances are 'marriages', as many executives view them, then it is accurate to say that most companies concentrate on the courtship phase, rather than on planning how to live on a day-to-day basis after the contract has been signed. Companies frequently make the mistake of thinking the contract is an end in itself. When alliances fail, they tend to blame it on faulty structure, not on poor management.

According to Jacques Meyer, international market planning director at AT&T, 'Putting together a venture contract is easy – making the alliance actually work is the real challenge.' In fact, consummating the alliance is only the beginning. The agreement will get you nowhere unless the alliance is properly managed. Success requires considerable time, effort and the right people. Although the words sound self-evident, one of the biggest stumbling blocks for ventures is that management often underestimates the necessary amount of energy and attention needed to manage cooperatively in a bilingual or multilingual cross-cultural situation. Robert Meredith, resident direc-tor for Xerox at Fuji Xerox, believed there can be no coasting period in a venture. Meredith said, 'An alliance can fall apart at any time – one day, one month, one year or ten years after signing the agree-ment. From the very first day, the partners must devote all of their energies and efforts to making the alliance work.'

8

How to get along: three guiding principles

Attitudes – how partners view and treat each other – shape the management dynamics within an alliance. No management techniques or tricks can substitute for the obligation of alliance partners to develop a basic understanding and respect for each other. But how? Certainly, getting along with executives from a competing firm is no simple task. And each venture is unique. Many of the challenges executives face in an alliance depend on factors such as the venture's structure, the personalities and egos of the managers and employees, the history of the competitive/collaborative relationship between the partners and external market conditions. None the less, several common themes emerged in the interviews with key executives. Based on their experience, several executives suggested ways to lay the foundation for a solid partnership by emphasizing a few simple but important guidelines:

(1) Treat each other as equals;
(2) Tap the support of the partner's senior management;
(3) Respect – do not fight – diversity.

Equality: the mainstay of a happy marriage

Many executives characterize alliances as marriages. To extend the metaphor, most marriages blossom when partners treat each other as equals. Equality is likewise crucial in corporate alliances. The particular challenge is how to create and maintain a relationship among equals.

Several companies, such as US-based Corning, believe that setting up a 50–50 joint venture is the most direct approach for ensuring a relationship of equals. According to Robert Ecklin, senior vice-president for the industrial products division at Corning, 'Management should not underestimate the symbolic value of a 50–50 venture to make co-operation work. Some MNCs mistakenly try to control alliances through a majority/minority equity split. However, most successful alliances are not managed or dictated by equity shareholdings. Instead, much of the success of a venture depends on the partners' ability to compromise on key issues. A 50–50 joint venture fosters such compromises and a give-and-take attitude. In essence, 50–50 joint ventures force the partners to try to get along.'

William Glavin, director of Babson College and former vice-chairman of Xerox, also adheres to a 50–50 philosophy. As he says, 'Some US firms constantly push for a 51–49 split, arguing the 51% entitles them to call all the shots. Yet, firms enter alliances as partners. Why not act as partners? Face the facts and run the business together in a 50–50 venture.'

As Kenichi Ohmae put it, 'Many ventures fail when executives believe they can control all operations by controlling the equity. But emotions (and partners) can never be bought with a controlling majority' (Ohmae, 1985). One US executive maintained that trying to use a 51–49 equity split as a means of securing control is the worst JV option: 'It is like saying yes, of course we are equals, but in reality, when there is a problem, not really.' Kenichi Ohmae argued that 'A need for control is deeply rooted. The tradition of Western capitalism lies behind it, a tradition that has taught managers the incorrect arithmetic that equates 51% with 100% and 49% with 0 percent' (Ohmae, 1990).

Shinichiro Yokoyama, manager of the international department at Nippon Sheet Glass (NSG), agrees. For instance, NSG has a long-standing relationship with US-based LOF Glass that includes several 50–50 ventures. In 1987, NSG purchased a 20% stake in LOF Glass, tipping the ownership balance in the partners' 50–50 joint ventures. Explains Yokoyama, 'We have a significant 50–50 venture in automotive glass in Kentucky. Officially, our 20% ownership of LOF Glass means the equity breakdown in the Kentucky operation is 60–40.' Yet Yokoyama believes it would be a serious mistake for NSG to exert its power over the operation just because it has a larger equity stake. NSG wants to operate the venture as a 50–50 partnership among equals.

Stephen Albertalli, Corning's recently retired director of investor relations, commented that 'Having a 50–50 or equal partnership is a cornerstone of Corning's joint venture philosophy. Even if actual equity ownership is not split 50–50, partners must reach decisions by consensus.' He concluded that 'Corning's emphasis on equality has been a key factor to its success in alliances. We regard ventures as marriages. It would not be a very happy marriage if problems were solved by one partner claiming to be bigger and more powerful.'

However, the equality philosophy can become a delicate issue. For instance, when Corning faced resistance in negotiations with Ciba-Geigy for a 50–50 venture in the medical diagnostics field, the Swiss giant argued one partner alone must carry the ball, whether through equity ownership, votes on the board, veto power, or the like. After considerable debate, Corning finally was able to persuade Ciba-Geigy of the merits of a 50–50 split.

Michio Naruto, senior vice-president and head of global marketing at Japan-based Fujitsu, finds the equality issue to be as much a state of mind as one related to the structure of the partnership. According to Naruto, 'Many US firms claim alliance participants never remain as equals, with one firm eventually taking a superior position to its partner. If management enters an alliance with this perception, it often becomes a self-fulfilling prophecy. However, at Fujitsu we do not agree with that attitude. We believe partners should go in and remain as equals.'

Nor is building a relationship of equal partners restricted to 50–50 ventures, for equality is as much a philosophical issue as a structural one. It also applies to alliances that involve several partners or to partnerships that do not entail the creation of a separate joint venture company. For example, the ICL–Fujitsu alliance underwent a radical change in 1988. Since 1981 the two partners have had a series of collaborative arrangements, including development projects involving mainframe computers, R&D projects and technical exchange programmes. A concerted effort to treat each other as equal partners set the tone for all cooperative ICL–Fujitsu endeavours.

As previously recounted, Northern Telecom purchased ICL's parent, STC, in 1988. To recap, Northern Telecom was not interested in the computer business and wanted to put ICL on the auction block. At this point Fujitsu faced the tough choice of either purchasing a majority stake in ICL or having its long-time partner fall into the hands of a competitor. In the end, Fujitsu purchased an 80% stake, with Northern Telecom retaining a 20% interest. As Naruto explains, 'Many critics regard the equity purchase as a straightforward acquisition in order to further Fujitsu's forays into Europe. However, Fujitsu views its relationship to

ICL as an equal partnership. Technically, ICL is a subsidiary of Fujitsu. Yet Fujitsu has no intention of changing our relationship as equal partners to a parent–sub hierarchy.'

As Corning's Ecklin observes, 'There is no end to the creative options available to fashion an environment within the alliance that emphasizes equality.' As mentioned before, Corning has a joint venture with Japan's Mitsubishi group in manufacturing pollution-control equipment for stationary emissions. Within Mitsubishi two separate companies were involved. Mitsubishi Petrochemicals held worldwide patents on technology for stationary emissions. And Mitsubishi Heavy Industries led in marketing and manufacturing the pollution control equipment. However, since both firms formed part of the same *keihatsu,* the three partners created a venture in which Corning holds 50%, with the other half held 15% by Mitsubishi Petrochemcials and 35% by Mitsubishi Heavy Industries.

Fujitsu's Naruto cautions, however, that equality must be based on solid ground. He urges that alliances must start as a marriage of equals, with each partner holding an important trump card, whether it is technology, market access, manufacturing expertise, human resources, or in another area. Whatever its competitive advantage, each partner must remain competitive in its own field; otherwise the responsibilities and burden of the venture may become skewed and the alliance suffer. In fact, some analysts suggest that the myriad of problems between Chrysler and Mitsubishi in the late 1980s stemmed primarily from Chrysler's eroding competitiveness. As one expert noted, 'At the end of the day, Mitsubishi had no need for a weak sister (partner).'

Ford also emphasizes the importance of partners remaining equally strong. According to a Ford executive, the strength of any alliance rests on the capabilities of the partners, even if this requires helping each other out in difficult times.

The equality issue is perhaps most critical in the distribution of profits and benefits from an alliance. According to Jon Elmendorf, former president of Westinghouse Energy Systems (Japan) and currently Westinghouse's director of environmental compliance, no alliance will survive if one partner is making a bundle of cash while the other partner is receiving only meagre benefits. All the partners in an alliance must have mutually comparable gains in order for the agreement to work. The concept of gains also applies to the many potential intangible benefits of an alliance, such as exposure to a partner/competitor's management and manufacturing practices. Executives and employees working in a competitive alliance – particularly from Western firms – must try to assimilate as many new skills and ideas as possible from partners. Certainly, gaining knowledge of and exposure to a partner's management techniques is in fact a key objective for most Asian partners/firms. According to Paul Drenkow, a Ford executive involved in the

Ford–Mazda relationship, 'It is no secret that Toyota wanted to learn how to manage and operate in a US environment from General Motors in the Nummi venture. GM indeed taught them very well. There is nothing wrong with the Japanese using alliances for learning purposes, but US and other firms should be cognizant of this goal and attempt to follow this example.'

Tapping the powers of the top brass

Much of any alliance executive's ability to treat his counterparts within an alliance as equals often depends on the response of senior management. Having the visible commitment and support of top management to an alliance can send a strong signal to the employees assigned to a venture to get along and make the venture work.

For example, Jean Bilien, president of CFM International, a 50–50 joint venture between General Electric of the US and French-based Snecma to produce commercial jet engines, recalled how the support and persistence of both partners' senior management was instrumental to CFM's success. As Bilien explained, the germ for a venture to develop and launch new commercial jet engines originated from personal chats between the CEOs of Snecma and GE, who had strong common interests and experiences.

Rudimentary proposals finally led to the creation of a joint venture in 1969, but the venture did not receive its first order until eight years later. Bilien admitted that 'Not having an order for the first eight years made the situation quite tense. There were plenty of people on both sides of the Atlantic who did not want the venture.' Endless complaints and nitpicking between employees of the two partners resulted, yet the venture survived, primarily because of the determination and support of top management. 'Without the support of top management,' concluded Bilien, who has been involved in the project since 1975, 'CFM International could have never continued for eight years without a single order. Once senior management sends a message that it wants an alliance, managers learn quickly how to make the deal work.'

Alexander Giacco, former chairman of Hercules and Himont, agreed. According to him, 'There will always be some divided loyalties and a not-invented-here syndrome within lower management ranks. Senior management support is a must in order to curtail the inevitable carping and jabs in the early stages of a venture.' William Glavin, president of Babson College and former vice-chairman of Xerox, emphasizes that senior management's support must remain consistent, and evident, throughout the life of a venture. Says Glavin, 'There were times during the 1970s and 1980s during which perhaps 60 to 70% of the Xerox employees dealing with Fuji Xerox did not trust their Fuji counterparts or want to work with them. However, we never flinched at the top and remained strongly committed to the relationship.'

Open support from senior management can be particularly invaluable in equity links and alliances in which the partners have a multitude of projects and ventures. Howard Hill, partner at Pepper, Hamilton & Sheetz and former legal counsel at Chrysler, said top management's support is an important adhesive binding the Chrysler–Mitsubishi relationship. In addition to Chrysler's minority equity position in Mitsubishi, the Chrysler–Mitsubishi arrangement has also included joint ventures, component-supplier links, marketing and distribution contracts, and the like.

With so many links, remarked Hill, some in-fighting within a specific project is not unusual. Lower-level employees in one project often do not have the vision to see beyond the current conflict. In such instances the long-standing ties and support of senior management provide an important balance. As Hill observed, senior management looks at the long-term strategic importance of an entire relationship, whereas a project manager is under stiff short-term pressure to produce results.

Lino Piedra, senior executive at Chrysler and former chairman of Diamond Star Motors (DSM) – once a 50–50 mid-sized joint Mitsubishi–Chrysler auto venture and now a 100% Mitsubishi entity with marketing ties to Chrysler – says that both Chrysler and Mitsubishi often go one step further than just demonstrating top management's support, by involving senior management directly in important projects.

Corning's Albertalli illustrates the importance of senior management in its Corning–Asahi alliance, which dates back to the 1930s. 'Suppose a venture manager on either side goes to his boss, complaining about how Asahi or Corning is trying to cheat on the project. Most likely, the senior manager will benefit from a longer relationship and keener understanding of the other partner. He can then say, "Wait, something is wrong. Neither Corning or Asahi operate with those tactics. Either you are not listening or you do not properly understand the situation." In effect, senior management can then help to put the venture back on track.'

However, not all members of senior management in alliances will enjoy decades of working together. Certainly, the operational and strategic challenges of running an alliance do mandate having business meetings and close contact between senior management during the year. In addition, executives such as H.P. Appleby, vice-president at Himont, suggested organizing a few social gatherings each year for senior management, to encourage closer links at the top. An open, friendly relationship at the senior level should then filter down through the ranks. Shinchiro Yokoyama of Nippon Sheet Glass points out that his firm plans at least two strictly social activities annually with its partners, LOF Glass of the US and UK-based Pilkington.

Similarly, a US MNC and its two Japanese partners, which are both part of the same *keihatsu*, plan an annual three-day meeting that is a mix of business and pleasure. Said an executive with the US firm, 'Having an opportunity for the top three executives in each company to meet and reaffirm their commitment to the relationship is a principal aim of the event. Of course, within the lower management ranks, we often wait with trepidation for the outcome of the meeting, wondering what new ideas for cooperation these guys will dream up. At the same time, however, such meetings can be extremely useful.' The minutes of the meeting are distributed throughout the three firms. As the US executive noted, 'We frequently find references of support for a given project that has been encountering strong resistance from the Japanese side. We can then say to our Japanese counterparts, "Look at the minutes. Your chairman fully supports this project".'

Manage – do not fight – diversity

Step inside your partner's shoes

Perhaps the most important cue that senior management can give alliance executives is to demonstrate and emphasize the need to understand, rather than oppose or try to change, any differences in the partners. According to one executive, 'The most important guideline for getting along in an alliance is to analyse the actions and/or positions of your partner from his perspective, rather than from your viewpoint. Do not make value judgements. What is needed is curiosity, openness to change, flexibility and, above all, respect for his situation.'

Yotaro Kobayashi, chairman and CEO of Fuji Xerox, believes that most operational and strategic issues become less cumbersome once each firm takes the time to understand the competitive dynamics and operating constraints facing its partners. Naruto at Fujitsu also believes this a golden rule for alliances. According to him, 'The first step in alliance management is to understand your partner's/competitor's situation. What are his internal operating constraints in areas such as financing, technology, manufacturing, human resources, geographic expansion? What are the external factors, such as the threats and opportunities he faces in the market? Then, once you know his situation, you can better appreciate his position on issues and the options available to him.' Yokoyama of Nippon Sheet Glass also finds that an awareness of his partners' difficulties – whether these are short-term financial pressures or problems with labour unions – can improve a relationship and make conflicts easier to resolve.

In fact, Jefferson Kennard, director for Fuji–Xerox relations at Xerox, shows how an appreciation of their contrasting management philosophies helped Fuji and Xerox overcome the common dividend dilemmas between the US and Japanese firms. As he says, 'It is general knowledge that US MNCs stress high dividend payouts, because of pressure from Wall Street and institutional investors, while Japanese shareholders accept low payouts, in return for profits reinvested for growth. Yet complicating this phenomenon was the fact that our partner Fuji has one of the most conservative dividend policies among Japanese MNCs. At an annual rate of 7 to 8% of earnings, Fuji Photo has the lowest dividend payout ratio among all the major Japanese firms listed on the first tier of the Nikkei Exchange. Xerox, however, has an average payout of 70 to 80%. In some cases, Xerox has paid out 100%. So here we have one of the most conservative Japanese MNCs teaming with one of the most liberal US firms.'

Despite these differences, the two firms have had no disputes regarding dividends. Kennard says that 'Both sides make an effort to understand the philosophy and pressures behind each other's dividend strategies. For instance, Fuji knows a significant portion of Xerox stock is held by institutional investors. If Xerox cuts its dividends, those funds may bail out immediately, sending Xerox's stock price down.' Similarly, Xerox understands Fuji Photo's long tradition and philosophy of low dividends. The US firm knows it cannot push Fuji to accept very high levels. By understanding the constraints on both sides, each partner is more willing to opt for the middle ground: Fuji Xerox dividends generally hover around 30% of earnings.

Lino Piedra, former chairman of Diamond Star Motors, finds that most problems in ventures are usually not problems at all. In fact, he considers, 'It is generally a lack of understanding between the partners. For example, foreign executives frequently complain about Japanese decision-making styles. Foreigners usually quip "the Japanese will never give a straight answer to a problem." Even the definition of the problem indicates to me a failure to appreciate any nuances between the operating and management styles of Japanese and Western firms. In most cases, the issue is simply that the Western executive is not getting an answer to what he thinks is the problem. His Japanese partner most likely views the situation differently, and is responding to a separate problem.'

Piedra recalls a comparable problem at DSM with Mitsubishi. As is common in most US operations, Chrysler routinely implanted some reporting procedures at DSM. Yet what Chrysler considered traditional controls greatly offended Mitsubishi, which felt that its US partner suspected it of cheating. But as Piedra says, 'When I explained the issue to Mitsubishi, my main aim was to demonstrate how the controls were routine in the US rather than motivated by suspicion. I used an analogy of airline controls. I asked, "When you pass through a series of controls before boarding a plane, do you get offended?" Well, I then explained how the reporting procedures at DSM were the same concept as the airline controls. Once they understood the rationale for the reports, the problem was eliminated.' Piedra advises that firms can circumvent many hassles by grasping differences in decision-making and operating styles, specifically how each side analyses an issue, what information is needed, the steps required to make an informed decision, who the key decision makers are and so forth. 'This simple exercise will eliminate much of the insecurity and frustration of coping with "too many unknowns" with the Japanese.'

Tim Leuliette, director of ITT Automotive in the US, considers the ability of different alliance partners to grasp and exploit the diversity among partners as perhaps the greatest challenge and benefit of an alliance. He argues that the greatest strength of an alliance comes from the different contributions and skills of each partner. How the firms in an alliance combine these assets and give real meaning to the word synergy is the toughest challenge.

The first step is to recognize the different levels of diversity in an alliance's partners. Leuliette believes that cultural differences fall into three main categories: by industry, by corporation and by nation. In each area, management needs to take the time to understand the main characteristics. For example, consider the differences in industry sectors. ITT Automotive frequently teams up with automobile manufacturers, yet it is an electronics firm, with an entirely different market and strategy from that of an auto company. The partners work better together once each firm understands the sectoral differences in lead times, production cycles, product cycles, cost structures, supplier networks, markets, customer profiles and the like.

The same dynamics apply in regard to corporate cultures. MNCs need to take the time to understand the organizational hierarchy and personal dynamics within their partner's company. For instance, what is its leadership style and corporate philosophy? What are the expectations and obligations of its employees? How is its power base shared, and how are decisions made there? What is expected in presentations, in collecting business data and in analysing competitors and markets? Finally, adds Leuliette, when you cap these differences with the cultural challenges of having, say, a German or a Japanese partner, the situation can be overwhelming. All these constraints tend to identify and shape the environment of an alliance.

Drenkow of Ford agrees, but adds a qualifier. 'When firms ally with a partner overseas, most executives tend to focus on the more obvious national differences. Yet my experiences underscore the need to analyse other aspects, particularly corporate cultures.' For instance, Ford's corporate culture encourages employees to operate as independent self-starters. Managers seek to develop several project proposals simultaneously. On some occasions, Ford managers would organize meetings to discuss their ideas with Mazda. Yet Ford managers' practice of using Mazda in brainstorming sessions on different cooperative proposals strained the alliance. Mazda mistakenly would consider the ideas as already having official Ford management approval, since Mazda would never approach Ford or any other partner with an idea until the project had official management approval. Hence, Mazda would take the time and effort to officially review the idea, only to be frustrated in the end when Ford management did not approve the idea. Eventually, both sides met to discuss their differences in management styles and iron out a communications strategy to eliminate problems and cultural clashes.'

References

Ohmae K. (1985). *Triad Power: The Coming Shape of Global Competition.* McKinsey & Co., Inc. Reprinted with permissions from The Free Press, a division of MacMillan Inc., p. 178

Ohmae K. (1990). *The Borderless World.* McKinsey & Co., Inc. Harper Business, a division of HarperCollins Publishers, p. 119

9

Conflict and change: how partners cope

Most MNCs concede that conflict in alliances is inevitable, given the rich diversity of capabilities, cultures and constraints of each partner. In fact, a certain level of conflict and competition can be healthy. For instance, according to an executive involved in a European/Asian alliance, 'Both partners privately try to foster some competitive tension between the various functional groups cooperating on projects in R&D, product development and marketing, even though neither side would admit this fact. Each partner has complementary strengths and weaknesses. With a little dose of competition, each side uses its partners' competitive skills as its own private benchmark to match or exceed.'

Whether conflict is deliberately planned or not, most alliance practitioners find that managing some level of tension is part of the regular challenge of living with an alliance. Yet success depends on maintaining a delicate balance between having a certain amount of conflict and not allowing the problems to swell and hamper progress. This chapter first offers some pointers from alliance executives on how they manage and resolve conflict, then examines two case studies: how Fuji Xerox and Xerox manage the competitive tension between the two entities, and how Westinghouse and Mitsubishi revamped their alliances to accommodate changes in the relationship and to sidestep future problems.

Seven steps to a better marriage

Conflicts are never easy to solve, least of all when they occur in a cross-cultural alliance. However, some experienced executives have offered a number of suggestions on how alliances can tackle such problems.

Employ a 'shoot the messenger' strategy

Howard Hill, a Detroit-based lawyer and former legal counsel at Chrysler, suggests a novel strategy often used by Chrysler for resolving conflicts and deadlocks. According to Hill, 'When partners reach an impasse, we suggest a dispute resolution in which both partners must send a deadlock notice to senior management at their respective parents. In the notice, the alliance executive asks the CEO or another senior corporate representative to select three dates on which he would be available to meet with his counterpart from the other partner to resolve the problem. What happens is that no executive wants to be the messenger with bad news that signals to the CEO "I have failed or I am not smart enough to solve problems". Nor are some CEOs particularly sympathetic, adding to this feeling of "shooting the messenger as a way to eliminate the problem". Consequently, what usually transpires with this technique is that alliance executives will work unbelievably hard to solve any disagreements to avoid getting the parents involved.'

Have alliance executives jointly set milestones

According to Glenn Gardner, former chairman of Diamond Star Motors (DSM) and current manager for the LH programme, partners should jointly set specific operating milestones for the ventures. For example, both Gardner and Yoichi Nakane, the Mitsubishi-appointed president for DSM, mutually agreed to a specific launch date for DSM. As Gardner says, 'We had an unbelievable number of operating hurdles to achieve our launch date.' Yet the necessity for the launch broke many impasses. Gardner notes that 'Both Nakane and I were determined to meet our goal.' In some respects Gardner likened the relationship to a marriage, saying that 'While some decisions in a marriage are a straightforward 50–50 effort, other problems may require an uneven split: 70–30, 60–40, 65–35, etc. We both realized that certain issues required one side to defer to his partner.' In most cases Gardner needed to defer to Nakane, who was primarily responsible for operations. Thus, says Gardner, 'I was not about to push for a stronger role and risk derailing the project.'

Gardner found that a strategy of jointly setting a specific goal for a venture can encourage partners to be flexible when resolving problems. However, the same partner cannot always give in to the other. Gardner says, 'I would never argue on an operational problem when it was a critical milestone that threatened the DSM project. However, in less critical areas I would stand firm. I did not want to appear as a mere pushover on all issues. By fighting on the ancillary issues I could build respect and equality, yet not endanger the venture's progress.'

Steer the alliance clear of the goals and strategies of the parents

Jean Bilien, president of CFM International, views conflicts and overlap between a venture and its parent organizations as a potential minefield of problems. From its inception, says Bilien, a venture must steer clear of parent operations in strategies, geographic expanse, product lines and so forth. In fact, Bilien attributes CFM's success to its maintaining a distinct separation between the venture and the parents' business lines. For instance, many of the difficulties and tensions in the Rolls-Royce–Pratt venture of forming International Aero Engines to manufacture V2500 engines stemmed from competitive conflicts with the parent organizations. The V2500, a competitor of CFM's own products, also competes directly with two Pratt engines – the JTAT 200 series and the Pratt 2037, as well as Rolls-Royce's RB211 engine. As another industry executive notes, 'Every time there is an international competition, all the project managers are there, contesting head-on with each other. Not only does the tension make managing the venture and relations with the parents strenuous, it can hamper productivity. Nobody wants to share information or new developments.'

Prepare alliance managers

Ford takes a proactive stance by offering a regular dose of training on how executives manage alliances and minimize problems. According to Paul Drenkow, a Ford executive active in the Ford–Mazda relationship, 'We realized a few years ago that many conflicts and headaches in the Ford–Mazda alliance, which spans over 30 projects, could be eliminated if we applied a consistent set of management principles to projects. Many of our problems in the relationship stemmed from unclear or misread signals between the two partners.' As a result, Ford and Mazda jointly developed a basic set of operating principles for the alliance. Separately, Ford also conducted a detailed assessment of how the company could operate more effectively with its partners, particularly Mazda. This effort led to the establishment of a three-day programme christened the Japan

Business Association. The seminar, held in Tokyo, is designed for existing and future managers of alliance projects. This programme gives courses on joint Ford–Mazda principles, internal Ford guidelines on how to work with foreign partners, how to negotiate and structure alliances, how to handle pricing, capital requirements, and budgets, how to operate in Japan and its culture and acceptable business practices. Drenkow said that 'While mishaps still occur – particularly given Ford's corporate complexity and its relationship to Mazda – the programme has helped to reduce problems and confusion.'

Eliminate product overlap

In addition to removing conflicting goals, Don Dancer suggests that partners must be willing to eliminate any product overlap before launching an alliance. For instance, in the GE–Fanuc link the two parties had complementary strengths in different product lines, GE in programmable logic controllers, whereas FANUC clearly led in computerized numerical controllers (CNCs). At the same time, however, GE did have a CNC product line. Both sides worked to phase out the overlap. As Dancer insists, 'Ventures cannot have competing products. This can foster animosity among employees from either side. While the "not invented here" syndrome initially can nurture resentment among employees when products are discontinued, the ill will dissipates once the venture progresses. Much of the success of the alliance will rest on how well firms address areas of obvious conflict in products, strategies and regions.'

Tap a seasoned alliance coordinator to mediate

According to Michio Naruto, senior vice-president and principal liaison for ICL–Fujitsu relations at Fujitsu, differences occasionally require some intervention from executives having many years of experience with a given partner. Naruto, who has been involved in the ICL–Fujitsu relationship since its inception in 1981, is often asked to intervene when misunderstandings or problems between divisions threaten the relationship. For example, he recalls a recent product link in which ICL planned to purchase a Fujitsu keyboard for one of its systems. The ICL engineers requested their counterparts at Fujitsu to test the quality of the product by hitting the same key 50 million times. Says Naruto, 'The request implies an abnormally high usage rate. It is unreasonable to think that someone would actually press the same key 50 million times, unless of course you work for the IRS. Consequently, the Fujitsu engineers were very upset and resented the demand. I then participated in the discussions to help convince the ICL division that they did not need such an excessive guarantee.'

Remember – flexibility is a virtue

Market and environment conditions change, and partners must be adaptable. Although a contract may legally bind partners together, many multinationals warn that a rigid adherence to an agreement can sound the death-knell of an alliance. When the partners to a European/UK alliance finalized the contract, the chairman of the Japanese company remarked that if the partners ever had to refer to the contract, the venture had failed. According to the CEO for the European company, 'When partners haggle over a contract and strictly hold each other to its terms, it is not collaboration but an original equipment manufacturing deal.' For instance, after the contract was signed, the base rate for product prices in the agreement shifted tremendously. Yet rather than enforce the contract prices, the partners met to determine a more equitable arrangement.

Tackling conflict and change in two different alliances

Most alliances rely on a variety of methods to tackle problems such as those described above, but some close-knit alliances have also installed formal channels to resolve differences and fortify strengths. The following two cases are examples of how some companies manage conflict and change. The material first examines the wide-ranging relationship between Fuji Xerox and Xerox, with their interwoven ties in R&D, manufacturing, product lines, marketing and services. This analysis highlights how the two firms tackle daily problems and resolve longer-term strategic issues. The second case looks at how two partners, Westinghouse and Mitsubishi, managed to overcome problems by dramatically overhauling the alliance.

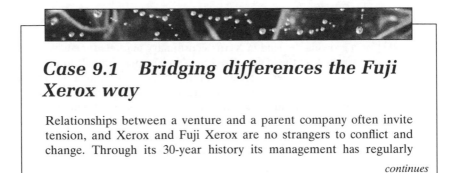

Case 9.1   Bridging differences the Fuji Xerox way

Relationships between a venture and a parent company often invite tension, and Xerox and Fuji Xerox are no strangers to conflict and change. Through its 30-year history its management has regularly

continues

---

continued

applied a healthy mix of flexibility, compromise and communication to keep the relationship on track. In particular, both firms encourage direct and frequent meetings between the various functional groups to minimize conflict. According to Robert Meredith, resident Xerox director at Fuji Xerox, 'Both firms have always made an effort to closely coordinate operations and strategy. Management emphasizes direct meetings and contacts between the different management levels and functional areas. Neither side ever wants to tie the groups up in knots with extra layers of bureaucracy and central coordination.'

The efforts and open relationship between Fuji Xerox and Xerox notwithstanding, market changes and operational ambitions threatened to unleash a host of new threats. These challenges prompted management to revamp the relationship with new strategic directions and more structured communication links. Yotaro Kobayashi, chairman and CEO of Fuji Xerox, and Paul Allaire, CEO of Xerox, commissioned their functional heads and corporate planners to form the Co-Destiny III task force in 1990. This device, conceived by Kobayashi, offers an avenue where senior management on both sides can meet to discuss strategy, goals and the long-term future and direction of the relationship. The main problems faced by the Co-Destiny III task force included a number of areas.

The South Pacific region   Fuji Xerox wanted to expand its Asian markets. The original technology and marketing contracts gave Fuji Xerox responsibility for Indonesia, South Korea, the Philippines, Taiwan and Thailand. Rank Xerox held responsibility for the South Pacific region: Australia, New Zealand, Singapore, Malaysia, China, and Hong Kong. According to Hideki Kaihatsu, senior managing director and chief staff officer at Fuji Xerox, 'Fuji Xerox encountered a number of obstacles from the arrangement. First, much of the potential business from Japanese MNCs was lost in the South Pacific area because of no direct presence of Japanese marketing and technical managers. Second, manufacturing inefficiencies abounded; knock-down kits often were shipped from Fuji Xerox to the UK for assembly and then re-exported to Asia.'

Miniaturization   A global push toward miniaturization exacerbated tension in the low-priced end of the market. Market analyses indicated a growing demand in Xerox's customary markets for smaller products, which were the mainstay of Fuji Xerox's operations. Traditionally, there had always been a broad split in product and regional responsibilities between the two entities, with Fuji Xerox in the low end of the market for office products like small copiers, personal facsimile machines and small printers in Asia, while Xerox concentrated on the middle and high portions of the market (medium-and large-volume copiers and office machines) in North America. The miniaturization boom meant that

continues

continued

both firms had to determine how they could maximize their investment yet also work out a role for Xerox in the low end of the industry.

This new problem illustrated to Xerox and Fuji Xerox how a venture's very success can present new challenges. Throughout the 1980s, as Fuji Xerox greatly expanded its technological capabilities and functional resources, its operational and strategic links to Xerox proliferated. According to Kobayashi, between 1980 and 1988 Fuji Xerox's sales to the Xerox group grew from $32 million in 1980 to $620 million in 1988. In 1980 some 30% of the small copiers sold by the Xerox group had been designed and developed by Fuji Xerox. By 1987, 94% were sourced from Fuji Xerox. Consequently, neither Fuji Xerox nor Xerox could afford to reduce Fuji Xerox's role in the low-end market. Yet Xerox needed equally to pursue its own ambitions in small-sized office products, to protect its home turf. In essence, the Co-Destiny task force had to blend Fuji Xerox's existing low-end predominance with Xerox's new needs, without incurring any wasteful duplication of effort. Complicating matters was the fear of encroachment and the resentment that can surface among employees when ventures' and parents' ambitions conflict.

Maintaining a united front Both firms were eager to map out the long-term vision, goals and strategic intent of the partnership for the 21st century. Senior management wanted to fine-tune their strategies to present a united front against the competition. Indeed, the competition, particularly from Canon, was formidable. The Harvard Business School case on Fuji Xerox and Xerox states the following (Gomes-Casseres and McQuade, 1991):

> 'From 1980 to 1989, Canon's total sales grew from $2.9 billion to $9.4 billion, a growth rate of 14% per year. Canon's R&D spending grew even more rapidly at 24% per year, from $77 million to $525 million. [Further,] by 1989, Canon was no longer primarily a camera company – 40% of its revenues came from copiers, and 20% from laser printers.' While Canon has a stronghold in the entry level of the copier market, traditionally a weak area for Xerox but the focal point for Fuji Xerox operations, Canon's long-term strategy places a high priority on the higher end of the product spectrum. In fact, the Japanese firm has been channeling substantial investments into building a stronger presence in the mid- and high-volume copiers, Xerox's mainstay. 'Canon's goal was to become a $70 billion company by the year 2000, implying a 22% annual growth rate in the 1990s. A significant portion of this growth was projected to come from Xerox's heartland – high- and mid-volume copiers and printers.' 'Although Canon spent less than $600 million on R&D annually, compared to Xerox's $800 million and FX's $300 million, [Canon] has introduced twice as many products as the Xerox group.'

continues

continued

With their alliance, Xerox and Fuji Xerox certainly believe that one plus one equals at least three, if not more. Yet true partnerships are not built without effort, and the management in this case sought to reinforce links between the two entities to exploit fully their strengths and synergies and ward off the competition. For Fuji Xerox and Xerox a fluid organizational structure to exchange information, ideas and people was a crucial weapon to ward off unnecessary internal conflicts and fend off external competitive threats.

How solutions were found

According to Jefferson Kennard, director for Fuji Xerox relations at Xerox, the Co-Destiny task force worked diligently for over a year on the issues. The efforts paid off with the following resolutions.

In regard to the **South Pacific region**, Fuji Xerox paid approximately $500 million to acquire operational and strategic responsibility for that area. Management recognized early on that it needed to handle delicately the transference of power and responsibility from Rank Xerox to Fuji Xerox. In particular, the firms were eager to lessen the impact on managers, employees and existing customers in the region.

To solve these problems Fuji Xerox established a new company in Singapore. The president of the operation is Japanese, but all other staff were recruited locally or were transferred from former Rank Xerox marketing locations in the region. The principal language in the office is English. As Kennard said, 'We targeted Singapore to simply put a new face on the company. We also wanted to minimize any potential anti-Japanese sentiments by locating within the region and encouraging a company culture that mirrors the local environment, not the Japanese ownership.'

With respect to the **miniaturization** issue, a recent summit meeting between the heads of Fuji Xerox and Xerox inaugurated a new Fuji Xerox–Xerox joint venture. According to Kennard, it is the first joint venture created by the parent and child in the 30-year relationship. Its aim is to collaborate in the low-priced end of the market. The entity, Xerox International Partners Ltd, is a 51–49 venture with headquarters in Palo Alto, California. The venture will market on an OEM basis Fuji Xerox-designed, developed and manufactured printers for the low end of the market. The partners targeted printers first because this is the fastest-growing segment in office equipment. The venture may eventually expand its cooperation to include other low end products such as multi-function devices. There may also be future cooperation in such additional functional areas as R&D and manufacturing. Kennard points out that Xerox is the majority partner because the venture is located in the US and the Connecticut-based MNC will take the lead in marketing. However, the president of the venture is from Fuji Xerox.

On the united front, research by the Co-Destiny III task force reinforced the critical importance of communication at all levels, to reduce

continues

continued

conflict and boost competitiveness. Faced, however, with fierce competition and the likelihood of even greater links and overlap in the alliance, the incidence of problems was likely to increase. Confronted with these risks and threats, the Co-Destiny task force decided to officially formalize the communication efforts. This formal recognition has sent a strong signal to all management ranks, giving executives on both sides a clear mandate to work together as teams.

The new communications system is comprised of the following meetings and programmes.

Co-Destiny task force　Fuji Xerox and Xerox created the Co-Destiny process, for which there have been three separate task forces during the past ten years, to offer an opportunity to plan jointly for the future. The task force, which includes senior executives from all functions, is formed when either side feels the need to re-evaluate the long-term goals and direction of the partnership or in response to unusual pressures in the environment. There is no regular schedule or plan. As Fuji Xerox's Chairman and CEO Kobayashi says, 'The emphasis is on what the two firms will do together. The idea is to look at the world and decide how we can best maximize our strengths and minimize weaknesses to prepare for the 21st century.'

Presidential summit meetings　The CEOs of Fuji Xerox and Xerox meet semi-annually to review strategies and operations. The two executives and their direct reports map out long-range plans for different products, markets and functions.

Functional meetings　The heads of every function meet with their counterparts twice a year, at which meetings the executives design their respective one- and five-year plans. Each plan has a corresponding set of action items and goals. In particular, the functional heads analyse and incorporate elements from the presidential summit agenda in their documents. The proposals for each functional group are then presented to senior management. Once approved, most of the action items then require regular face-to-face meetings between lower-level employees, as well as frequent exchanges of personnel.

Resident directors　Each company has an in-house resident director to encourage close contact in the relationship. There are three principal roles for the resident director:

(1)　To be cognizant of the enormous variety of cooperative activities in all functions;
(2)　To spot the salient issues and channel them to the appropriate executives and decision makers;
(3)　To identify and create synergies where both sides could benefit.

continues

continued

Personnel exchanges As does the resident director programme, personnel exchanges offer an excellent opportunity for employees to develop their own working relationships and agendas. By 1989, well over 1000 young high-potential Fuji Xerox employees had spent three years each as residents at Xerox, and some 100 Xerox employees had done the same at Fuji Xerox. In addition to these longer-term transfers there are approximately 1000 visits per year from managers and engineers to each other's locations.

Case 9.2   *Westinghouse and Mitsubishi strengthen their alliances*

According to management expert Peter Drucker, many corporate liaisons can get into serious – and perhaps critical – trouble when they succeed. Good examples of this type of problem are the dynamic, complex alliances between Westinghouse US and two powerhouses in the Mitsubishi group – Mitsubishi Electric (Melco) and Mitsubishi Heavy Industries (MHI). Their successes created new difficulties. Yet the solid relationship and commitment between these partners enabled the three MNCs to enter a new cooperative era in the Mitsubishi–Westinghouse relationship.

The Westinghouse–Mitsubishi alliance dates back to licensing agreements forged in the 1920s. Over the years, the partners have built up an army of cooperative links in R&D, product development, manufacturing and marketing. However, changing global market conditions and pressures on the partners for new strategies placed the complex of alliances in jeopardy. This case study looks separately at how the firms revamped the relationship to preserve the alliances between Westinghouse and Melco and between Westinghouse and MHI, since they faced different obstacles.

Westinghouse–MHI breathe new life into alliance
Westinghouse and MHI have long enjoyed a classic licensing arrangement in steam turbine and gas turbine technology. As is often the case in such a licensing relationship, however, the student eventually accumulates as much knowledge as the teacher, jeopardizing the deal. During the mid-1980s, MHI's lower-level engineers in particular became disillusioned with a relationship in which the Japanese firm paid

continues

continued

royalties for Westinghouse technology that MHI had greatly advanced. Westinghouse equally acknowledged that the licensing partnership was outdated, because of the new product and technology innovations achieved by MHI.

Yet senior management at both companies still wanted to preserve the relationship, for several reasons. For one thing, global market conditions were tough, and both sides believed they would be more effective competing as partners rather than alone. Also, technically MHI could not use the technology once the licensing agreement had expired, since licensing is a rental and not a transfer of ownership. In addition, MHI and Westinghouse wanted to build on many years of a good relationship. Both managements felt they could achieve new product, market and technological breakthroughs by working as strategic partners.

Consequently, as the agreements came up for renewal MHI and Westinghouse worked out a new direction and vision for the alliance. When the agreement covering steam turbines came up for renewal in February 1989, the partners replaced the old licensing agreement with three new contracts that are completely without royalties. As Jon Elmendorf, former president of Westinghouse Energy Systems (Japan) and current director for environmental compliance at Westinghouse in the US says, 'The agreement took effect in March 1989, even though we actually did not sign the deal until September. It took us an extra six months to iron out the mechanics of the alliance.'

The key features of the new agreement include the following.

Business cooperation   MHI and Westinghouse agree to jointly develop and advance technology together. The agreement also covers cooperation in product development. The partners further identified plans to create partnership strategies to build a global presence and cooperate in marketing on a case-by-case basis where such cooperation would enhance competitiveness.

Technology cooperation   The partners will collaborate in R&D, either in the same research labs or at their own separate locations. However, all R&D efforts and patents will be jointly owned by MHI and Westinghouse. The contract also granted MHI rights to use the Westinghouse technology in perpetuity.

Organizing communication links

When MHI and Westinghouse designed their new arrangements, both sides realized that alliances need constant attention and maintenance, so they created a series of committees to accompany the new partnership and foster close contacts. 'Our main aim,' says Jon Elmendorf, 'is to encourage direct relationship between the different managers and engineers. We want to avoid a single point of contact, because problems

continues

continued

are much easier to solve by talking directly with peers.' The three committees include, among others, the following.

A steering committee   Top management at MHI and Westinghouse meet semi-annually to discuss the alliance and evaluate the direction and strategy of the partnership. The partners aim to have a frank discussion on key issues: what each firm expects from the alliance; how the partnership can improve competitiveness; how rival firms react to the new liaison; and an outline for one-, two- and 10-year agendas for the different activities and operations.

A technology committee   This committee brings together engineers and managers from MHI and Westinghouse to discuss products, technology and new strategies. There is no formal schedule for meetings, but the engineers are encouraged to meet frequently.

A marketing committee   The marketing team pools executives from both partners to brainstorm on how to build market share and prise open new markets. As with the technology committee, the marketing group is encouraged to meet regularly.

Alliance in gas turbines mirrors new strategy

Following the success of the new MHI–Westinghouse relationship in steam turbines, the partners decided to adopt the same strategy for gas turbines. Even though that licensing agreement did not technically expire until 1992, senior management signed a similar set of agreements for gas turbines in July 1991.

The decision to move quickly has paid off. As Elmendorf notes, the new MHI–Westinghouse global strategic partnership recently won the Yu Yu twin cities project in Korea to build two new power plants. Westinghouse will act as the lead vendor, with MHI as its partner.

Westinghouse and Melco level the playing ground

Riding on the successful changes in the Westinghouse–MHI relationship, the two firms set out on the same road in mid-1991. Initially, a corporate umbrella agreement between the senior management of Westinghouse and that of Melco constituted the keystone of the alliance. The umbrella accord included a cluster of Westinghouse technologies licensed to Mitsubishi. Royalty and other fees from the technologies were paid directly to Westinghouse senior management and later disbursed internally to the different divisions. According to Elmendorf, the agreement functioned smoothly for years. Mitsubishi obtained the necessary technology to build a big business in the power-generation industry. On its side Westinghouse received a steady stream of revenue and also expanded the geographic scope of its technology. Yet turbulent global market conditions and changing corporate objectives and strategies threatened to unbundle the closely-knit relationship.

continues

continued

Several developments placed the umbrella agreement in jeopardy. First, Westinghouse's markets for power generation in the US were shrinking, while the Asian markets were expanding. It did not make sense for Westinghouse to push on while its markets floundered. As one Mitsubishi executive said, 'It was never a case of one partner being dumb while the other was savvy. The world changes, markets change. And companies must react.'

Consequently, Westinghouse refocused its energies from working with mature, low-growth industries such as certain areas of power generation toward higher-growth segments. Key businesses, particularly the transmission and distribution (T&D) section, were sold to competitor Asea Brown Boveri (ABB). Westinghouse also withdrew its participation in a 50–50 joint venture with Melco in high-voltage power circuit breakers. Other sectors were restructured and downsized. The amount of business connected to the umbrella agreement fell from a high of 50 projects to only a handful. Yet the royalties had already been paid by Melco and disbursed by senior management, leading to tension at lower levels when projects ran aground.

A second factor jeopardizing the umbrella agreement is that the licensee/licensor relationship became obsolete. Elmendorf points out that Mitsubishi had clearly advanced the technology. The Japanese firm had developed many improvement patents as well as introducing new technologies and products to the market. Much of the resentment among Mitsubishi engineers stemmed from their desire to operate on a level playing ground with Westinghouse. And other executives concurred, saying that there comes a time in any prosperous licensing relationship when the two sides must operate as equals, to keep problems and tension from suffocating the relationship.

The power of equals

Subsequently, both partners worked to transform the alliance from a licensee/licenser relationship to a global strategic partnership. Westinghouse and Melco allowed the umbrella agreement to expire when it came up for renewal in April 1991. Instead, they replaced it with a series of agreements covering products, sourcing and relationships.

Products The partners listed several product areas in which they agreed to collaborate in R&D, new technology and product development, manufacturing and marketing. Their products cover the field for large rotating electric generators that are either hydrogen- or air-cooled. To strengthen the new relationship, Melco recently established an office in Orlando, Florida, the operating centre for Westinghouse's power-generation businesses. The two partners also exchanged engineers, with one Melco engineer working in a Westinghouse plant in Orlando and two Westinghouse engineers transferred to Melco facilities in Japan.

continues

continued

Sourcing   After Westinghouse shed several low-profit businesses in power generation in the late 1980s, the US MNC faced serious gaps in its product line for the construction and maintenance of power plants. Therefore, Westinghouse and Melco signed a series of supplier agreements in which the latter acts as principal supplier for equipment such as transformers, switch gear, and so on.

Relationship   Mirroring the MHI–Westinghouse deal, both partners were committed to working together worldwide. Management also wanted to encourage as much cooperation and communication as possible between all levels of management and engineers to help reconcile previous differences and problems. Hence, Melco and Westinghouse also adopted the three-committee strategy of steering, technology and market committees to nurture cooperation and compete as partners in the global marketplace.

Reference

Gomes-Casseres B. and McQuade K. (1991). *Xerox and Fuji Xerox*, case 391-156. Boston: Harvard Business School, 1991. Copyright © 1991 by the President and Fellows of Harvard College, p. 13

10

The foundation for management success

Finding the right mix of management ingredients for success can be quite daunting, particularly since each alliance has its own unique needs and talents. In an effort to improve the success ratio for today's alliances, multinationals offered a number of managerial suggestions. In this chapter we examine some of the crucial components for maintaining a competitive alliance – designing a solid management and human resource base, fostering close communications links and reducing the risks of competitive cooperation.

Addressing human resource issues

Find me a leader: who is Mr Right?

Success in alliances depends largely on the character and leadership qualities of the executives charged with running the venture. Lino Piedra, former chairman of Diamond Star Motors (DSM) and senior executive at Chrysler, emphasizes how the venture leader must have a clear code of ethics and understand all of his obligations. According to him, one cannot overemphasize a leader's duty to ensure that his venture's management team and employees know what game the alliance is playing and where the goals are. The CEO has the unenviable task of building a management and employee team around the alliance's mission. He or she must set the direction, then communicate it to the work force.

Alexander Giacco, former chairman of Hercules and Himont, offered this opinion, 'All partners must be absolutely comfortable with the CEO. He particularly emphasizes the need to find an executive who will give equal weight to all the partners' needs and interests. If the venture leader comes from one of the parents, he must be careful not to spend too much time with management from his parent company. Other partners may begin to believe his position on venture issues is swayed. Their trust and support for him and the venture will dwindle.'

Stephen Albertalli, recently retired director of investor relations at Corning, offered a suggestion on how Corning avoids the problem when an alliance CEO appears to spend too much time with his parent company. Parent firms should give a venture's management and board of directors ample decision-making powers. This permits them to act immediately on many issues, rather than first having to consult the parents. Added Albertalli, 'If a venture's management frequently has to return to the parents for authorization, the alliance executives will begin to analyse the problem from the parents' perspective. Risks then increase that alliance decisions [will] mirror the parents' rather than the venture's interests.'

According to Glenn Gardner, programme manager for the LH programme at Chrysler and first chairman of DSM, 'The alliance CEO sets an example to all venture employees. And if the CEO does not first look after the interests and goals of the venture – even when they may conflict with parent interests – then there is scarcely a chance to create a management team that supports the venture's goals and ambitions.' Yet the task can seem insurmountable. The unwritten rule for alliances is that most MNCs still expect venture executives to safeguard the interests of the parent company. Consequently, there is a built-in conflict which venture management must learn how to balance.

Piedra finds that the task of balancing a venture's interests and the ambitions of the parents is a critical problem for venture leaders. As he says, 'Jobs at more senior levels are usually not well-defined. Hence, there is greater latitude for interpretation and innuendos, further complicating roles, responsibilities and decisions. For instance, at venture board meetings the alliance's health and prosperity is a top priority – but this may not be the case at a partner's individual corporate strategy meeting. Senior venture executives must be able to deal with both pressures. In fact, if an executive has any plans to return to the parent company, he or she better figure out how to manage the dichotomy.'

Besides balancing the interests of parent and venture, venture leaders must be able to cope with a host of other challenges. Tim

Leuliette, president and CEO of ITT Automotive, says partners must find executives who possess a portfolio of skills to manage and exploit the partners' differences. In this regard, Piedra cites the following character-istics desirable in alliance leaders: independence; self-reliance; ability to work well away from the day-to-day direction of headquarters; adapt-ability; ability to get along easily with others; and being able to 'go with the flow'. On the latter point Piedra says, 'I do not mean in the sense of being weak willed. Instead, the Japanese have an expression, "hard like water". It refers to how water is incompressible and will mould to what-ever container is used. This implies qualities of being firm yet flexible enough to adapt to different needs and environments.' In fact, adds Piedra, the complex roles and responsibilities require an alliance's leader to understand clearly who he is, what he represents and what his obliga-tions are to the other partners besides his parent company, as well as the objectives of the venture.

Leuliette adds that alliances need leaders who do not want to manage a global business from the centre. Instead, he points to how former chairman Lee Iaccoca managed Chrsyler. Iaccoca said 'I manage by walking around.' Logistically, it does make it rather difficult to adopt this strategy if the venture has operations in 20 countries. But Leuliette points out that ITT Automotive manages its ventures with a philosophy of 'Don't come to us, we'll go to you'. For example, for monthly venture conferences senior executives organize the meeting in a different location each month. This offers an opportunity to meet and interact directly with local venture employees and management.

Eric Mittelstadt, president of Fanuc Robotics – formerly a JV with General Motors – emphasizes the need to maintain very 'proactive leadership'. As he said, 'As the venture leader of GMFanuc Robotics, my top priorities were to build and maintain trust and foster a team spirit among employees and also with the parent companies. I needed to be consistent in my actions and words, since they sent important signals to employees.'

For instance, GMFanuc had a unique relationship with both its parents. With GM the venture acted as a supplier for robots. There was also some collaboration in R&D and technology with GM's internal robotics research area. With FANUC the venture cooperated on a variety of projects in research, technology and product development. FANUC also acted as a supplier to GMFanuc for important products and components. Mittelstadt remarked that the dynamics of a buy/sell relationship versus cooperative R&D and technology projects are quite different. Yet they overlap and influence each other.

For instance, GMFanuc sourced approximately 25% of its robots from FANUC, the world industry leader and largest producer of robot-ics, which obviously has better operating margins. Mittelstadt offered the following scenario. GMFanuc would bid for a high-volume, fiercely competitive order. In order to win it, profit margins were on the low side. Yet suddenly complaints and resentment would swell when venture engineers grumbled about FANUC's earnings. For instance, said Mittelstadt, 'I would hear jabs about how FANUC was earning 18% after taxes on sales while the venture did not even come close to those levels. Indeed, the margins were true, but I needed to intervene to explain why. FANUC was the world's largest manufacturer of certain robots, such as computerized numerical controllers (CNCs). Obviously, it reaped considerably greater economies of scale. I actively worked to squash the complaints immediately and offer proof with concrete examples of when FANUC gave us a break on pricing to win a deal. Unless top management stays on top of these issues, they are like sores which can fester. New rumours circulate and the situation can lead to insurmountable problems. Ill will grows and impacts all areas of the alliance – R&D, technology, product development, etc. For me, putting out these fires was my most challenging and important job.'

In recalling his experiences at the helm of DSM, Gardner emphasizes the importance of displaying honesty, commitment and fairness without exception. As he says, 'Most employees will take their cues from senior management. If the leaders are not consistent, this will give lower-level management and employees ample ammunition to resist building a cooperative team spirit in the venture. There were instances in which DSM employees from both partners were dishonest and unfair, creating an array of problems. Yet neither the Mitsubishi-appointed president – Yoichi Nakane – nor I flinched. Had we not been firm in our actions and policies, employees would have quickly spotted the inconsistencies and reverted to their old bad habits.'

According to Mittelstadt, 'The CEO of any venture must actively demonstrate his full trust and support for the venture and the parents. This encourages teamwork within the venture and with colleagues in the parent companies.' Added Leuliette, 'Partners must find leaders, not just managers. A manager tells you what to do. A leader shows you how to do it.' This advice is doubly important in alliances where fear and anxiety about dealing with a partner/competitor provide fertile ground for fostering mistrust. However, the real challenge is often to find executives with both leadership and management qualities. Some executives argue that a venture's leader must also possess the management skills to tackle the day-to-day hassles and obligations of running a business. Several firms find it easier to build leadership teams. For instance, some alliances place two or three individuals at the helm to both lead and manage: for instance, the power is shared by two directors at the Nippon Sheet Glass/LOF Glass joint venture in Kentucky. Similarly, at Siemens Electronics in the US, three executives function together as the president's office.

Concluded Leuliette, 'Today's leader must be a team player. Nowhere is the need greater for a team approach than in an alliance. In the past, there were two types of leaders. First, there was the cigar-chomping, limousine chap who made all the decisions without consulting anyone. Second, there was the poor fellow who was incapable of making any decision; he was immobilized by turf fights and corporate politics. Neither one has a place in an alliance. Today's alliance leader will say to his team, "Okay we need a decision by two o'clock. Either I make it alone or we can do it together."'

Build a solid management team

A CEO's ability to manage with a team strategy depends on recruiting the appropriate executives for the management crew. Not every executive is suited to work closely with counterparts from different national and corporate cultures. On the one hand, companies need to select executives with the skills and know-how to propel the operations of the venture forward. On the other hand, such executives may not necessarily possess the requisite diplomacy to effectively manage the often delicate relationship and interactions between the various alliance partners. In their search for talented alliance managers, several MNCs zeroed in on individuals with some of the five following qualifications:

Find the technician who is culturally well-versed

According to many venture executives, it is critical to find people who can manage the marriage successfully over time. This does *not* mean just finding a mid-level executive who manages technology. The management skills require a fairly high-level individual who understands the company and the culture in which the alliance will operate. A crucial goal of the alliance manager is to secure trust, respect and influence with the partner. This task is made easier if the manager is a culturally sensitive individual who is broad-minded enough to promote both his own and the ally's culture.

Pick managers with strong potential for upward mobility

According to Lino Piedra of Chrysler, the people initially appointed to a venture send a strong signal of the partners' support and commitment. Tim Leuliette agreed. 'If you appoint a manager who is later promoted to a very senior position within the parent company, this can significantly motivate venture employees.'

Above all, executives caution against relocating mediocre employees to alliances, particularly given the growing importance of alliances to many MNCs' global strategies. Robert Ecklin, senior vice-president for industrial products at Corning, says Corning seeks high-potential entrepreneurial types. 'While it is very difficult for me to assign some of my best and brightest, it is a mistake to try to cut corners when launching a venture. The gravest error is to assign the village idiots.' Echoed Stephen Albertalli, 'You can be sure Corning never assigns any stumblebums to its joint ventures.' In fact, said Howard Hill, a Detroit-based lawyer, 'Assigning "the son of the chairman's best friend" or "poor Bob from accounting because no other division will take him" is a quick way to ruin a venture.'

Seek a good listener

As a US executive who works closely with his firm's Japanese partners explained, it is essential that a manager be willing and able to listen – *and* to take the time to understand what the partner is trying to say. Based on his experience in Japan, he has found that the Japanese do not communicate information in the same manner as their US counterparts. 'Thus,' he remarked, 'you have to look for the answers in different ways. If you rely on a combative approach, you never hear anything, and the Japanese will quit trying to talk to you.'

Match executive talents to venture conditions

Jacques Meyer of AT&T said his company first seeks to match the talents and skills of the executives with the venture's needs and mission. For instance, a cash cow obviously needs a very different type of executive than a fast-growing business. A Clark Equipment official pointed out how the various stages of a venture frequently mandate different executive talents. For example, when Clark and Volvo established their 50–50 JV VME Construction Equipment they needed executives skilled at consolidating and restructuring the construction equipment operations of both partners. He remarked that 'It is a painful and difficult task to close plants, relocate employees, prune product lines, etc. The tasks require executives with specialized skills and capabilities on how to downsize and trim a business. Yet once the restructuring is over, the venture switches into a growth mode. The alliance now needs executives with the vision and talents to expand the business and uncover new market opportunities. Sometimes partners are lucky [enough] to find all of these qualities in the same executive. In most cases, however, a venture needs two sets of management teams.'

A well-respected liaison

Alliance executives should have credibility with the organizations of both (or all) allies. The most serious organizational problem one US MNC (Company A) has encountered with a Japanese partner is finding a high-level Japanese national to serve as second in command. Company A searched for an executive with sufficient authority and responsibility to command the respect of both US management and its Japanese partner. In this regard, the US MNC felt that the manager should be a Japanese national to act as an effective liaison with the Japanese partner, but the desired candidate should also come from its own ranks or he would not be seen as speaking for the US firm.

Staffing ventures: where to look

In general, staff for ventures can come from one of three pools – corporate headquarters, outsiders and subsidiaries. Many ventures examined in this book drew people from corporate headquarters to staff their alliances. Other multinationals preferred to draw their alliance personnel from local and regional subsidiaries, as this can usually be done at less cost than transferring headquarters personnel. US Company X believed this practice helped it integrate venture products and operations into its global businesses. By using personnel from the subsidiaries, the firm could create continuous three-way communications and coordination among the three principal elements of its global strategy: parent headquarters, local and regional subsidiary operations and its alliances.

Said a Company X executive, 'If a joint venture is located in or near our foreign partner's headquarter operations, the local firm traditionally contributes the majority of lower-level staff. Our input may be key strategic decision-makers, such as the president, the CFO and marketing director. But we are kidding ourselves if we think that we really control and operate the JV with a handful of executives. We believe we can boost our position in the venture by requesting that some lower-level management and operational positions be filled by staff from our subs in the country.' An added plus: the alliance provides valuable training opportunities for subsidiary personnel.

Executives such as Meyer at AT&T suggest companies do not restrict their recruiting efforts to local subsidiaries. Instead, they emphasize the merits of tapping local management talent. As with wholly owned operations, this places the venture on the right track to prise open regional market and business opportunities. Recruiting local executive talent also encourages the alliance to develop a culture of its own, different from that of its partners. Moreover, in emerging markets where the operating environment can be a unique challenge, local executives will help the alliance weave through a maze of government, regulatory and cultural issues.

At Tambrands' venture in Ukraine to produce and sell Tampax tampons and sanitary napkins, management worked to replace expatriates with local managers as soon as possible. As Tambrands' Paul Konney explained, having a local general manager to understand how the bureaucracy works, analyse political changes, interpret any new regulations and hire and manage workers can make a big difference. In particular, Tambrands' venture manager has been instrumental in building a dedicated work force. As Konney said, 'It can be difficult to motivate workers who are accustomed to getting paid regardless of whether they work or not. The venture's local general manager offered a unique solution to motivate workers: build a cafeteria and offer free meals.' Since Ukrainian food supplies have been unreliable, many workers were eager to work for Tambrands to get steady meals. In fact, Tambrands regularly shipped different foods from the US and Europe to the workers' cafeteria. Tambrands' local managers also helped to resolve the company's housing problems. It was very difficult to find proper accommodation for any visiting executives or expatriates on temporary assignments. Tambrands finally acquired a house and cut it up into several apartments. The venture's Soviet managers were important players in finding an appropriate residence, negotiating the transaction and overseeing the renovations.

Communications: setting up the channels

Executives rank effective and continuous communications as one of the most important ingredients in managing *any* type of venture. Developing a solid communications system helps to foster the trust that executives regard as essential for alliance success. Although trust is a soft word, the consensus among managers from Europe, the US and Asia is that *any alliance is meaningless unless the partners can build mutual trust.*

Maintaining good alliance communications requires a lot of hard work and planning – and even then it is difficult. Communications problems occur within a single organization, but in a multilingual, multicultural one, there is considerably more room for dissension and distrust. Even minor language difficulties can transform a slight error into a huge problem. A Ford alliance manager summed up his own experience, saying, 'Misunderstandings occur day after day, no matter how hard you try to sort them out.'

Laying the cables

The multinationals surveyed for this book cope with communications problems through a variety of mechanisms. In many alliances, companies have established a clear communications infrastructure, detailing the contact points in each partner's organization. Japanese MNCs, like Mitsubishi Electric Corp., often have their overseas subsidiaries serve as a primary communications vehicle for their overseas partnerships. Matsushita generally follows this practice but notes that companies should be flexible, since the communications needs for a particular venture may require direct contact with headquarters.

Most alliances establish regular meetings at various levels. Frequent staff visits and exchanges may also be encouraged. Most companies recommend frequent meetings at which operational and technical staff can review whether the alliance is on track toward its stated goals and objectives. A few companies also have formal, cross-cultural, cross-corporate training programmes. Some alliance makers argue that such cross-fertilization is the most effective way to facilitate communications, assess progress, solidify relationships and resolve problems. Finally, there are a few alliance courtesies that, when observed, improve trust. For instance, companies such as UK-based ICL and FANUC of Japan make a point of trying to keep their respective partners informed of their other alliance activities or pending new projects.

In many of the alliances examined in this book, the partners have spent considerable time and effort in building a solid communications network. The next sections of this chapter present different corporate examples of how some companies structure and manage communications and information flows between parents and alliances. The material here on communications strategies is separated into two groups, beginning with how some MNCs manage communications that cover multiple alliances with the same company. Given the complexity of some of these alliances, it is necessary to look at the links from all angles, not just the parent–alliance ones. Communications crisscross between alliance managers from both partners on the same project, and come through direct contact between both partners' senior management or between the alliance managers at one partner and senior executives at the other company. These alliances frequently involve an equity link, such as in Ford–Mazda and ICL–Fujitsu. This chapter's final section outlines how MNCs like AT&T and Corning manage multiple alliances with a number of partners.

Multiple links with a single partner

Ford–Mazda

As cooperative links and business flourished between Mazda and Ford in the 1980s, Ford re-evaluated how management could more effectively organize communications. Paul Drenkow, a Ford executive closely involved in the Ford–Mazda relationship, explained how their implementation of a communications and management process progressed over two steps.

First, in 1986 Ford realigned its Japanese operations, transferring responsibility for the Mazda relationship from the Asia-Pacific division to a newly created North Pacific Business Development Office (NPBD) under the Corporate Strategy Group, headquartered in Dearborn. Drenkow said the transfer was a significant change signalling Mazda's growing importance to Ford. Under this transfer the head of the Corporate Strategy Group reported directly to Ford's chairman. This arrangement continued until October 1989.

In 1989, Ford uncovered two management impracticalities: trying to manage alliance relations with Mazda out of Dearborn, and managing parent–venture links with other Asian partners from Ford's Australian operations. This recognition triggered a corporate reorganization whereby the alliance management with Mazda ventures was transferred to Ford's Tokyo office, which was considerably expanded. As Drenkow noted, 'Asia represents one of the greatest opportunities and challenges for Ford. Similarly, some of our toughest competitors are Japanese. It really did not take much thought or analysis by Ford management. Put simply, we said if Ford is going to be a global auto business, it must compete with the Japanese and build a long-term presence in Asia. Well, with those objectives there is no better location than Japan.'

As a result, at end-1989 Ford established a corporate vice-presidential office in Tokyo to coordinate communications and issues between Mazda and Ford as well as with the US auto giant's other Asian partners. A key feature of this arrangement is monthly management meetings between the Ford vice-president and the president of Mazda. At these meetings senior officials work together to identify opportunities for new projects and address difficult issues. Added Drenkow, 'I emphasize, however, that the monthly meetings are not designed to be problem solvers. We encourage Ford divisions to maintain direct contact with their Mazda counterparts and resolve any problems at the project level. Only when there is a more serious problem or deadlock is the issue referred to senior management.'

Reporting to the Ford vice-president in Tokyo is an alliance-coordinating office in Hiroshima, which combines the various groups representing Ford's activities with Mazda. This office has a manager for each project to coordinate with Ford headquarters and the director of each project. As Drenkow outlined it, 'Project team leaders are always located at the operational base of the project or venture. The Hiroshima manager assists the team leader in coordinating activities and communication with Mazda. Of the roughly 30 Ford–Mazda projects, each venture has some representation in Hiroshima.'

Westinghouse–Mitsubishi

Westinghouse has a wide variety of functional agreements, joint ventures, cooperative R&D and marketing arrangements with two main Mitsubishi companies: Melco and MHI. The partners divide the relation-

ship into three separ᷄   ᷉estinghouse links in
power generation, a sᷓ   ᷍estinghouse alliances con-
centrating on fossil fuel ᷓ   ᷍d steam turbines, and a third,
MHI–Westinghouse broad᷄   ᷍uclear energy.

Internally, Westinghousᷓ   ᷍y Systems contains three separate
divisions that work directly witᷓ ᷍eir Mitsubishi partners and the specific
ventures. Within each division the management encourages direct
communication between the engineers and the executives working on
different projects. To complement these communications channels,
Westinghouse Energy Systems has a large office in Tokyo whose main
function is to support the relationships, encourage greater contact, identify trouble spots and seek new areas of cooperation.

ICL–Fujitsu

The prospects for greater cooperation heightened with Fujitsu's
purchase of a majority stake in ICL in 1989. Said David Dace, recently
retired technical director of collaboration at ICL, 'The two firms have
worked closely since 1981 in R&D and technology development associated primarily with two mainframe computer projects. The equity investment now paves the way for the partners to forge even deeper ties in
technology and R&D as well as add new links in products and marketing.
Prospects for closer ties, however, have forced management to refine its
communcations approach.'

As Dace explained it, experience has proven that the most effective
strategy for managing projects and resolving conflicts is direct contact
between the engineers or executives involved in the project. Michio
Naruto, senior vice-president and head of global marketing at Fujitsu,
remarks that 'In some instances, we may have as many as 20 projects
with an equal or greater amount of direct contact between project
team managers.' On average, Naruto estimates that at least 30 Fujitsu
employees in each function or division may meet each month via
teleconferencing with ICL managers. And the holding of monthly
technology development forums means that an average of 100 engineers
travels back and forth monthly to meet and review progress. As the links
proliferate, Fujitsu and ICL want to maintain a dose of control without
hindering the growth of personal relationships at lower levels.

David Dace likened the ICL–Fujitsu strategy of using contact points
at all levels of the organization to a gatekeeper concept that basically
operates as a system of checks and balances. Day-to-day operational
issues are handled directly between the ICL–Fujitsu executives or
engineers leading a project. Complementing this activity are gatekeepers
charged with working out a long-term strategy and direction for the partnership and with addressing any serious operational roadblocks. The
gatekeepers are as follows:

Summits for chairmen

Senior management of ICL and Fujitsu meet at least twice a year for both formal discussions and informal gatherings.

Strategy coordinator

Michio Naruto, who wears several management hats at Fujitsu including chief coordinator for links with ICL, Amdahl and other partners, schedules a teleconference with Peter Bonfield, ICL chairman, three or four times a week. Their discussions focus primarily on strategy, corporate direction, product development and potential acquisition targets rather than operational issues.

Tactical coordinator

ICL expanded its original one-man coordination unit to include coordinators for important functions and technologies. For example, a technical gatekeeper focuses on identifying opportunities for new technology projects, while other executives are charged with specific product lines, manufacturing, and so on. Once a venture has been established, operational responsibility rests with the project team. When necessary, the coordination unit offers assistance on strategic or operational issues that threaten to derail a project or damage the overall alliance.

Swapping personnel

The two partners have exchanged personnel to strengthen communications. A Fujitsu executive transferred to ICL reports directly to Peter Bonfield. The main responsibilities of this executive are to assist on strategic issues and serve as in-house liaison with Fujitsu. To Fujitsu, ICL sent two executives – a technical expert and a product-development executive – to coordinate projects and identify new areas and opportunities for collaboration. Recently the firms each swapped ten engineers, to further strengthen ties and communications.

Multiple links with multiple partners

Many firms like AT&T and Corning operate with a wide network of partners and ventures. Given the complexity of managing multiple partners, most firms delegate the principal communications and management responsibility to the division. However, as much as central management's intervention is criticized in alliance management, executives concede that some oversight is important to avoid conflicts of interest. For example, central coordination can help firms steer clear of instances when different divisions might strike separate collaborative deals with fierce competitors or when units commit resources or operations to a project that falls outside of the overall corporate strategy and direction.

Here's how Corning and AT&T set the internal specifics for communications. First, Corning, which garners 37% of its revenues from alliances, emphasizes a decentralized approach. Each Corning division is equipped with its own functional capabilities for R&D, engineering, technology development, manufacturing, marketing and so forth. As self-contained units, the divisions can seek and manage their own ventures. Says Robert Ecklin, senior vice-president and general manager for industrial products, 'Corning has a simple set of principles on alliance management for the divisions. The first rule is that each alliance or venture must have a mentor or champion within the division. His or her principal responsibilities are to keep abreast of the venture's progress and report to senior management. Second, divisions manage their own R&D and technology development. As a division uncovers new technologies or innovations, the mentor must analyse how any of these new breakthroughs impact the venture. He must then ensure that the alliance receives the appropriate technology enhancements. There is also a central R&D group that conducts basic and applied research for the divisions. (Whenever the central group undertakes a project, it must have a customer at the division level.) A venture can also subcontract – via the division and mentor – for specific R&D work from central research.'

Ecklin observes further that 'Direct venture/division management is simpler and more effective than trying to have one corporate umbrella group manage all functional and operational aspects of different alliances. There is, however, a senior management committee – the group of 30 – that meets at least once a year to review the status and direction of Corning's internal operations and its outside partner activities.'

Having an oversight committee intervene whenever divisions might want to enter into alliances with competing partners is particularly useful. As Ecklin notes, 'Corning is still small enough as a company that communications within divisions are fluid. Plus, many executives – such as myself – have worked in most Corning divisions. This rotation offers firsthand exposure on market and competitive conditions. Consequently, many executives know which companies and/or partners to avoid. However, it can still happen; a division is tempted to enter an alliance that could threaten another venture. The senior management committee then plays a key role in resolving these issues.'

AT&T, the US telecommunications giant, follows tactics similar to Corning's. With AT&T, venture responsibility rests primarily at the division level, with a few important exceptions. First, says Jacques Meyer, international market planning director, 'Management distinguishes between tactical and strategic alliances. When an alliance has broad implications beyond one division, then management responsibility is jointly shared by the divisions and corporate staff. While divisions handle daily and operational issues, close contact with senior corporate staff on strategic and other important issues is maintained.'

'Other ventures,' adds Meyer, 'such as the AT&T–NEC link to develop new generations of superchips, do not have implications beyond AT&T's Microelectronics division. Hence, Microelectronics manages the relationship, with little interference from corporate headquarters.' Moreover, with most small ventures – under $25 million – divisions are free to seek alliance partners and structure the deal themselves. Operational units also have greater independence in their alliance activities after they meet their corporate capital requirements. Each division is responsible for contributing X amount of capital to the corporate coffers. Once a division reaches its quota, unit management has significant latitude on how it may use additional revenues and capital.

Of course, there are limits. If a proposed alliance or venture does not further AT&T's long-term corporate goals and directions or involves a hefty investment, AT&T's corporate alliance coordinating unit gets involved. AT&T concedes that its central oversight team is useful, yet management realizes that divisions sometimes don't share the same viewpoint. As Meyer recognizes, 'Where you sit colours your perspective. If you are a division trying to close a deal, you may not appreciate the "full benefits" of corporate involvement. However, as a global company headed toward the 21st century with many potential opportunities and tough challenges, a system of checks and balances is necessary to keep AT&T on the right track.'

AT&T also minimizes conflicts by encouraging regular contact and communications at various corporate levels. Adds Ramesh Barasia, vice-president for marketing, AT&T Network Systems, 'Despite AT&T's size, the company still manages to operate as a community in which different units come together and share information at many points.' The strategy officers of all units meet at least once a month to discuss their activities and new ideas. Regional presidents – such as the CEO for Europe – form part of a global operations team that also meets monthly to discuss strategy and alliance issues. The global operations team is the second-highest decision-making authority in AT&T, reporting directly to the chairman. Regular communications among individuals on the team play a key role in building a synergistic global strategy for AT&T.

Managing the risks of competitive cooperation

Companies should never forget that their allies are often also their competitors. The task can be daunting because it involves a delicate balancing act: a company tries simultaneously to foster a mutually trusting relationship and to guard its flanks. Many savvy MNCs involved in alliances recommend some of the following strategies to minimize the danger of collaborating with competitors:

Foster mutual dependence

Ensuring continued reliance provides an important protective shield. For many ventures involving technology, most companies ensure that know-how and technology exchanges are a two-way street. Other MNCs point out that the greater the number of links between partners, and the greater the reciprocal needs for each other's markets, capital and technology, the less likely it becomes that one partner will turn around and stab the other in the back.

Many alliance makers also maintain mutual dependence by ensuring that they always provide some value added. Joel Marcus, partner at Los Angeles-based Brobeck, Phleger and Harrison, offered an example of an alliance between two US MNCs (Company C and Company D). Company C was responsible for developing and manufacturing the product that Company D would distribute and sell in the US. The latter, however, requested a second source of supply in case its partner encountered any business or financial difficulties. In response, Company C – which was obviously interested in preserving its technological lead – provided a second firm with only partial know-how. This way, the second supplier – which was subsequently acquired by Company D – still needed to rely on Company C for some bits of the technology.

Keep close tabs on the venture to ensure the objectives and goals of the partners do not diverge

Unless partners agree on a schedule for reviewing the progress and status of a venture, alliances risk derailment. Indequate control and regular monitoring triggered the downfall of the NEC–Varian link. Years ago, Varian Associates (US) established a JV with NEC to manufacture and market Varian's semiconductor-making products in Japan. According to Varian, 'Problems and the firm's loss of technology were a result of Japanese regulations restricting foreign firms to minority ownership. NEC, with 51%, took responsibility for staffing and managing.' Without any direct involvement in overseeing the venture, Varian did not know until it was too late that NEC had a different agenda. Added a Varian executive, 'After operations started, we later realized that the NEC staff's goal was not to sell Varian products; they were interested in acquiring the know-how and technology behind them.'

Establish an alliance coordination unit

The decade-long alliance between ICL and Fujitsu has matured to include a complex network of communication links at all levels within both organizations. In fact, management has consistently encourged direct personal contacts between employees to strengthen the relation-shop and minimize problems in a specific project. The multiple interfaces also encourage the flow of ideas, boosting the knowledge and skills benefits of collaborative endeavour. At the same time, however, both partners have maintained limits, primarily through the work of central co-ordinating groups or 'gatekeepers'. Gatekeepers hold a critical role in the control and dissemination of information. Many other executives concede that an extra dose of protection can come from having a central liaison group to monitor and control who works with the partner and what information is shared.

Ensure all employees understand the risks

Perhaps one of the greatest roles for alliance coordinators is to inform all employees of the risks of collaboration. An attorney with Fujitsu noted that sometimes the best technology transfer occurs when two engineers have a beer together after work. Yet, engineers must know the limits on how much information is tradeable and what is proprietary. For instance, remarks Jean Bilien, president of CFM International, 'The venture is in the business of developing and manufacturing commercial jet engines, not sharing proprietary technology. Engineers on the project clearly understand the boundaries on what know-how and technology is exchanged. For instance, General Electric's system of cooling blades for commercial jet engines is highly proprietary. There is no way an engineer would be foolish enough to discuss this matter openly.'

Similarly, MNCs must carefully manage the contradiction between encouraging camaraderie among venture employees yet ensuring that too much friendliness does not result in leaks of valuable technology and know-how. 'Too much collegiality should set off warning bells to senior managers. CEOs or division presidents should expect occasional complaints from their counterparts about the reluctance of lower-level employees to share information' (Hamel et al., 1989). Senior manage-ment clearly must convey the objectives and risks of collaboration to all employees. If alliance managers are not properly informed of the risks, information may pass to a partner/competitor simply because senior management failed to impress upon them the high stakes of a competi-tive/cooperative relationship.

Pay attention to questions as well as answers

When Boeing set up a JV with Mitsubishi Heavy Industries, it was terrified that the Japanese company might get its hands on Boeing's expertise at designing airplane wings. So it monitored all the requests for information and discovered that instead of wings, Mitsubishi was zeroing in on Boeing's project management skills. That knowledge helped

Boeing stay in control of how much know-how it should let slip. And it gave Boeing's managers a valuable insight into Mitsubishi's assessment of its own strengths and weaknesses (The Economist, 1988).

References

The Economist (1988). With allies like these... 19 Nov. p. 59

Hamel G., Doz Y.L., and Pralahad C.K. (1989). Collaborate with your competitors – and win. *Harvard Business Review*, Jan.–Feb. 1989. Copyright 1988 by the President and Fellows of Harvard College, p. 138

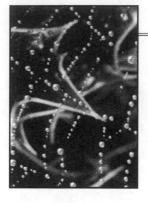

11

Gearing up in operating functions

The heart of most alliances is the sharing of responsibilities for different functions. In this sense, key fields of cooperation are research, product development, production and marketing. This chapter examines how a variety of alliances tackle the obstacles in these critical areas.

Teaming up for R&D

Collaboration in R&D is frequently cited as one of the driving forces and advantages of entering ventures. By sharing resources in an alliance, companies can better cope with the escalating costs and risks of research, access a wider pool of talent, avoid expensive duplication and speed up product introduction. Several firms interviewed consider joint R&D programmes vital to their success in securing global market leadership. Generally, the alliance tackles a specific project or business segment and the partners limit the technology exchanged. In a few cases, notably where the allies have an equity tie, collaboration occurs across a wide product spectrum and information is openly exchanged.

Cooperation can be structured in various ways. In some instances, the participating firms prefer to conduct research separately at their own facilities, then share the fruits of their labour through a steady flow of information and personnel exchanges. Other alliances, such as the Siemens–IBM–Toshiba chip link, prefer to bring all researchers and engineers together at one site. Depending on the scope and objectives of alliance partners, cooperative research pacts cover a broad spectrum. In some ventures, cooperation is limited to a simple exchange of information. In others, partners undertake different aspects of the R&D process based on their respective technical and organizational strengths. Alternatively, where complementary technology is involved, partners sometimes work on different ends of a product spectrum. In some of the most ambitious projects, partners set up and finance a joint design office.

Siemens–IBM–Toshiba extol virtues of working side by side

When structuring their billion dollar, multi-year alliance to design a 256-megabit (Mb) dynamic random access memory (DRAM) chip, IBM, Siemens and Toshiba insisted on having engineers from the three partner companies work together at the same facility. Dr John Kelly, an IBM executive involved in the alliance project, cites several reasons why the partners wanted to conduct research jointly at a single location. First, previous relationships among the partners offered proof of how well the companies could work closely together. Siemens and IBM had been working together on the design and development of the 16 Mb and 64 Mb DRAMs. Siemens also had long-standing ties to Toshiba in a variety of chip projects, including the development of 1Mb DRAMs. In addition to manufacturing links, Toshiba and IBM had been collaborating on the development of 'flash' memory chips, a unique chip that retains stored information when the computer's power is turned off.

Second, IBM had recently built a state-of-the-art research facility in East Fishkill, New York. The cost of building the new facility was close to $1 billion. Neither Siemens nor Toshiba had made any investments in new research facilities. By using the East Fishkill facility, IBM could share its hefty investment costs while Siemens and Toshiba could access a brand-new facility at a lower cost than establishing their own respective research sites. Third, the partners analysed many options on how to structure and organize development alliances. Conducting the research separately at partner operations yielded few cost benefits. Communications is another problem when partners partition the work. In the end, said Kelly, 'We decided that integrating the work was the most cost- and time-effective.'

Each partner contributes an equal number of staff and management personnel. The total number of engineers for the 256 Mb DRAM project is 150, with each firm contributing approximately 50 researchers. For most engineers, the duration of the assignments to the project ranges between two and four years. In an effort to build on existing camaraderie and ties, many individuals assigned to the project previously worked together in some of the other IBM–Siemens–Toshiba collaborative endeavours.

All engineers work for one common management team. Alliance managers can select engineers from any of the three participating companies to work on a particular phase of the project. Within each partner organization is a personnel manager to assist in transfers back to the parent company and any other career issues. A sophisticated data and communications system allows the three partners' parent operations to access data and information directly from the East Fishkill project. Senior managers responsible for the project within the three participating firms meet monthly to review progress. These managers then meet quarterly with corporate executives to evaluate progress, strategy and goals.

Sematech boosts global market lead of US players

Threatened by the growing dominance of the global semiconductor industry by Japanese companies, the US formed an industry/government consortium – Sematech – for the research and development of new generations of chip technology. Established in 1987, Sematech has 11 corporate members – Advanced Micro Devices, AT&T, Digital Equipment Corporation, Hewlett Packard, IBM, Intel, Motorola, NCR, National Semiconductor, Rockwell and Texas Instruments – plus the US Department of Defense (DOD). Sematech's mission was to revitalize the US chip industry. Thus far, the strategy is producing results: statistics from the Semiconductor Industry Association (SIA) indicate that US semiconductor firms now have 43.2% of the global market for microchips while Japan holds 41.6%. This is a reversal of trends in the late 1980s. In 1988, US firms had a meagre 37% while the Japanese boasted 51% of the global market.

In terms of governance, each of Sematech's corporate partners can appoint one voting member to the board. The DOD's board member has no voting rights. The board sets strategy and outlines the consortium's one- and five-year goals. Board members meet quarterly to review progress. Sematech's board also holds an annual strategy summit to prioritize goals. Once goals and strategy are set, responsibility for daily operations is held by a four-member executive management team. The technical officer of the four-member team is usually selected from one of the Sematech partners. All research is conducted at the Austin, Texas headquarters. In some instances, engineers will be temporarily assigned to work at different suppliers' operations. To date, Sematech's operations include over 800 engineers, both direct hires and 'assignees' from partner companies. Each corporate partner is required to contribute a certain number of engineers, based on the company's size. Members can also send additional engineers for training at Sematech. However, prior approval from the management committee is required. And Sematech is not obliged to accept everyone. Once a project is completed, the technology is then disseminated to all corporate members. At the end of 1994, Sematech will transfer 0.25 submicron technology capabilities to all partners. Such technology is capable of producing 256 Mb DRAM memory chips. Each Sematech partner is then free to implement the technology as it chooses.

Allying to hasten product development

In most industries, speed – accelerating the time to market for new products – can give companies a formidable edge over competitors. In the electronics industry, one company says 'Accelerating the pace of new product introdution can be a matter of life or death.' As pressure mounts on firms to slash product development times and costs, many companies seek to combine their complementary strengths in collaborative ventures. By pooling their technological might in an alliance to develop a new cluster of computing technologies, IBM, Motorola and Apple are setting the stage for a potentially huge new market. Partnerships with suppliers is a key feature in Chrysler's new 'platform' product development strategy. By including suppliers up front in the product development process, the US auto company reduces development time and boosts its ability to provide a steady flow of quality products. Chrysler expects to deliver more new vehicles over the next three years than it did in the past 20 years. By frequently churning out quality products, Chrysler can enhance its position as an innovative market leader. Below are profiles of how alliances play a key role in product development.

IBM–Motorola–Apple pool technology might in Power PC pact

In a direct challenge to Intel's hegemony over the global microprocessor chip market, IBM, Motorola and Apple pooled their technology to develop the Power PC microprocessor chips. Based on IBM's Reduced Instruction Set Computing (RISC), the Power PC technologies provide a tremendous boost in power, performance and computing capabilities.

Named Somerset – after the county where King Arthur's knights legendarily put aside their swords to join the Round Table – the Power PC chip venture works at a new Austin, Texas-based design centre owned and managed by IBM and Motorola. Somerset's $1 billion development costs are shared jointly by all three partners. Each partner holds an important piece to the new technology puzzle: IBM brings its invention of the Power RISC architecture; Motorola supplies vital technology on the external structure of chips, plus its capabilities for volume production of microprocessor chips and know-how for creating a single chip version of the Power PC chip; and Apple contributes its software technology and expertise, namely the support and application of software for the Power PC microprocessor chips.

All three partners contributed engineers, know-how and technology to the project. However, since Somerset primarily focuses on the hardware technology – the development of the Power PC microprocessor chips – the influence and contributions of IBM and Motorola are greater than Apple's input. Of the 300 engineers working in Austin, most of the individuals come from IBM and Motorola.

Somerset is organized around the project's four key products – the Power PC chips 601, 603, 604 and 620. For each chip, there is a corresponding research and product development team. Two co-directors, one from IBM and another from Motorola, oversee and manage the four projects. The four projects progress at different stages, thereby allowing for some overlap and exchange of personnel. The 601 chip – used in Apple's Power Mac personal computers and IBM's RISC system 6000 computer servers – is already in volume production. The 603 chip – designed for notebook computers because it consumes less power and does not overheat quickly – is in the manufacturing stages but is not yet ready for volume production. Somerset recently completed designs for the 604 chip – a more powerful chip than the 601 and 603 – and the 604 model is now in the 'sampling' phase. Work on the 620 – a chip designed for high-end users – should be completed by year-end. Once a chip is ready for volume production, the design is given to IBM and Motorola's internal design operations to make the appropriate parts and equipment to launch volume production. Separately, IBM and Motorola market and sell the chips to computer manufacturers. For instance, both partners compete to supply Apple with the Power PC chips necessary for the latter's new line of PowerMac computers.

While the original Power PC microprocessor technology developed by Somerset is owned by IBM and Motorola, new enhancements or product derivatives developed independently by any of the partners is owned solely by that company. For instance, suppose IBM creates a new derivative by embedding the Power PC microprocessor chip in one of its computers. This design and new product is owned exclusively by IBM.

And Somerset is only the beginning

The venture's ambitions do not stop at developing new superchips. The partners also want to create a vast new industry around the Power PC technology. As part of their strategy, IBM and Apple are planning to develop a uniform operating standard to eliminate any incompatibilities between the new IBM and Apple Power PC systems. Within the hierarchy of computer technology, the Power PC microprocessor chip forms the foundation for new Apple and IBM computer systems. Yet each company also has distinct operating systems for their computers; Apple Power Macs run on the company's traditional System 7. The IBM 'RISC PCs' – which will be released shortly – will be capable of running on a number of different operating systems. This includes OS/2, NT, and Solaris. Through a complex process called emulation, the IBM RISC PCs will also run on DOS and Windows. Currently, Apple's System 7 is incompatible with many of the operating systems planned for the IBM RISC PC. Yet the partners plan to create a common 'reference platform' or 'prep specs' to remove any differences and allow users to freely link IBM and Apple Power PC computer systems. By creating a new uniform operating platform, the partners can build a broad support and customer base for the Power PC technology. Their efforts will be supplemented by the creation of a new industry organization as well as the establishment of broad links with hardware and software manufacturers.

Suppliers play key role in Chrysler's new product strategy

Chrysler's reorganization of car and truck operations into autonomous product development teams or 'platforms' mandates significant changes in a host of activities. Perhaps nowhere is the challenge greater than with supplier links. Building strong supplier ties is fundamental to Chrysler's objective of ameliorating quality and speeding the introduction of new products to the market. Yet the task of developing new supplier links can acquire even greater complication in other markets, such as Mexico. (See Box 11.1.) Below are some of the approaches of the platforms to build and manage a new supplier network:

Direct dial: supplier to product development team

Within the platforms, the suppliers actively participate up front in the design and development of the vehicle. Within the platform team, there is no single individual assigned to 'oversee' all supplier relations. Said G. Glenn Gardner, head of the LH platform at Chrysler, 'I would like to eliminate the word "liaison" from the English vocabulary. At LH, the different team members who are responsible for various components or systems also directly manage the alliance with the supplier.'

Approximately 70% of the components and systems for a new vehicle come from outside suppliers. Chrysler's platform teams are responsible for the development of the entire vehicle but key parts – such as exhaust systems, steering gear, instrument panels, and seats – are designed, engineered and tested by the suppliers. In most cases, the technology and design of the different parts is usually owned by the supplier, with Chrysler securing an open licensing pact to use the component for as long as necessary.

The suppliers usually have their designers and engineers work on-site at Chrysler's R&D and design premises. Some suppliers, who have design and engineering operations within the Detroit area, prefer to go back and forth between their offices and Chrysler's design centres. 'Certain suppliers, though fewer and fewer,' said Gardner, 'still believe they must do the research and design work at their own headquarters.'

Keep it simple: eliminate dual sourcing

The LH program has eliminated all dual sourcing of parts to reduce its network and reinforce management and communication ties with key suppliers. This allows both manufacturers and suppliers to develop a closer and more direct relationship. Gardner figured that the LH platform has reduced by over one-third the number of suppliers traditionally required to build an auto.

Gardner estimated the reduction by calculating the fall in shipping points – the number of different shipments entering the factory. Said Gardner, 'An assembly plant for a car may average 600 different shipping points. Of course, this does not mean 600 different suppliers since some automotive parts firms may provide a wide variety of different parts. Nonetheless, the LH team reduced the number of shipping points to 250.'

Experiment with modulization

According to Roy Sjoberg, head of the Viper project, full assembly of an auto can require 3000–5000 different parts. The Viper team's goal was to simplify the design and assembly of the vehicle by reducing the number of end items being shipped to the factory. Their success depended considerably on the close ties between the Viper team and its suppliers. 'Working with our suppliers,' says Sjoberg, 'we decided to experiment with modulization, in which suppliers are required to pre-assemble various parts together before shipping them to the plant.' This drastically cuts down on the error rate, minimizes the number of suppliers required, improves quality, and eliminates the need for large plants. As a result of modulization, the Viper car has only 674 parts. Plus, the Viper team drastically cut the plant space necessary to manufacture the car. While the average length of an assembly line to manufacture autos extends 2.5 miles, the Viper line is less than 700 feet.

Remember who is the final customer

Pricing remains one of the major challenges with suppliers under Chrysler's new platform strategy. Negotiating more competitive prices for components can be tough. According to Gardner, 'We continually work with the suppliers so that they view the individual who purchases a vehicle as the final cusomter rather than Chrysler Corporation.'

Box 11.1   The US–Mexican supplier dilemma

As Chrysler garners greater competitive strength from new organizational techniques, challenges await in how to export its novel management strategy abroad. In particular, the North American Free Trade Agreement (NAFTA) has placed Mexico centre stage.

Management is working diligently to accommodate or blend two rather divergent paths. First, its 'platform' strategy requires managers from all functions as well as outside suppliers to work side by side in the design and development of a new vehicle. Jon Maples, director of procurement and supply for Chrysler explained, 'With our new product development strategy, we have suppliers working in-house with Chrysler engineers four years before we even build the new vehicles.' In fact, the upfront involvement of suppliers was one of the key reasons why Chrysler was able to develop the LH models at one-third of the cost of its competitors and in three years versus the average four–five year gestational period for the design of a new vehicle. Second, however, are local content rules which require 34% Mexican content in all vehicles in the first year after ratification of NAFTA. This necessitates a well-established local supplier network in Mexico.

These two major forces put increased demands on Chrysler's supply base. Concluded Maples, 'Our dilemma is how do we balance the contrasting needs of having our suppliers both in Mexico and the US. With "platform" engineering, we really need all of our key suppliers – including our Mexican ones – to collaborate with us in the US and interact closely with our engineers during the development of the vehicles. At the same time, however, we must develop a world-class supplier network in Mexico to satisfy local content requirements.'

Strengthening the supplier network for Mexico

One of the most significant changes under platform engineering is in the actual design of a vehicle's components. In the past, auto manufacturers employed a 'build to print' approach. An auto manufacturer would design the requisite part for a vehicle and then hand the blueprint to a supplier to recreate. According to Maples, a company basically could hand the print to any competent supplier around the world to manufacture. However, 'platform engineering' requires the supplier to actually design the part. The component thus becomes the proprietary design and technology of the supplier. Yet is the US supplier willing to hand over its proprietary technology to a Mexican firm so that Chrysler can satisfy the 34% local content rule?

While some of Chrysler's suppliers – such as PPG Industries – have been in Mexico for over 50 years, many of Chrysler's other US suppliers

continues

continued

have a limited or no presence. Consequently, key US suppliers are going to have to choose between licensing the technology for their components, seeking a local Mexican partner to jointly manufacture the parts, and setting up independent operations. Each strategy has its advantages and disadvantages. First, licensing is the least expensive but also the riskiest since the licenser has limited control over its proprietary technology. Setting up operations is the most expensive yet also affords the greatest control over the technology. The middle road – strategic alliances – is one which Maples expects most suppliers to select. Through its direct contacts and efforts with local auto parts firms, Chrysler is also working to secure greater participation by its Mexican suppliers at its centralized R&D centre in Auburn Hills, Michigan. Said Maples, 'We invested substantial resources to build a vast design and development complex – 4.5 million square feet under glass – so that there is plenty of room for everyone.' Chrysler wants its Mexican suppliers to understand and participate in the platform development process so that the new vehicles also incorporate any unique demands for the Mexican market.

Breathing new life into managing supplier relations

With some novel techniques, Chrysler is nurturing a new management approach to supplier relations within its Mexican operations. According to Maples, the critical role played by outside suppliers in the 'platforms' requires Chrysler to take a much stronger, more proactive management stance with suppliers. Yet similar to other overseas subsidiaries, this hands-on style is quite a departure from the historical way in which Chrysler de Mexico has managed its suppliers at arm's length. Consequently, Chrysler is working with its Mexican staff to instill a philosophy in which suppliers are managed as partners.

Traditionally, Mexico has been structured along conventional practices in which many aspects of supplier relations were part of the manufacturing or engineering group. Engineering – not a separate procurement group – was responsible for supplier quality. However, this approach tended to foster an adversarial relationship between the suppliers and production. Without a comprehensive approach to managing supplier quality, the production people would tend 'to inspect' the quality of the part once it arrived at the assembly plant or when the component was already on the line. Yet if the quality of the part was deficient, production was disrupted and the supplier/manufactuer relationship soured.

Instead, Chrysler is transferring a new approach to Mexico in which a unique supplier development group manages the relationship. Explained Maples, 'With the platform strategy, Chrysler's procurement and supply group – and its corresponding staff members within each of the different platforms – owns the relationship with the supplier.

continues

continued

> Procurement tells the suppliers when to ship parts; we arrange the shipment; we monitor the quality; we pay for the tooling; we negotiate the pricing and commercial terms; we have a materials supply system in which we monitor and track the delivery and use of parts to avoid any excess inventory or waste; and we outline the production schedule for the assembly plants. From every angle, there is no such thing as "inspecting" quality. Instead, we ensure that the supplier has the quality designs and manufacturing processes to make it impossible to produce a defective part.'
>
> Finally, added Maples, some companies may try to cement a business relationship by offering equity to a supplier. Yet equity buys nothing. Instead, Chrysler wants to encourage commitment among its Mexican suppliers with a philosophy of 'shared destiny'. 'What is important,' added Maples, 'is that neither the manufacturer nor the supplier views the alliance as a static commitment.' Instead, Chrysler views its supplier relationships in Mexico as a dynamic ongoing exchange of information and ideas. Said Maples, 'Rather than giving a supplier a chunk of equity, we emphasize flow management in which assets – people, ideas, goods and services – are flowing back and forth.'
>
> According to Chrysler, equity is often a factor in Japan's *keiretsu* whereby the supplier will then only provide materials and parts to its parent company. Yet under the Western entrepreneurial spirit, corporations do not want to use equity to restrict a supplier's business to the parent company. In fact, in North America, equity can be a hindrance. The supplier may lose other customers, thereby losing its economies of scale and lowering its profits. A North American *keiretsu* succeeds when manufacturers and suppliers are bound together through the exchange of ideas and long-term commitments, not static equity participation.

Production and manufacturing

In many of the ventures examined in this book, the benefits garnered in the manufacturing/production arena were a major impetus behind the partners' interest in collaboration. The alliances exemplify some strategies on combining manufacturing prowess and production capabilities in order to clinch a leading market position. For instance, neither Siemens or IBM alone wanted to shoulder the $800 million costs for a chip fabrication plant in Europe. Instead, the two partners split the costs of expanding IBM's existing plant at Corbeil-Essonnes, France to accommodate the two partners' pact to jointly manufacture 16-megabit DRAM chips. The two companies jointly manage and control the production.

Cooperation is limited to manufacturing. Output from the facility is split between the two companies – either for internal use or for sale to third parties.

Trends also point to a growing flexibility when using alliances in manufacturing. In a major study by the Iacocca Institue of Lehigh University on how the US can regain its manufacturing excellence in the 21st century, one-time, project-specific ventures are fundamental to achievement of a new system of agile manufacturing. The report emphasizes the need for inter-firm cooperation through alliances. The study presents ideas on the need to create a network to link all US factories. The factories would use this network to form short-term, narrowly focused partnerships to satisfy an immediate goal or need of the marketplace. Once the specific project is completed, the venture is then disbanded.

In a number of case studies examined in this book, the partners split production responsibilities along each company's area of expertise. Obviously, this strategy enables the alliance to best exploit the complementary strengths of the partners; it is also the most expedient and cost-efficient way to launch a product:

CFM International

In this 50–50 joint venture established by US-based General Electric and France's government-owned aircraft manufacturer, Snecma, to build a new generation of medium-sized aircraft, the French company manufactures the low-pressure turbine at its headquarters, while GE makes the high-pressure turbine in the US. After the turbines are finished, each firm sends one-half of its production to the other, thereby creating a set of engines in each country. Each company has full responsibility for the quality of the engine half it produces.

The division of production between two countries is a potential bureaucratic nightmare for many companies. But in the case of CFM, the venture benefited from having resident representatives of the partner constantly on hand. The venture also profited from a joint certification procedure operated between the US and French aviation authorities. Each agency accepts the other's word as a stamp of approval for the quality and safety of the half of the engine made in the US or France.

Ford Aerospace

In order to win the Intelsat V project, which entailed the design and construction of 15 advanced civil communications satellites, Ford Aerospace built a seven-company global team. When forming the consortium in the early 1980s, Ford sought the participation of Marconi Space and Defence Systems (UK), Mitsubishi Electric Corp. (Japan), Selenia Spazio (Italy), Messerschmitt-Bolkow-Blohm (Germany),

Aerospatiale, and Thomson-CSF (France). The task of dividing and coordinating manufacturing responsibilities among seven partners in six countries is nothing short of tremendous. Ford Aerospace relied on two approaches: it gave the partners considerable autonomy, and simultaneously it installed a communications system to monitor and coordinate the complex activities of all partners.

The partners hammered out an agreement outlining the component and technological contributions of each firm. Each assumed full responsibility for designing, manufacturing and testing its equipment and had complete liberty in the selection of subcontractors. As prime contractor, Ford undertook the overall spacecraft design, fabrication, test and launch support. Ford prepared detailed technical specifications, statements of work and interface control documentation for each team member. After three design and management readiness reviews with each team member, the hardware was fabricated and tested. The hardware was then shipped to the Ford Aerospace Space System in Palo Alto, California, for final assembly and integration into the spacecraft.

To keep communications smooth across the board, Ford Aerospace established subsystem managers for each team leader providing day-to-day management and direction. Further, Ford resident management specialists were established at each team member's facilities to assist in the required hands-on coordination.

Ironing out production kinks: Fujitsu and Alcatel cite dos and don'ts of licensing

Reaping the full benefits of licensing largely depends on how a company structures, manages and executes the actual technology transfer. Skilful management of a licensing agreement's three key elements – documentation, training and support – ensures the licensee's ability to effectively exploit the technology, minimizes the licenser's costs and maximizes its revenues. Careful attention to these points can also plant the seeds for deeper collaboration between the licensing partners. Fujitsu of Japan and French-based Alcatel have developed tactics that allow them to operate successful licensing programs.

First things first: finding the right partner

A manager for advanced industrial projects at Alcatel's advanced manufacturing technology centre in Brussels offered an important licensing guideline: the better the licenser knows the licensee, the greater are the chances for success. Some firms also say taking an equity stake in a prospective licensing partner can solidify the relationship and enhance the chances for success. It also can open up business opportunities in other areas where the partners may also have complementary strengths. Further, the equity link can act as a strong deterrent against any unfair infringement or use of the technology.

The path for finding the right licensee is beset with obstacles. Companies must take the time to seek a licensee with which the licenser can build a relationship. Even before official negotiations begin, Alcatel – which has successfully licensed its technology in some tough and highly protected telecommunications markets – will visit the licensee to discuss its objectives and motivations for the deal, evaluate its technical talent, components and raw materials, and assess the regulatory environment. An analysis of the potential licensee and its home base will yield important information on how to structure the financial arrangements for the technology. Will the licenser receive an upfront payment or running royalties? How much money does the licenser want the licensee to invest in the venture? Does the licensee have the resources? How will the transfer of additional technology be compensated? What is the quality of the licensee's factories, sales and marketing staff, distribution outlets, and so on?

Information obtained in any early visits, says Alcatel, is instrumental in structuring a well-targeted proposal to win the contract and later tailoring the documentation, training and support operations to suit the licensee's specific needs.

Although particularly useful in developing countries, precontract visits can be a good planning tool for cross-licensing between companies in industrialized countries, says an executive with the advanced products division at Fujitsu Microelectronics. The executive, who worked on Fujitsu's cross-licensing arrangements with Ungermann Bass and Sun Microsystems, offers other key operating details to consider when drafting documents or designing training and support:

Documentation

Specify language for technical documents

The Fujitsu executive recalled an experience with his former employer. The firm licensed technology to decontaminate nuclear reactors to a French company, but neither partner specified the actual language of the technical documents. The arrival of English manuals, which the French firm's engineers could not comprehend, created tension between the partners and delayed implementation of the technology.

Avoid literal translations

Only a technically astute individual with strong language skills should serve as translator. The Fujitsu executive recalled another experience: in an intercorporate transfer between an Asian subsidiary and his division, both sides agreed that the documents would be in English. The technical manuals arrived in literal English translations that were incomprehensible.

Emphasize quality, not quantity

Most documentation in technology transfers tends to be voluminous. A succinct 12–15 page summary of the technology and the transfer process will often be more useful than 15 binders.

Is that feet or metres?

Unless licensees, particularly from the US and UK, clearly specify the measurement system of the technical documentation, this small detail can create scheduling problems. Licensers ideally should agree to provide the technical documentation in both their own and the licensee's measurement systems. 'Failure to provide documentation in a form with which the licensee is comfortable can jeopardize the transfer process by making a very difficult task even more difficult,' said Fujitsu. Further, conversions should be prepared early in the process; the potential error rate is much greater when engineers work furiously at the last minute to convert feet to metres and ounces to grammes.

Timely delivery of documents

Fujitsu and Alcatel recommend that the delivery of documents coincides with the official launching of the training programme. If documents arrive six months before the training team, says Fujitsu, the material will be stale or forgotten, leading to a less-effective training programme.

Training

Rely on top-down approach

Fujitsu and Alcatel are proponents of a top-down approach to technology transfers. The first training sessions should address senior technical and management executives at the licenser's site, showing them the advantages of the technology and an overview of the transfer process. The next phase is a more comprehensive on-the-job training for mid- and lower-level engineers and technicians at the licensee's site.

Have a training strategy

Loosely structured training is one of the biggest culprits behind cost overruns and operating bottlenecks. Companies should map out a training package that outlines the structure, focus, format and participants for each session and includes training and testing materials. 'The more interactive, hands-on and multimedia the training sessions are,' said Fujitsu, 'the more effective will be the transfer.' Strict parameters should be set for the official training period to prevent its dragging on endlessly, chipping away at revenues and draining the licenser of critical resources.

Pick trainers, not technical gurus

Not all top-notch engineers are automatically gifted with training skills. Alcatel devotes time and resources to improving the training and communications skills of engineers selected to serve as trainers.

Encourage informal information exchanges

Cultural barriers and communications difficulties can impede even the most well-conceived plan. Fujitsu tries to nurture close ties between the training team and the licensee's engineers by encouraging after-work activities.

Support

Adopt a hands-on approach

Problems in licensing deals often crop up because the licenser thinks he need only transfer the technology and then sit back and wait until the profits start to roll in. Yet trying to get something for nothing usually results in a very short-term benefit: the lack of involvement may do irreparable long-term damage to the brand or trademark. Instead, a licenser must take a very communicative, open approach with licensees. For instance, some licensers ask for three-year business plans, actively participate in the formulation and implementation of marketing strategies, and work closely with operations to ensure that quality standards are upheld.

Install telephone 'hot lines'

Once the documents have been sent and training completed, continued support must be provided to answer innumerable questions and enable the licensee to effectively exploit the technology. This support, however, should be well defined and restricted to specific individuals. Plus, firms need to clearly spell out the payment terms and precise conditions for providing ongoing information and know-how. Otherwise, a few phone calls here, a few there, can add up to an expensive amount of engineers' time and erode any profitability from the deal.

Fujitsu assigned staff to telephone 'hot lines' to answer requests. Fujitsu recommended this approach because it 'provides a clear channel of communication for the licensee,' and it also 'funnels queries to defined contact points, thereby releasing other members of the licenser's technical staff from time-consuming support activities.'

Provide regular updates

Most agreements stipulate that licensers must provide any changes or improvements to the technology for a limited period of time. Fujitsu, however, suggests that providing this information on a regular basis not only ensures that the licensee will continue to utilize the technology in the most productive manner, but may also foster opportunities for future collaborative endeavours.

Marketing: the perils, the profits

While a number of problems can surface during R&D or production, many companies say the real mud-slinging between partners occurs in the marketing arena. In fact, marketing ventures can be so delicate that alliance practitioners prescribe a rigorous analysis of a partner's marketing capabilities before making any commitments. Box 11.2 details how some alliance-makers cope with the challenges of developing a synergistic marketing strategy.

Cultivating marketing synergies

Here are five techniques recommended by experienced alliance-makers on how partners can develop a synergistic marketing strategy:

(1) *Don't cannibalize the market*   According to the marketing director at Intel Corp., companies involved in alliances must find ways to maximize the complementary nature of the relationship and minimize direct competition. This means making sure that your partner is opening new markets and not simply competing head-to-head for the same customer base. If the venture ends up cannibalizing the original market, the most probable outcome is a price war, and any alliance yielding such a result is doomed to a short life. Certainly, fighting over the same customer base triggered the downfall of the Tandy–Apricot venture. (See Box 11.3.)

Box 11.2　Marketing alliances under the microscope

As a start, sizing up your partner's marketing prowess in advance can reveal problem areas and where the alliance later needs to focus its marketing energies. For cross-marketing and -distribution agreements, the feasibility team responsible for analysing a potential partner's capabilities should include a number of sales and marketing executives in addition to other functional executives. Below, alliance practitioners offer some pointers on judging marketing capabilities:

Cover all of the basics

The group's analysis will concentrate on the partner's distribution capabilities, advertising strategies, client base, and so on. Market research should include an extensive examination of the product's pricing structure, customer demand, servicing requirements, and so on. The team may also want to ask for customer lists and conduct firsthand interviews with clients to accurately test the product's acceptance.

Don't be fooled – networks vary for different products

In addition to examining a potential candidate's overall distribution strategy, the team may wish to look at its network for each product. A company may have a tremendous market presence in one area but be weak in other product lines. For example, AT&T has a high profile in the telecommunications market but does not enjoy the same reputation in computers. In the mid-1980s, Olivetti was disappointed in AT&T's ability to sell the Italian company's personal computer in the US, forcing the two companies to abandon the computer-marketing partnership for the US.

Don't believe everything you hear

A rigorous evaluation of the strengths and capabilities of potential candidates can be a real life-saver. One US office equipment manufacturer (Company A) was considering a cross-distribution agreement with another MNC (Company B). Said a Company A executive, 'We requested customer lists from Company B. The data revealed some disturbing evidence; actual sales volume and product position were not what Company B claimed. We also did our own sleuthing. Much to our dismay, we discovered that the company's market position was not even close to what it had originally told us. Our analyses further indicated steep marketing costs associated with Company B's products. Consequently, we dropped the alliance idea.'

(2) *Clearly delineate marketing responsibilities along product and geographic lines*   This will help both to prevent market overlap and preclude the dangers that partners will pursue the same customer. In a five-year pact between a US company and a European firm to develop and market the former's 25 different bipolar and high-voltage circuits, marketing responsibilities were clearly defined. The US MNC covered its home turf, while the European company used its extensive worldwide network (33 sales offices plus 200 distributors) to market the US-made products globally.

(3) *Organize a global partner network*   AT&T's recent pact with Unisource – a venture between the Swedish, Dutch and Swiss national telecommunications carriers – provides the crucial European piece to AT&T's global Worldsource puzzle. Worldsource – an international partnership offering telecommunications services and products to multinational companies – includes such key Asian partners as Japan's KDD and Telstra, the Australian national operator. With national champions in key regions and companies, Worldsource is poised to launch a major marketing campaign for the growing international corporate communications business.

In its efforts for the worldwide launch of its private satellite data communications products (PACTnet), the US firm, Harris Corp., made sure it found a partner for each key region. In Europe, Philips NV had distributor rights for the PACTnet, while Matsushita of Japan covered the Asian turf. In the US, Harris and AT&T jointly provided the Ku-band satellite business communications service. For Canada and Latin America, Harris retained marketing rights.

(4) *Utilize captive-customer relationships*   In some alliances, success in marketing can receive a boost from the partners' ties to their parent organizations. Yet some executives are sceptical of relying on parent firms as captive customers in the long-term. The head of the former GMFanuc venture in robotics said alliances must avoid the 'big brother' syndrome. It can often produce more damage than reward. It can result in what he terms the 'malicious obedience' syndrome and gives factory managers an easy scapegoat for all operational problems.

He recalls a front page *Wall Street Journal* article on a new GM Cadillac plant in which the GMFanuc robots went beserk, smashing windows and painting each other. However, there were many other more serious operational kinks and problems than the robots. Yet everyone focused on the robots. The robots became an easy scapegoat for all of the factory's problems. Consequently, from the venture's inception, GMFanuc Robotics worked hard to decrease reliance on parent company sales. The venture's business as a supplier of robots to GM factories dropped from a high of 75–80% in the early years of the venture to 30% in 1991.

(5) *Gain an 'in' with the Japanese MNCs operating abroad*   Some US and European MNCs find that their Japanese partners help them clinch orders from Japanese MNCs operating outside of their home territories. Having a Japanese partner in an alliance has helped several US and European companies develop customer ties with foreign subsidiaries of Japanese companies. In the case of LOF Glass, its 40-year relationship with Japan-based Nippon Sheet Glass helped the US company become the automotive glass supplier to Toyota's Nummi venture in the US. (In Japan, Nippon is Toyota's long-time supplier of automotive glass.) In the GE Fanuc Automation joint venture, GE points out how FANUC has been instrumental in opening doors at Japanese companies with operations in the US.

Box 11.3   Competing distributors sabotage Tandy–Apricot link

The failure of a 50–50 JV between Apricot Computers and Tandy Corp. (AT-Computer World) provides a lesson for other MNCs on the importance of developing synergy between distributor networks of alliance partners. Established in February 1985, AT-Computer World was designed to create a network of 90 retail outlets in the UK and four other European countries. Although the partners claim the JV's collapse in January 1986 stemmed from a downturn in computer sales, a closer look indicates that the reason may have been poor planning plus inherent organizational conflicts between the distributor networks of the two companies trying to penetrate the same market.

The UK served as the JV's departure point. Each partner contributed £1.5 million to transform 13 Tandy Computer Centres and 16 Apricot franchises into new AT-Computer World outlets and to establish a headquarters and distribution facility in Birmingham. In addition to the UK, the venture was slated to tap new markets in Belgium, the Netherlands, France and Germany. The five-country operation would have required a £9 million investment, consisting of £3 million from each partner and £3 million in loans.

continues

continued

But the JV strategy never made it across the English Channel. A major stumbling block was the venture's inability to iron out kinks in distribution. For Apricot, the investment and organizational planning that was required to set up a retail chain in mainland Europe similar to the UK's seemed too ambitious. Instead, it suggested that the partners rely on distribution agreements already established by Apricot.

This arrangement did not work well for Tandy. The partners had agreed that the local Tandy outlets would sell Apricot equipment and software. In addition, the Apricot distributors would continue to sell a full range of company products. Tandy's management soon discovered that these distributors were acting as competitors – not partners. Tandy stores simply stopped selling the Apricot products.

Examining events in the Netherlands revealed the roots of the dispute and highlights how two partners pledged to cooperation met head-on as competitors. Apricot sold computers there through a distribution agreement with Systel Automatisering BV. Some 150 dealers composed the network, including Pro/AM, Systel's wholly-owned retail chain. About 55% of Systel's turnover came from Apricot products and software.

Systel also acted as a supplier for Tandy. A Tandy salesman reported that the US company's outlets had to order specialized software from the Dutch distributor. Systel then turned around and approached those Tandy customers for whom they were supposed to be developing software and undercut Tandy's computer prices. Tandy dealers retaliated by stopping the sale of Apricot computers.

Systel denied the allegation and argued that Tandy's local strategy of selling hardware without offering software in the package undermined Apricot's potential market. Pro/Am added that Tandy's reputation in Europe hindered the venture since the firm was associated with the sale of game computers. When it tried to market the Apricot business computer, customers did not take Tandy seriously.

Who withdrew?

Systel argued that a software package that was easy to use saved money. If a salesman sold a computer without software, negotiations would be prolonged by discussing the software. The time wasted could be spent selling a computer to another prospect. According to Systel's owner, his company withdrew from the supply agreement with Tandy – not the other way around – since it received too many software-related complaints from customers.

Tandy disagreed. According to the general manager of Tandy's European HQ in Brussels, the problems it had with Apricot were not confined to the Netherlands. 'None of our European outlets ended up selling Apricot products for long. We had some problems with the software and with the availability of language programs – not all users' English was that good.'

continues

continued

Since the January termination date, the partners have disbanded the Birmingham distribution site. The 13 JV-owned stores were retained by Tandy as part of its retail network; the 16 franchise stores went to Apricot; all 29 stores retained the name AT-Computer World.

Deferring to local partner breeds success for Xerox

Success usually requires partners to concede marketing responsibility and control to the company with an 'insider's position' in key markets. For instance, Xerox's decision to allow Fuji Xerox significant leeway to work out its own marketing strategy for Japan and other Asian countries has paid off handsomely. As Yotaro Kobayashi, Chairman of Fuji Xerox says, 'Xerox traditionally relies on the marketing might of a direct sales force. In Japan, however, we realized that we needed to complement direct sales and marketing efforts with additional tactics. A direct sales force works very well for large cities with a high concentration of customers in a limited area. Yet in many other areas of Japan the market and customer base is scattered. A direct sales force is neither effective nor cost efficient. Moreover, firms should aim to establish a local presence in these areas because local allegiances in Japan can be very strong.'

Fuji Xerox designed a unique alliance strategy to operate as a local throughout many regions in Japan, by teaming up with a strong local partner. To date, Fuji Xerox has 26 different marketing ventures spanning many regions and cities in Japan, including Hiroshima and Kyoto. As Kobayashi says, 'Many of the ventures consistently rank within the top five locally in traditional Japanese corporate popularity rankings, compiled annually to pinpoint both national and local favourites.' Riding on its success in Japan, Fuji Xerox has exported this alliance strategy to other countries, including the Philippines, Korea, Indonesia and Taiwan. Fuji Xerox applies the following three standards when selecting partners and structuring a deal:

Emphasize compatability and capability

Kobayashi says that Fuji Xerox's management applies the same partner-selection and management criteria to all its marketing ventures. In essence, he notes, 'We want partners with solid local distribution capabilities and a strong reputation. We seek partners with whom we can build a relationship based on mutual trust, compatibility and mutual benefits.'

The ventures are 51–49

With Fuji Xerox assuming majority control, this policy is consistent with Xerox's global policy of securing an extra measure of control in smaller ventures to safeguard Xerox's trademarks and image worldwide. The local partner appoints the chairman and executive for administration. Fuji Xerox nominates the president and local general sales manager. Fuji Xerox assumes primary responsibility for strategic and operational issues, particularly since its partners are unfamiliar with the dynamics of the document processing business. Within Fuji Xerox the management appoints a liaison to assist the management of the local marketing venture.

Partners' activities lie outside office equipment

Fuji Xerox has a wide variety of partners: department stores; wine and beverage companies, such as Suntory; construction firms; stationery stores; petrol stations; a 200-year-old paper company that originally specialized in making folding paper for kimonos but now produces computer paper; and the world's largest safe manufacturer, Kimohira.

Apple seeks licensing pacts to expand market share

Companies frequently employ a licensing strategy to boost market share and acceptance of new technologies. For instance, Apple Computer formed a task force to develop licensees for its new line of Power Mac personal computers. The licensing team is charged with developing licensee partners worldwide. The licensing task force reports directly to Apple's CEO, Michael Spindler, underlining the task force's key role in Apple's global product strategy. Officially, Apple expects to make announcements on key technology licensing deals within the next 12 months. Unconfirmed reports, however, say few US computer manufacturers have shown interest so far. Some analysts attribute the delays to Apple's careful screening and selectivity in identifying strong, potential licensees. There appears, however, to be strong interest in Asia. John Floisand, president of Apple Pacific, said Apple is talking with dozens of Asian firms, such as Taiwan's Acer. He says Asian-based computer-makers are keen on the idea, thanks to Apple's success in Japan, where it is No. 2 in the market. 'We can basically pick our licensees', says Floisand (Rebello, 1994).

How two corporate heavyweights manage market tensions

This final case on the trials and tribulations of the Westinghouse–Mitsubishi Heavy Industries (MHI) alliance in the global nuclear energy market captures the management challenges facing partnerships in the marketing arena. The Westinghouse–MHI partnership offers telling insights into how two powerful MNCs manage a complex net of co-operative links yet simultaneously compete against each other in key markets.

The foundation for this alliance dates back to the 1960s when Westinghouse licensed its nuclear energy technology to MHI. Through the years, this licensing agreement has been supplemented with additional links in marketing, plant design and construction, and engineer-exchange programmes. At the same time, the two MNCs are free to compete in key markets, even Japan. In Japan, Westinghouse and MHI both sell nuclear energy products and services to Japanese utilities. In other words, while Westinghouse and MHI collaborate in nuclear energy via their licensing and other arrangements, they also compete in certain product segments in Japan. In fact, claims Jon Elmendorf, former president of Westinghouse Energy Systems (Japan) and current director for environmental compliance at Westinghouse in the US , 'The Japanese customers want us to compete. Even though the competitive market tensions can make the relationship strenuous, Japanese utilities, such as Kansai Electric, would be very upset if we did not continue as rivals.'

According to Elmendorf, the Japanese utilities want Westinghouse to compete as independent suppliers, for several reasons. First, MHI enjoys a monopoly position as the sole Japanese MNC to have pressurized water reactor (PWR) technology. [In nuclear energy there are two basic types of technology – PWR and boiling-water reactors (BWR). PWR is a Westinghouse-developed technology; BWR originated at General Electric (US).] In BWR, the Japanese market has two indigenous competitors, Hitachi and Toshiba, as well as General Electric. In PWR, without Westinghouse there is only one company: MHI. As Elmendorf observes, 'From a utility's point of view, it is too risky to entrust the design and construction of a nuclear energy power plant to one firm. Similar to any advanced science or critical technology, an independent verification is highly recommended. Consequently, the Japanese utilities have an abiding interest to keep MHI and Westinghouse independent.'

Disagreements over the future direction of nuclear energy further complicate the market tensions between allies MHI and Westinghouse. The aftermath of the nuclear disaster at Three Mile Island in the US triggered new concepts about passive nuclear energy technology. Westinghouse is now leading a new project called the AP600 programme that is funded by the US Department of Energy. The principles of this programme centre on relying on such natural safeguards as gravity to minimize the dangers and damages in an accident. Elmendorf explains that 'At Three Mile Island, damage would have been considerably less had the plant operators done nothing when the crisis erupted. Instead, their reaction made the disaster worse. The AP600 programme is designed to create technology that is operator proof. Even if a plant operator reacts improperly to a problem, the plant will automatically employ its natural safeguards to protect itself and lessen any damage.'

MHI has shown little interest in such new passive technology, partly because of the technology's size limitations. Currently, the new technology can only be applied to small nuclear plants up to 600 megawatts. Given the geographic constraints of Japan, most Japanese plants are a minimum of 1000 to 1300 megawatts. As a result, MHI emphasizes new evolutionary designs based on conventional technology, while Westinghouse backs passive technology, in addition to the large evolutionary designs. MHI is nevertheless under pressure from Japan's utilities to get involved in the new technology. In this regard the Japan Atomic Power Company recently funded a Westinghouse research project on passive technology in which MHI, under pressure from Japanese utilities, agreed to participate. Elmendorf says the passive technology is advancing to accommodate larger plants, in the 1000-megawatt range. As the technology advances further, MHI will probably offer greater support. Until then, however, the different partners' separate technology paths add extra tension, particularly since the Japanese utilities have offered Westinghouse some financial support.

Balancing market competition and global pressures to ally

Faced with these obstacles, it is little wonder that managing the MHI–Westinghouse relationship in nuclear energy can be challenging at times. As Elmendorf says, 'MHI is not happy that we are active in their home market. Plus, at present, we are at odds on the direction of the technology, with their prized Japanese utility customers sometimes siding with us. So I guess one asks, Why do we still stay together? Why not just make a clean break and save ourselves plenty of headaches? Well, there are many compelling pressures in the global economy to remain as allies – steep development costs, customer preferences, formidable competition – and the need to support nuclear energy as a viable alternative for utilities. And the importance of these factors is likely to increase with time rather than decrease. This makes it even more imperative that we make the alliance work.'

Other key driving forces behind the Westinghouse–MHI alliance include:

Market conditions and formidable competition

A combination of weak demand created by a scarcity of nuclear energy markets in today's global economy and excess supply from an assortment of powerful global competitors like GE, Hitachi, Toshiba, ABB,

Framatom and KWU makes it impractical to abandon the alliance and compete against each other. Elmendorf says that 'It makes no sense to beat our heads against each other when we already face such stiff competition. We are much wiser to stick together and jointly compete for new global markets.' In fact, the two partners recently signed a series of new country-specific cooperative marketing pacts. Thus far, MHI and Westinghouse have mapped out separate agreements for Indonesia, Taiwan, mainland China and the UK to compete as a team for nuclear energy projects.

What the Japanese market wants is also critically important. Elmendorf explains, 'As much as the Japanese utilities complicate the MHI–Westinghouse alliance by insisting that Westinghouse provide an alternative to MHI in the local market, they would be extremely upset if we decided to sever all ties. And ultimately we, the MHI–Westinghouse alliance, must do what the market wants in order to succeed.'

Stiff development and technology costs

Nuclear energy shares the same financial plight as the fields of aerospace, semiconductors and pharmaceuticals. In the nuclear area the development and technology costs are phenomenal, often in excess of $1 billion per project. Few companies harbour the resources to shoulder such a financial burden alone. Hence, it is in the interests of both MHI and Westinghouse to preserve the alliance in order to retain their positions as technology leaders.

Mutual need

The divergent approaches to nuclear technology reinforce these partners' mutual needs and potential benefits of maintaining a partnership. Clearly, MHI has a great deal of technical knowledge of plant construction and engineering. Elmendorf also credited MHI's manufacturing excellence to its premier position as a key supplier of vital components – reactor vessels, steam generators, pressurizers and tanks – for nuclear plants. Westinghouse for its part has broader capabilities and experience in the underlying nuclear technology. In addition, its state-of-the-art advancement into passive technology provides the alliance with an important edge against other competitors.

Relying on conflict maintenance

According to Elmendorf, 'In spite of all the nice agreements and commitments to work together, alliances inevitably run into problems and conflicts. Fundamentally, it is very difficult to get two sovereign MNCs, each with a great deal of pride, to cooperate in business. Partnerships require dedicated efforts by management to build and support personal ties and open communication at all levels.' To help in this regard, Westinghouse and MHI emphasize direct links between employees at all levels, rather than trying to coordinate and manage relations through a single point of contact. As Elmendorf acknowledges, 'We probably have one to two problems that surface daily. In some instances, they are misunderstandings. Other cases are fundamental disagreements. In any event, we persuade individuals to meet and discuss the issues directly with their peers. Sometimes the problems are resolved. In other instances, they simply agree to disagree. Yet whatever the outcome, we want to ensure that issues are not ignored and allowed to fester. Building personal contacts strengthens the cooperative bonds and allows us to keep everything out in the open.'

Checklist

There are countless issues and strategies to consider when teaming up in such key fields as R&D, product development, production and marketing. While each venture has its own preferences and needs, alliance strategists should consider some important questions when mapping out their operational tactics:

- How will partners divide work in an R&D project?
- Should the research scientists and engineers work side by side at the same site or work independently at their own facilities?
- If alliance researchers work separately, how will information and technology be shared?
- How will partners share the fruits of an R&D project? How will new technology be disseminated to the partners' operations? Are the partners free to use the technology as they may choose?
- How will partners manage the product development process?
- Based on the respective strengths of each partner, what specific contributions must each participating company make to the product development venture?
- How will management organize the product development projects?
- How will ownership of any new products and technology be divided among the partners?
- What is the role played by suppliers in new product development?
- How will partners incorporate suppliers into the product development process?

- What are the management challenges of unique manufacturer/ supplier links in the product development process?
- Who manages supplier relations during the product development stages?
- How does management include overseas suppliers into new product development strategies and processes?
- How can management reorganize the supplier network to develop closer ties with principal suppliers?
- In manufacturing alliances, how will partners split production responsibilities?
- How will the venture coordinate and manage the different production activities in a manufacturing pact?
- In licensing ties, have the partners addressed the three key elements of documentation, training and support to streamline the technology transfer process?
- What documentation will the licenser provide? Have the partners agreed upon and specified a common language and measurement system for the documents?
- Will the delivery of documents coincide with the launching of a licensee training programme?
- Have the partners mapped out a formal training programme? What are the key features of the programme?
- Who will act as trainers? Will senior management inaugurate the training sessions?
- What ongoing support will the licenser offer? Is the assistance clearly defined and organized?
- Are there any agreements to provide regularly any changes or improvements to the technology?
- Have you adequately assessed your marketing partner's strengths and weaknesses?
- Have you analysed your potential partner's distribution networks and marketing strategies for specific products?
- Have you done your own sleuthing rather than just relying on data provided by a potential partner?
- Will the marketing alliance target new customers or just cannibalize existing markets?
- Have marketing responsibilities been clearly delineated?
- Does the alliance have a presence in all key regions of the global market?

- Have you adequately weighed the benefits and costs of relying on captive customer relationships by targeting sales to parent organizations?
- How can Japanese partners help in gaining sales with Japanese multinationals operating abroad?
- Will the local partner take the lead in marketing strategies to boost credibility and success?
- How can a company design a global licensing strategy to build market share and acceptance of new technologies and products?
- How can partners manage the delicate balance between cooperating with competitors in some markets and competing against them in other markets?

Reference

Rebello K. (1994). A juicy new apple. *Business Week,* 7 March, p. 90

12

Using alliances to build knowledge and skills

Learning tops the list of alliance objectives

Competing in today's global economy requires companies to question continually existing corporate practices and experiment with new ideas and skills. Learning and acquiring the 'best practices' of competitors is one of the best ways to shake up lethargic corporate organizations. What better opportunity is there than to learn directly about a rival's operating and strategic advantages by assimilating this information through a competitive alliance?

The constant flow of information in an alliance potentially offers both far-reaching benefits and risks – information gained may also mean information lost. A partner will want equally to enrich his knowledge and competitiveness from the alliance. Many alliance critics argue that Western firms lose out in alliances with Japanese partners because the latter are said to always walk away with greater benefits; Japanese companies work hard to gain as much knowledge as possible. In fact, says Dr C. K. Pralahad, professor of business at the University of Michigan, 'Asian and Western firms tend to adopt different attitudes on alliances. Many Western firms consider it unethical to try to assimilate the skills of their partners. But that is the problem. Absorbing new ideas should be a key underlying objective for all ventures.'

Adds Pralahad, 'Western firms are anxious to demonstrate their expertise; they are eager to act as instructors to teach their Asian partners. Yet Asian companies are not insulted; they are quite comfortable with the roles. As the "students", they stand to gain valuable information.' Similarly, Western partners need to impress upon alliance executives the critical value of operating as students.

This chapter examines the dynamics within both an alliance and parent organizations that can either encourage or impede the flow of information. Joseph L. Badaracco, Jr, provides alliance practitioners with an important guiding principle (Badaracco, 1991a):

'In a world of strategic alliances, the idea of a firm as a medieval fortress that invents, owns, controls and finances all of its critical assets has faded. A better image for many companies today is the Renaissance Italian city-state. These tiny sovereign bodies evolved and prospered in turbulent, dangerous, confusing times. Their boundaries were open and porous. City states competed and cooperated with each other, often at the same time. The leaders of city-states such as the Medici of Florence raised diplomacy to a high art as they forged and managed a complex changing network of strategic alliances.

If we imagine that firms resemble city-states, a new perspective emerges. In this view, a company no longer has a vested interest in building up barriers that protect it from the outside world. Instead, its strength lies in its openness to ideas from outside. Knowledge has become the currency of modern economic competition, and a company must seek to acquire it through every means possible.'

Learning through good alliance management

The following four cases illustrate how Ford, Chrysler, Xerox and General Motors have been developing their own venture management strategies to boost the enormous knowledge benefits available from competitive alliances.

Chrysler ceded control to Mitsubishi Motors in the Diamond Star Motors (DSM) venture in order to learn management skills it could transfer back to its own operations.

Ford used its alliance with Mazda to improve its manufacturing competitiveness, mirroring some of the designs and organizations in Mazda factories, and learning how to manufacture to the Japanese company's rigorous standards and strengthen supplier relations.

GM, as a result of its failure to gain knowledge in Japanese manufacturing and human resource management from Toyota in the NUMMI joint venture, has developed guidelines for use in future alliances.

Xerox, through such ventures as Fuji Xerox, has gained skills and knowledge that have allowed it to improve its own quality standards.

Chrysler: effecting change the DSM way

When Chrysler joined forces with Mitsubishi Motors Corp. in 1986 to create Diamond Star Motors (DSM), a principal objective of the US auto company was to gain firsthand knowledge about Japanese management and manufacturing principles. Chrysler deliberately ceded management control for daily operations to Mitsubishi to learn how that firm handled the complex engineering, functional and operational tasks involved in launching and manufacturing a new range of mid-sized models. While financial problems forced Chrysler to sell its 50% DSM shareholding in October 1991 to raise capital, new agreements still enable Chrysler employees to work inside DSM and learn how the Japanese manage and organize auto operations. In its efforts to learn from Mitsubishi, Chrysler employed the following five tactics to broaden its knowledge base.

(1)   Adopt a top-down commitment

Most of the knowledge and skills gained in an alliance are at the lower levels of an organization, yet G. Glenn Gardner, former DSM chairman and current general manager for the LH platform at Chrysler, emphasizes how senior management needs to participate actively. In particular, top management must clearly convey to venture employees why learning is a key objective, and how to obtain good information. For instance, some firms offer their venture employees competitive comparisons between their own in-house and a partner/competitor's operations, to illustrate dramatically the benefits and reasons for remaining open to new operational, organizational and strategic techniques. A demonstrated commitment from senior management can play a decisive role in making venture employees eager and receptive to acquire new skills and knowledge in an alliance.

(2)   Encourage company-wide visits

Chrysler senior management insisted that its employees at all levels and within all divisions make an effort to visit DSM. As Gardner explained, 'Within Chrysler there was strong interest about DSM from both proponents and opponents. Some Chrysler managers came to DSM to genuinely understand how and why the Japanese could design, develop and manufacture a new car in a fraction of the time and expense US auto firms required. Yet, there were also the opponents who refused to believe that DSM could provide them with any new insights. Whether it is the not-invented-here syndrome or simple arrogance, some managers strongly resisted the learning idea. Plus, DSM's location away from Chrysler headquarters made it difficult for employees to go there. The complicated logistics of travelling from Detroit to DSM's Illinois location provided foes with an easy excuse why they could not visit the venture's site. While most executives point to the many advantages of siting a venture away from partner operations, it's also hard for employees to travel there to tap the potential benefits and knowledge. Slowly, however, as DSM produced positive results, many opponents either disappeared or changed their opinion.

'For instance, former Chrysler chairman Lee Iacocca came to DSM on three occasions and asked how frequently Chrysler managers were visiting to take advantage of the unique learning opportunity.' As Gardner admitted, 'On the first visit of Iacocca, I had to lie a bit. But by the second and third visits, I could genuinely tell Iacocca that many different divisions were actively involved in learning from DSM.' Unfortunately, the strongest resistance came from the engineering division, the very same area from which Gardner had come. Gardner acknowledged that 'It was unbelievably frustrating. My own former colleagues did not believe DSM had anything to do with engineering. Yet, DSM provided the perfect example of the Japanese process-driven design and development of a new car. The venture offered evidence of how to structure and manage the links and interrelation between all activities – engineering, design, manufacturing, suppliers, etc. – in developing new car models.' However, resistance within the engineering division was costly. The head of engineering at Chrysler was replaced, and his successor then used DSM as a model to reorganize the engineering division.

(3)   Map out a training programme in advance

Gardner suggests companies should work with their partners to design an appropriate training schedule. For example, it took close to nine months before Mitsubishi agreed to allow having trainees. As Gardner described the process: 'We had offered to pay all the costs incurred by the training project and accommodate Mitsubishi in all areas to avoid any disruptions to DSM's operations. We also agreed to set some limits; trainees would stay for a minimum of 18 months to avoid a constant influx of people. However, I could tell my Mitsubishi counterpart [DSM president Yoichi Nakane] still resisted the training idea. Finally, Nakane's boss in Mitsubishi Motors resolved the problem. For Japanese executives, the word "training" means to teach. It is a formal job. Hence, Nakane was grappling with how he could balance the formidable task of designing and building a new auto plant to manufacture a new range of mid-sized cars with the responsibility of teaching Chrysler trainees from parent headquarters. Once I explained that the Chrysler employees were coming to observe and learn, and there was no obligation to provide formal teaching, we moved ahead with the project.'

(4)   Identify high-potential managers

Selecting high-calibre individuals for training can help to overcome resistance both from the partner in the venture and within parent headquarters. For instance, one of the first trainees at DSM was a very promising engineer who secured a high-level position within manufacturing after training at DSM. As Gardner observed, 'Everyone at DSM, particularly the Mitsubishi-appointed staff, were ecstatic and extremely proud of the guy. It helped to build greater enthusiasm for future trainees.'

(5)   Seek individuals with open minds

There is only so much that management can do to encourage venture employees and trainees to learn as much as possible from their tenure at an alliance. Ultimately, success depends on how willing and open the individuals are to learning new ideas and skills. Alliance managers' individual curiosity is an important success factor. Japanese firms encourage employees to ask lots of broad questions as a means to procure wide-ranging and valuable information. Western companies should do the same.

Learning produces results: the LH and Viper examples

With the five steps outlined above, Chrysler tapped its unique ties to DSM to revitalize operations and earnings with new management and organizational techniques. Thus far, the results are impressive: first quarter 1994 net profits reached $938 million, a 77% increase over the previous year's first quarter. Profits per vehicle also outpace Chrysler's Detroit competitors – of the 2.5 million cars sold by Chrysler in 1993, each auto had an average profit of $848 – versus $26 for General Motors and $158 for Ford. Sales analyses of the LH sedans – Eagle Vision, Dodge Intrepid and Chrylser Concorde – indicate many purchases are import trade-ins.

Yet Chrysler's impressive results did not occur easily or overnight. The implementation of the new concepts and techniques has suffered from the inevitable kinks that surface when re-engineering a company's structure. (See Box 12.1.) None the less, the US company's tactic to reappoint DSM executives and trainees to positions within Chrysler where they could instigate and promote change was an important first step. For example, after Gardner's term as chairman of DSM he was appointed to manage Chrysler's vaunted LH program. New techniques learned from DSM and outsiders also contributed to the successes and milestones achieved with the Viper.

According to Gardner, 'Within a large corporation such as Chrysler there are always ways to hide errors. Yet a joint venture is completely exposed. Management cannot hide anything. Chrysler now has a benchmark in which managers can test operations. No longer can employees say, "Well, my operation or project is different." Management can respond, "How? Let us go to DSM and we will make a direct comparison, apples to apples." DSM eliminates excuses.'

In fact, LH and Viper car project managers continue to make frequent visits to DSM to check their progress, and compare operations, processes and strategy against that of DSM. The strategy is working: Gardner and Roy Sjoberg – manager for the Viper project – point to some significant changes and breakthroughs both within the LH and Viper programme and companywide:

Leaner, cross-functional project teams

Chrysler reorganized its car and truck operations into 'platforms' – flexible, autonomous product teams of cross-functional experts. Whereas engineering or manufacturing units had previously worked independently on the same car project, they now worked together. The LH platform and the Viper project organization consist of cross-functional teams. Using 'platforms' produces substantial savings in human resources. The number of employees involved in the LH project was 800, substantially lower than the industry norm of 1400.

Shorter lead times

Said Sjoberg, 'Bringing together all functional managers streamlines commmunications, thereby reducing the risks of error and minimizing the number of re-engineering changes required. Consequently, quality is better and teams are able to cut the time required to develop and produce new models. For instance, the average gestational period for a new vehicle in the US and Europe approximates 4–5 years. Yet the LH team – which designed four different models with entirely new engines and transmissions – completed the work in a little over 36 months while the Viper was completed in 36 months. Pilot test runs of the LH vehicles commenced a full 15 weeks ahead of schedule, mirroring the same schedule as DSM. The difference, as Gardner noted, is that the LH team was all-American.

Uniform objective

According to Gardner, by pulling all experts together on one team – from design, engineering, manaufacturing, marketing, purchasing, and so on – everyone automatically concentrates on the same goal – developing a premier product that mirrors consumers' needs and wants. This goal may sound simple and obvious. Yet the company previously was hampered by functional fiefdoms in which different department heads had their own internal agendas and ambitions. Plus, cross-functional teams are highly motivational since they give power and control to the managers and engineers actually doing the work.

Fewer test vehicles

The LH program only used 44 test vehicles, as opposed to the traditional norm of 100. As Gardner noted, 'We used only 30 at DSM so I said, why not?' Certainly, the change produced significant cost savings. The average cost of a test vehicle is $400,000, a figure which does not even include maintenance expenses. Hence, the reduction in test vehicles translated into a saving of $22 million. Plus, the test vehicles passed the crash test the first time, a significant milestone for Chrysler.

Simplifying assembly operations

The LH platform mirrored DSM's practice of framing the auto body in one station. Explained Gardner, 'In the past, each part of the auto body – side assemblies, roof assembly, rear assembly, underbody, etc. – were framed at separate work stations. Of course, each station added its own variations, thereby increasing the number of errors and readjustments required. By adopting the DSM strategy of one station, we improved the quality of the vehicles and drastically reduced the time required for assembly.'

Lower costs for supplies and raw materials

When the LH project team first presented its specifications for dies, the suppliers, as an example, quoted a die at a price of $1.5 million. LH refused to pay this amount, since the cost of dies at DSM approximated $850,000. The suppliers tried to argue that the DSM quotes were from Japanese sources, but when the LH team provided evidence that the DSM suppliers were US companies, this forced the prospective LH die supplier to re-evaluate its bid. As Gardner said, 'We finally agreed to a price of $900,000. We did not reach $850,000 – as DSM did – but the price was significantly below the original $1.5 million quote.'

American-style *neimawashi* (consensus making)

Gardner said that 'The LH team adopted many of DSM's operational and decision-making tactics during the project. For example, in the past I would get project managers together for a meeting and say, "Okay guys, we have to make a decision in two hours." If we did not reach a decision in two hours, I was impatient. I would say, "Stop the nonsense and fix this problem fast." Yet, I learned from the Japanese consensus-making, or *neimawashi* decision-making style at DSM. Now, I have greater patience. I let meetings run as long as possible until we have everyone on board. Decisions are much more effective and implemented with greater ease.'

Box 12.1   Putting ideas into practice

Acquiring new skills and knowledge from alliance partners is just the beginning. The real challenges occur when management then tries to install and gain acceptance for these novel techniques within its own company. Consider some of the problems Chrysler faced:

Manage ebbs and flows in human resource needs   Notwithstanding the savings in human resources – the LH platform at its peak used 800 people versus an industry norm of 1400 – Gardner considered the constant fluctuations in the human resource requirements of cross-functional platform teams as one of the greatest challenges. He said, 'Obviously, the design and development of new vehicles require substantial resources and expertise. Yet once the product development cycle matures and the cars reach continuous volume production, fewer resources are needed to manage and oversee the production process.' For instance, the LH platform now consists of only 50 people to oversee production and another 50 engineers who are responsible for making incremental changes so that the vehicles continue to comply with federal environmental standards. For Gardner, the challenge has always been how to downsize the team and re-orient vital resources and talents to jobs that are both challenging and motivational. In fact, coping with constant changes in a team's size and needs has been a key obstacle and the reason why many US companies have been unsuccessful in adopting a cross-functional team approach throughout the corporation.

The LH platform is coping with the problem by phasing in new assignments as older projects reach volume production. Once the LH vehicles were ready for volume production, most team members moved to a new project, the JA models. Noted Gardner, 'Slightly overlapping projects within the same platform is certainly helping to re-allocate resources with fewer complications. However, I would be lying if I said that we had this challenge completely behind us.'

Adjust to new decision-making processes   According to Sjoberg, auto companies traditionally have relied on a serial logic pattern to address the different milestones in the design and development of an auto. Problems and issues were addressed sequentially A-B-C-D-E-F, etc. Management could take the time to tackle the individual concerns of each function separately. With cross-functional teams, added Sjoberg, 'You are suddenly going from A to D to F back to B, etc. In other words, management must address the needs and demands of all areas – design, engineering, manufacturing, purchasing, marketing, sales, suppliers, etc. – simultaneously.'

Plus, some groups – such as manufacturing and engineering – are not used to having to listen and deal with problems and issues outside

continues

continued

their own domain. Sjoberg likened the challenge to the crumbling of the Berlin wall. 'On both sides, there are Germans. Yet they think, behave and act differently. The same applies to the traditional walls that have separated groups such as engineering and manufacturing. They may all be engineers but they think and operate very differently.'

Organize structure to spread new knowledge and skills   Encouraging the flow of information and ideas between different platforms is instrumental to Chrysler's success in adopting cross-functional teams throughout the company. Added Sjoberg, 'With cross-functional teams, we have eliminated the barriers that traditionally separated and hampered communications and cooperation between different functions such as design, engineering and manufacturing. It is now critical that we do not resurrect new walls between the different platforms for Oldsmobile, Buick, Pontiac, etc.'

Chrysler is employing several tactics to build cooperation between different platforms and nurture the exchange of ideas and experiences. First, management has set up unique 'tech clubs' for each area or function – such as power trains, steering systems, brakes, and so on. Managers responsible for power trains from all platforms meet on a regular basis to share their thoughts and problems at their 'tech club'. Periodically, the tech clubs also invite outside experts or companies to present their viewpoints and approaches.

In addition to the tech clubs, some managers and engineers act as 'missionaries' and rotate jobs between the different platforms. By transferring between various vehicle platforms, the 'missionaries' can bring a wealth of their experiences on previous car projects to new assignments. Added Gardner, 'Missionaries also are a great tool when a particular project needs to downsize its team.' All individuals have the chance to work as missionaries. If a new job opportunity is available on a particular platform, the transfer is negotiated and agreed upon by the platform leaders and the employee under consideration.

Finally, Chrysler has a few core research groups. According to Gardner, some engineers have a very narrow and preferred area of technical expertise. They find it difficult to work within the broad scope and responsibilities of a cross-functional team. Consequently, said Gardner, 'Engineers in these core technology research groups – in areas such as engines, transmissions, and electronic systems – regularly move among the different vehicle platforms and provide assistance in their area of expertise. By rotating between the different platforms, these technical experts also transfer vital information and technology.'

General Motors: 10 steps for transferring knowledge

A major setback for General Motors was the US company's failure to create an organizational structure that would help the US auto giant learn from its Nummi alliance. This proved a great disappointment, since GM had originally sought the Nummi alliance, a 50–50 joint venture with arch-rival Toyota, to learn firsthand about Japanese management principles in such key areas as manufacturing, inventory, labour–management relations and quality. A Massachusetts Institute of Technology (MIT) report concluded that the plant tours, videotapes and manuals GM relied upon had conveyed only a very partial understanding of Nummi's procedures. Joseph L. Badaracco (1991b) points out that GM's experience with Nummi led one of their executives to specify 10 steps crucial for transferring knowledge and capabilities:

(1)   Involve prospective users up front.
(2)   Encourage users to participate in the development of the technology.
(3)   Apply the new technology to a few critical problems before attempting to transfer it.
(4)   Package the technology so it is accessible to users.
(5)   Provide formal training in using the new technology.
(6)   Follow up to determine the effectiveness of the transfer process.
(7)   Provide users the opportunities to meet collectively and share their experiences with the technology.
(8)   Do not rely solely on written reports to sell technology.
(9)   Be willing to provide resources such as people, time and money to sell the technology.
(10) Consider transferring people along with the technology.

Xerox: fluid information channels with Fuji Xerox

Many Western companies concede that ventures with Japanese partners provide a unique gateway into understanding and assimilating Japanese techniques of quality control and other management tools. Similarly, Japanese firms can gain insight into how to apply their management techniques and manufacturing strategies in a US environment. Xerox and its Fuji Xerox alliance have capitalized on the advantages of having a continuous two-way exchange of people and ideas to strengthen competitiveness. Jefferson Kennard, director of Fuji Xerox relations at Xerox, cites Fuji Xerox's role as an 'agent for change' as its greatest benefit to Xerox. Fuji Xerox's early forays into quality control and management have served as a strong inspiration to Xerox.

Both Xerox and Fuji Xerox's efforts to boost competitiveness by sharing information and experiences have already produced positive results. Within their respective countries, several Xerox entities have received national quality awards: Xerox Mexico (1990), Xerox Canada (1989), Xerox France (1987) and Xerox Netherlands (1983). Moreover, both Fuji Xerox and Xerox (US) have received the national Deming and Baldridge awards, in 1980 and 1989, respectively. Kojiro Akiba, associate director and manager of the New Xerox Movement at Fuji Xerox, outlined the following nine important activities designed to encourage the exchange of knowledge and skills between Xerox and Fuji Xerox.

(1) Total Quality Control (TQC) benchmark teams

Xerox and Fuji Xerox jointly established a programme in 1988 in which the latter accepted functional teams from Xerox for additional training in quality control. The two companies inaugurated this programme with the first team coming from top management, led by Xerox president and CEO Paul Allaire to send a strong signal of support throughout the company. The first team included the director of each function. Following the senior management team, over 15 Xerox teams have since completed the programme. Xerox basically selects 20 individuals for each team, from marketing, manufacturing, engineering and so on. Most of the team members come from the middle- and senior-management levels. Approximately four teams go through the training each year. Team selection is not restricted to US operations; as Akiba pointed out, teams have also come from Rank Xerox and Xerox operations in Latin America, Asia and Europe.

The TQC benchmark programme, which generally lasts one week, features lectures from noted Japanese professors on quality management, plus discussions on operational techniques from qualified Fuji Xerox personnel. Trainees also spend time working with their Fuji Xerox counterparts to learn about the operational specifics of applying quality management. Fuji Xerox also organizes visits to university research labs and Japanese MNCs noted for quality control, such as Matsushita, Komatsu and Toyota.

(2) Resident quality director

Fuji Xerox's division responsible for quality, which is known as the New Xerox Movement, sends a senior staff manager to Xerox to serve as TQC senior adviser. This TQC manager is charged with assisting different Xerox divisions with their quality programmes. In addition, he serves as a primary liaison to ensure that new ideas and concepts on quality management are transferred and reach the appropriate Xerox individuals.

(3) Exchange programme

Fuji Xerox and Xerox exchange from 70 to 100 engineers annually to encourage the flow and exchange of ideas. The two firms also frequently centralize their operations for new research and product development projects. This enables engineers and scientists to work side by side, enhancing the flow of information. In the past, said Hideki Kaihatsu (senior managing director and chief staff officer at Fuji Xerox) Fuji Xerox and Xerox would split the responsibility for a particular development project, then coordinate activities from the separate locations. Now, however, management finds it more effective to use a single-point research centre by grouping all project team members at the same R&D location.

(4) Official presidential reviews

Xerox recently adopted Fuji Xerox's system of having annual presidential inspections. Each year, the president critiques the corporate-wide strategy on quality. Proposals submitted by each function on how divisional managers plan to improve or achieve total quality are analysed. At both Fuji Xerox and Xerox, the respective CEOs – Yotaro Kobayashi and Paul Allaire – give their written feedback on both the divisional proposals and the corporate strategy. During Xerox's presidential reviews Kobayashi frequently acts as adviser to Allaire, offering new concepts developed by Fuji Xerox or by influential Japanese management circles on quality.

(5) Send TQC professors

Fuji Xerox arranges temporary sojourns at Xerox of Japanese professors renowned for their expertise with TQC. These professors assist Xerox in developing and implementing in-house quality programmes. On average, Akiba says, two professors are sent to Xerox every three months.

(6) Worldwide information exchange

Different Xerox operations share information on advances in quality management through the company's internal system for electronic mail. The typical information traded includes novel concepts for benchmarking, improvements in customer service and new criteria for evaluating quality levels in various functions such as manufacturing and marketing. Often, the different Xerox operations trade around the results of their own internal benchmarking analyses for peer review by quality experts at other locales. Furthermore, Fuji Xerox frequently sends out news alerts and briefs on breakthroughs in quality management at Fuji Xerox or other Japanese MNCs.

(7) Arrange client visits

Fuji Xerox and Xerox frequently arrange customer visits for each other. For instance, Fuji Xerox has sponsored training sessions for many of Xerox's US clients. The curriculum for these week-long client conferences basically mirrors the seminar schedule for the internal TQC benchmarking teams. Client participants are also culled from senior management levels. For instance, the chairmen of both Procter & Gamble and Boeing led their own corporate teams. Other corporate participants include the US carpet firm Miliken & Company, which recently won the Baldridge award. The US Embassy in Japan also sent a training group from the US armed forces. Similarly, Xerox has hosted Fuji Xerox clients in the US. As Akiba said, many Japanese MNCs are interested in the organizational and management dynamics of implementing Japanese quality and other management principles in a US environment. For instance, Xerox recently received a team of executives from Toyota and its affiliates at its US headquarters.

(8)   Quality day

Both Xerox and Fuji Xerox annually hold a Quality Day, replete with conferences, presentations, training sessions and activities on internal quality efforts. During their respective quality events, the two parties exchange representatives to make a presentation. Separately, Xerox also has a Quality Day at least three times a month in which participants from the government, academia, clients and the document-processing industry gather with Xerox executives for various seminars and activities on quality.

(9)   Quality implementation teams

Throughout the global Xerox network, management has set up a pool of high-calibre executives to serve as its quality implementation team. The team meets at least four times a year at Xerox's US headquarters in Stamford to encourage close contact between quality experts. This closer personal contact facilitates information exchange throughout the year.

Ford uses Mazda links to strengthen competitiveness

According to Paul Drenkow, a Ford executive closely involved in the Ford–Mazda relationship, 'Many Western firms take a narrow view of alliances. Management tends to focus on the operating objective only – for instance, to jointly manufacture X product or component. Yet, what companies often fail to realize is that collaborative projects offer a unique opportunity to observe and learn about a competitor's tactics. Venture employees need to keep their eyes and ears open to learn as much as possible. And whatever new knowledge and skills an employee may assimilate, bring the know-how back to parent headquarters and spread it around.' Drenkow points to three concrete steps in Ford's strategy to boost competitiveness by tapping the knowledge and expertise of its long-standing partner, Mazda Motor Corp.

Seek supplier and technology ties

Ford's management has consistently sought opportunities to act as a supplier to Mazda for components and products to boost its internal inventory management and quality techniques. For instance, a new Ford factory began supplying transmissions to Mazda's Flat Rock, Michigan, plant in the early 1990s. Notes Drenkow, 'By forcing Ford's plant to supply transmissions to Mazda, management can learn how to operate under the stringent just-in-time and quality standards of Japanese manufacturers. Also, when constructing the new transmission facility, Ford arranged to have Mazda take responsibility and control for building a transfer line (critical machining and manufacturing operations in which engineers basically take a transmission mould and design the manufacturing line according to the transmission's specifications). The Ford engineers remained on the sidelines, observing and learning how the Japanese build transfer lines. Ford used similar tactics in constructing its Hermosillo, Mexico plant, for which Ford engineers obtained access to the blueprints for a state-of-the-art Mazda facility in Japan. (See Box 12.2.)

Working side by side with Mazda to build the Ford Escort in 1989 also revealed to Ford important management and organizational improvements, particularly with regard to suppliers. Impressed by Mazda's rigorous standards for quality and timeliness, Ford has since been adopting a tougher stance with its own suppliers. And, mirroring a trend among US manufacturers to consolidate their supplier networks, Ford plans to cut its 1200-strong North American supplier base to 900 companies by 1995.

Finally, Ford and Mazda recently established a component venture in Japan for climate control and air-conditioning systems. The venture, which will supply both Ford's and Mazda's factories, wed Ford technology with Mazda manufacturing expertise. As Drenkow says, 'We deliberately located the venture in Japan to adopt and assimilate as much know-how as possible on Japanese manufacturing practices.'

Reverse roles

In 1989, Ford and Mazda agreed to jointly design and develop a new range of small trucks. Mazda sought this alliance to cope with the 25% US duties on small-truck imports that made Japanese exports costly and uncompetitive. Ford, however, wanted to see how far it could stretch its capabilities to develop a vehicle for its Japanese partner. The venture began with a compact utility, the Ford Explorer and the Mazda Navajo. 'In fact,' says Drenkow, 'the project is the first time in which the traditional roles of a US–Japanese partnership have been reversed. In most cases the Japanese take the lead in developing a new vehicle.'

Yet the role-reversal provided a unique opportunity to learn how to develop a new vehicle under rigorous Japanese standards, and proved a tough yet rewarding experience for Ford. For instance, when a Mazda team came in early 1990 to review the first Navajo prototype, it was an eye-opener for Ford. 'The Mazda team festooned the Navajo with 400 triangular stickers colour-coded to indicate problems in everything from fit and finish to design, with criticisms scribbled on them. "After two days, there were so many stickers, you could hardly see the paint", recalls Phong T. Wu, head of the Ford team' (*Business Week*, 1992).

Yet the criticisms offered valuable lessons which were later transferred internally to other development projects. Moreover, in late 1991, the cooperation in this venture was extended to include small pickup trucks. Again, Ford assumed responsibility for the design, development and production of a small pickup for Mazda, as well as for its own product line. As Drenkow concludes, 'These projects mark a major milestone in the Ford/Mazda relationship in which Ford is now supplying vehicles to Mazda.'

Encourage technology forums

A few years ago, Ford operations in Europe and North America launched a series of technology forums offering engineers and executives from different operations an opportunity to meet and exchange ideas. Shortly after Ford inaugurated the series, its management realized that Mazda could provide an invaluable contribution. Hence, Ford's management met with its legal department to identify a list of technical areas in which Ford could talk openly with Mazda. Ford first zeroed in on the two important areas of paint quality and noise vibration and harshness (NVH), which basically refers to the rattles and squeaks customers hear in a vehicle. Drenkow points out that since Mazda joined the forums, Ford has made great strides in improving paint quality and NVH. Says Drenkow, 'Overall, for Ford, Mazda's involvement has highlighted the value of suggestions from workers. Many valuable Mazda improvements actually originate as ideas from plant employees. Consequently, Ford is also trying to pay closer attention to what workers say.'

Box 12.2   Hermosillo mixes the best of Ford and Mazda

When Ford sketched its plans to construct the Hermosillo, Mexico facility in the mid-1980s, management wanted to tap Hermosillo's unique advantage as a 'clean sheet of paper' to introduce new operating techniques. As a 'greenfield' site, Hermosillo provided the ideal setting to experiment with novel organizational and management approaches.

continues

continued

In particular, Ford was eager to draw on its long-standing links to Mazda Motors Corp. to implement some of the lean production techniques perfected by Japanese manufacturers. Installing Japanese tooling and manufacturing processes also made sense since the vehicles manufactured at Hermosillo – the Ford Escort and Mercury Tracer – were products of Ford–Mazda cooperation. In fact, these two vehicles – designed by Ford and engineered by Mazda – are representative of the strengths and successes of the Ford–Mazda marriage. To date, some Ford executives consider Hermosillo a model operation; the Mexican facility incorporates the best elements of both Mazda's and Ford's organizational philosophies and skilfully adapts them to a Mexican environment. Hermosillo's success has also served as an agent of change to motivate other Ford North American facilities to adopt similar techniques.

Using Hofu as a model

Ford management zeroed in on Mazda's Hofu facility as a benchmark when designing the Hermosillo facility for several reasons. First, Hofu manufactured light vehicles that were similar to the autos designated for the Hermosillo plant. The Japanese plant's production capacity was comparable to the Mexican plant's capabilities of approximately 160,000–170,000 vehicles per annum. Several Ford teams dedicated months to analysing various Mazda operating tactics. Starting with the Telesis study – a detailed analysis of hourly workers at Hofu – Ford was able to set productivity targets for the Hermosillo workers that matched those of the Japanese.

Thereafter, Ford organized a five-member team to analyse Hofu's salaried employees so that Hermosillo's staffing needs and resources equalled Japanese practices. Yet the salaried staff study yielded knowledge well beyond a mere understanding of staffing within a Japanese facility. According to one member of the Hermosillo Salaried Staffing Study team, the Hofu study was not just a model for how to staff Hermosillo but a bell-wether for how to operate Ford's other North American assembly plants. Following Hermosillo's success, Ford management transferred many of the same techniques to other North American assembly plants. Their use within North America is paying off. Recent ratings by the consulting firm Harbour Associates ranked Ford – and its 18 North American assembly plants, including Hermosillo – with the highest productivity of all indigenous auto manufacturers and Japanese transplants.

This case examines the techniques garnered from the Mazda Hofu studies and from Ford's own internal initiatives that provided the foundation for building a lean competitive facility at Hermosillo. Two important factors contributed to Hermosillo's successful implementation of a new management and organizational strategy. First, three of the individuals on the original five-member Hermosillo Salaried Staffing Study had been assigned to work on adapting the new ideas to the Mexican

continues

continued

plant. These three managers – who were definitely sold on the benefits of using the new ideas garnered from studying Mazda – acted as the champions of the new philosophy. Said one Ford executive, 'By appointing these three individuals as Hermosillo plant managers, Mazda's staffing and operations strategies were already halfway to Mexico.' Their enthusiasm and direct involvement eased the adoption of these new ideas at Hermosillo.

Second, Mazda was an important link in the smooth transfer of vital know-how and technology. During the first few months of production, approximately 15–20 Mazda engineers worked at Hermosillo to assist the workers and iron out any start-up kinks. Mazda also offered assistance when the workers were retooling the facility in 1990 for the new Mercury Tracer.

Designing a flexible facility

The concepts adopted by Ford for the Mexican plant included:

Combining stamping and assembly operations under one roof By having stamping and assembly operations within the same building at Hermosillo, Ford saves on transportation costs as well as any expenses incurred from parts damaged in transit. Management can also better match the supply of exterior parts, such as doors, to the needs of the production line, thereby reducing excess inventory costs. Placing the stamping and assembly operations under one roof also yields direct economies of scale in management and staff support.

Beginning with a versatile floor plan Hermosillo's versatile design makes it infinitely expandable, thus offering Ford the agility to respond quickly to changing market needs. Ford also purchased ample land surrounding the Hermosillo plant for future expansion. Within the floor plan, each operation is a dedicated section of the plant. Body and stamping operations are in the west side of the plant, the paint area is located in the centre or core, and the assembly operations are in the east. Should management want to expand any of the three areas, this layout enables Ford to knock down the absolute minimum number of walls and expand any particular operation vertically.

Using area management to organize operations Each of the three sections of the Hermosillo plant – body and stamping, painting, and final assembly – operates as a self-contained unit managed by independent teams. Area management entails a more holistic approach to production, encouraging workers to develop multiple skills and assume a more proactive hands-on approach to running the operations. Each area has its own engineering section that provides all the necessary activities to support production. This includes the handling of materials, budget performance analyses, process and industrial engineering, maintenance and quality. Having Hermosillo's production workers

continues

continued

responsible for their own quality control and maintenance on the assembly line is a significant departure from the traditional organizational style of auto plants. Hermosillo provided substantial guidance and training so that the workers could develop the skills to finesse the often complicated mechanical, hydraulic and electrical equipment processes related to maintenance.

Streamlining accounts payable with the single-chain method   One of the most interesting discoveries from the Hermosillo Salaried Staffing Study was how Mazda managed its accounts payable. At Hofu, Ford's team learned that Mazda's entire accounts payable department consisted of only five individuals. This compared with Ford's 500 across North America. Even after adjusting for Mazda's smaller size, Ford figured that its accounts payable organization was five times the size it should be.

Ford discovered that Mazda had a simple yet efficient system for processing accounts payable. Named the single-chain method by Ford, it is an invoiceless process that starts with entering purchasing information for supplies into an online database. When the parts arrive at the dock, the receiving clerk checks the database and enters the transaction into the computer system. The computer system then matches the goods received with the original request. After matching the order with the goods received, the computer automatically prepares the cheque, which is then sent to the supplier. There are no invoices to worry about since Ford has asked its vendors not to send them.

The single-chain method – which is used at Hermosillo as well as throughout Ford's North American automotive operations – has yielded tremendous savings, in time, money and human resources. Ford's former system had followed a circuitous route. When the purchasing department wrote a purchase order, it sent a copy to accounts payable. Later when materials control received the parts, it sent a copy of the receiving document to accounts payable. The supplier also sent a copy of the invoice to accounts payable. Accounts payable then had to match the purchase order against the receiving document and the invoice. If they matched, a cheque was issued. If not, a clerk would investigate the discrepancy. Most of the department's time was spent trying to solve mismatches. Now, however, Hermosillo's use of the single-chain method streamlines the factory's management and control over the timely delivery and payment of parts.

Brawn with brains

Many of the techniques for labour management at Hermosillo are key to the factory's productivity and market responsiveness. While some of the tactics were acquired from Mazda, Ford also benefited from Hermosillo's unique advantage as a greenfield site and also from its location in a non-industrial area of Mexico. Both factors make it easier to experiment with new management ideas:

continues

continued

Help wanted: no experience necessary   Hermosillo is located in the state of Sonora, a predominantly agricultural area. Most of the workers at the facility came from the agricultural sector and had no prior experience in the auto industry. Consequently, they were easier to train and more open to new ideas. One Ford executive considers the 'mañana' syndrome in Mexico a misnomer. Instead, he points out how many Mexicans are artisans. As a result of this background, the Hermosillo workers tend to be creative, willing to try new ideas, and craft tradespeople.

Boosting agility with one job classification   Since Hermosillo was a brand new facility, Ford was able to circumvent many of the requirements for different grades and job classifications within other North American assembly plants. Hermosillo uses only one job classification for hourly workers – technician. Having only one job classification offers considerable flexibility by allowing workers to develop and handle multiple responsiblities.

   A good example was when the plant needed retooling in 1990 to prepare for production of the Mercury Tracer. Initially, Ford had planned to have the Mercury Tracer manufactured only at Wayne, Ohio. Then, when management decided to allocate some production to Hermosillo, the company did not have the appropriate tools for the Mexican facility. Hermosillo was made inoperative for several months while management waited for the necessary retooling. However, rather than continue waiting, Hermosillo's workers decided to install their own tools. The workers removed the old set of tools and refitted the plant for the new Tracer model. Normally, union demarcations require auto companies to delegate this complicated task to outside skilled tradespeople. However, Hermosillo's single job classifications eliminates narrow job restrictions and thus permits workers to take greater initiative.

Setting productivity targets   The Hermosillo benchmarking studies established targets for the number of hourly workers and salaried employees so that Hermosillo's productivity matched the competitiveness of a Japanese facility. Consequently, the Hermosillo plant has a very lean hourly and salaried staff – 2440, including 2120 hourly workers and 320 salaried employees.

Nurturing workers with training   Training, training, training and lots of it has been a motto of Hermosillo from its inception. While the plant was being built, Ford recruited several hundred individuals and sent them to various Ford facilities in Spain, Belgium and the US as well as to Mazda facilities in Japan for on-the-job training. The on-site training was later reinforced with several weeks of classroom instruction. In total, this core group spent three–four months of 40-hour weeks in training prior to launching production at Hermosillo. This group was

continues

---

continued

then responsible for assisting in the training of the other workers. Complementing the initial training is management's effort to keep the Hermosillo workforce up to date on the latest quality and manufacturing techniques with ongoing workshops and seminars. The focus on training – combined with the advantages of one job classification – is churning out a highly skilled workforce. In fact, Hermosillo's assembly workers handle much the same tasks that Japanese workers are required to do.

Solicit input As part of its productivity push, Hermosillo encourages a continuous dialogue among employees within the plant as well as with other North American facilities. Long before Ford even plans production of a new model at Hermosillo, design engineers go to the Mexican plant to explain to the workers the design intent of the vehicle and how their jobs fit into the design process as well as into the responsibilities of the next team on the assembly line. The engineers also solicit any ideas or suggestions from the Hermosillo workers on how to improve the process for building a particular vehicle.

Besides helping with plans for new vehicles, workers are encouraged to offer their input while on the line. If a worker has a problem or has a better idea on how to assemble certain parts, he can just pick up the phone and make suggestions to the plant manager. Concluded one Ford executive, 'who knows better how to build a vehicle than the actual assembly worker?'

(*Source*: *Responding to Change in Mexico* (1993) © Economist Intelligence Unit, p. 30 and *Global Benchmarking for Competitive Edge* (1993). © Economist Intelligence Unit, p. 81)

References

Badaracco J.L. (1991a). *The Knowledge Link: How Firms Compete Through Strategic Alliances.* Boston: Harvard Business School Press, p. 13

Badaracco J.L. (1991b). *The Knowledge Link: How Firms Compete Through Strategic Alliances.* Boston: Harvard Business School Press, p. 145

Business Week (1992). The Partners. 10 Feb, p. 104

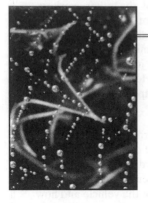

13

Dealbusters: why some alliances break up

This chapter reviews several reasons why the partners in some alliances go their separate ways, and their experience in doing so. Because it is often difficult to isolate a sole reason for a partnership divorce, cases are often discussed under one or more headings. Whether partners use an alliance as an exit strategy or simply one partner wants out, divorce does not signal failure. While some partnerships unquestionably do end bitterly, several executives argue fervently that a breakup does not automatically imply a flop. (See Box 13.1.) In fact, alliances are not required to continue endlessly – few do.

Tallying the successes and failures in 30 ventures

In a 1987 Economist Intelligence Unit report – *Competitive Alliances – How to Succeed at Cross-Regional Collaboration*, 30 alliance cases were examined in detail. Many of these alliances were partnerships among strong global competitors, such as AT&T, Chrysler, Ford, Fujitsu, Mitsubishi Heavy Industries, Nippon Sheet Glass, Corning, General Electric, General Motors, FANUC, Imperial Chemical Industries (ICI), Westinghouse, International Computers Limited (ICL) and Himont.

Box 13.1   Himont: success or failure?

When Hercules sold its equity stake in Himont – its 50–50 joint venture with Montedison to manufacture and market polypropylene worldwide – alliance sceptics quipped 'another corporate partnership fails'. Yet Alexander Giacco, former CEO of Hercules and chief architect of Himont, argued differently. 'An underlying motivation for all joint venture partners is to create wealth,' said Giacco. 'Analysing the success or failure of a venture should be based on its profits. Success should not and does not depend on whether the entity continues indefinitely as a joint venture.' Longevity is not a measure of success. In support of this argument, Giacco demonstrated how Himont did create wealth, clearly making it a successful joint venture.

In the early 1980s, Hercules was facing a serious dilemma. Its position as global market leader for polypropylene, a flexible plastic material used for both commercial and industrial purposes, was in jeopardy. One of its main rivals, Montedison, had just developed a novel technology that would radically change the production cost structure of polypropylene as well as pave the way for new product extensions. Montedison's technological breakthrough meant that Hercules would have to invest hundreds of millions of dollars to renovate its operations worldwide in order to retain its leadership position. Moreover, Montedison had embarked on an aggressive licensing strategy that was seriously undermining Hercules's position in the market. However, Hercules, with total capitalization of approximately $600 million at the time, clearly did not have the financial resources, much less the R&D capabilities, to meet Montedison head-on.

Hercules had two choices. First, management could opt out by leaving the industry. However, market conditions at that time were depressed, and the company probably would not have received more than $100 million to $200 million for the business. Furthermore, as Giacco argued, 'Market leaders usually do not just exit an industry'. Second, Hercules could ally itself with Montedison. Each company enjoyed a competitive advantage in the industry that the other lacked. Montedison had the technology, but no markets outside of Western Europe. Hercules had a sophisticated worldwide marketing network, yet lacked the technology and the resources to develop the necessary know-how in-house. So the two firms decided to form a joint venture and pooled together $900 million in assets to create Himont in November 1983.

As Giacco emphasized, 'With a joint venture, it is critical that one plus one add up to more than two – at least three, if not more'. The partners set out to achieve this high return with Himont and succeeded. Through research and technological breakthroughs, the venture added new properties and applications for polypropylene. In essence, said Giacco, 'We put the mystery back into a mature product. It went from

continues

---

continued

the mature, lower-priced end of the product curve over to the higher-priced growth side. We ceased being simply a resins company but became a materials firm.'

Further, Himont has grown worldwide to include over 3000 employees (20% working in R&D), 38 manufacturing plants and distribution capabilities in 100 countries. With a heavy emphasis on R&D and product development, Himont management made a commitment to earn at least $150 million per annum from new products. Moreover, in the early 1990s, Himont was a leader in the chemical industry with a return on equity of 38%.

Therefore, Giacco found it difficult to accept critics calling Himont a failure because it is no longer a joint venture. As he argued, 'Hercules' total capitalization in the early 1980s approximated $600 million. The US firm sold its 40% stake in Himont to Montedison for $1.6 billion. [Himont's management had already sold 20% of its shares to the public.] Given this return on investment on what was previously a mature, dead-end product, how can Himont be considered a failed venture?'

Of the 30 cases, four examples were reviewed after the alliances had broken up. Of the 26 fully operating alliances in the 1987 study, new interviews for this book revealed ten cases still in operation, ten alliances dissolved and the management for six cases declined to comment. These figures translate to a ratio of 38.5% of the firms remaining married, 38.5% deciding to divorce and 23% being reluctant to discuss the ventures. By analysing why partners in certain ventures went their separate ways, this chapter attempts to offer some insights valuable to other companies interested in alliance-making as part of their global strategies. The material also covers the details and the troubles afflicting a few other global ventures. Based on input from these alliance executives and other reference materials, there are a 'dozen dealbusters' to keep in mind on why some ventures break up.

A dozen dealbusters

Scenario 1: Changes in strategic objectives and focus

Recurring difficulties for many alliances result from changes in one or all partners' long-term strategic objectives. Given the dynamics of the global economy, few MNCs say that they manage to steer the same long-term course for a notable amount of time. In some instances, flexibility and perseverance to jointly tackle a given market may be enough to keep an alliance intact. In other instances, however, a partner may undergo such a significant overhaul of operations that existing ventures may no longer be economically feasible or sensible.

Take Westinghouse's forays into ventures with Mitsubishi and Toshiba. In the mid-1980s, Westinghouse and Mitsubishi created a 50–50 joint venture: Westinghouse Mitsubishi Power Products Inc. (WMPPI), designed to compete together in the volatile market for high-voltage circuit breakers. A few years after the venture's inception, Westinghouse switched its focus from mature markets toward new high-growth areas. This triggered restructurings in several of Westinghouse's traditional power-generation products and businesses.

As a first step toward exiting the industry, Westinghouse merged its transmission and distribution businesses into a $1 billion venture with Asea Brown Boveri (ABB). According to Roger Barna, former chief of WMPPI and current president of Mitsubishi Power Products, this alliance with ABB presented problems for WMPPI. ABB was a direct competitor to WMPPI in the market for high-voltage circuit breakers. Hence, the US Justice Department ruled that Westinghouse could not be party to both entities. Westinghouse then exited WMPPI, since it was significantly smaller than the ABB arrangement. Westinghouse's new focus also contributed to its decision to leave the Toshiba–Westinghouse Electronics (TWEC) venture for colour display tubes. According to Robert Kaemmerer, former executive at TWEC, the venture no longer made strategic or business sense to Westinghouse. Then, when TWEC reached phase two of its business expansion plan and required additional financing, Westinghouse withdrew rather than invest scarce capital in a business that did not fit its new strategy.

In the early 1990s, stiff global competition and poor financial results forced Philips NV to redirect its corporate strategy. Philips' new competitive mandate to focus on core businesses, such as consumer electronics, required management to shed or restructure countless businesses. Among the casualties were several important alliances, as for instance when Philips NV withdrew from the Mega-Project, a joint endeavour with Siemens to develop new generations of submicron chips. Even after their sinking nearly $1 billion into the project over the previous five years, Japanese and US rivals still beat Philips to the market with cheaper versions. Instead, sources say Philips planned to use outside suppliers for the chips necessary for its technologies or possibly set up new, tighter links with Matsushita of Japan. Neither did Philips' new strategy work for telecommunications. And when Philips' former joint venture with AT&T – APT Telecommunications – to manufacture and market telecommunications equipment in Europe needed additional capital from the parent firms, Philips withdrew rather than allocate scarce corporate resources to a nonstrategic business.

Similarly, General Motors' financial difficulties and management upheaval in the early 1990s forced the company to sell its interests in many venture activities in order to focus on its core vehicle operations. As part of the restructuring, GM sold its 50% share in GMFanuc Robotics to its Japanese partner at the end of 1992. Yet despite the breakup, GMFanuc Robotics is a good example of how divorce does not always translate into failure. In fact, GMFanuc was quite successful. With about $10 million contributed from the alliance partners for initial capitalization in 1982, management succeeded in building a global business in which cumulative sales topped $1 billion by 1990. The growth of GMFanuc Robotics also enabled the venture to push beyond Asia and North America into Europe. Using its own capital resources, the alliance acquired a UK company, expanded its German subsidiary and established new operations in France, Italy, Spain and Sweden. The venture was also the only company in the North American robotics industry that had positive cumulative earnings throughout the tumultuous 1980s.

Scenario 2: Changes in corporate leadership

There is a distinct correlation between changes in corporate leadership and the charting of a different company course with new goals. In fact, changes in top management frequently precede new strategic plans and ambitions. For instance, once Jan Timmer had taken the helm of Philips NV, he did not waste time in shedding unwanted ventures and operations, such as the cooperative R&D Mega-Project with Siemens or an alliance with Whirlpool in white goods. Similarly, Alexander Giacco – managing director of Axess and former CEO of Hercules – timed Hercules' withdrawal in the late 1980s from its 50–50 joint venture with Montedision – Himont – to coincide with his retirement as head of Hercules. In fact, Giacco outlined the four pillars of his philosophy on the pivotal role of CEOs in beginning and ending an alliance.

(1) The CEO must really want the venture, because too many lower-level executives and employees will resist cooperation. Alliances need this high-level commitment up front to survive.

(2) The seed for cooperation is often planted through informal and personal contacts between corporate leaders, illustrating the unique value and importance of personal relationships to a venture.

(3) Since cooperation is fuelled by the commitment and personal ties of the partners' leaders, CEOs must terminate the alliance before they depart or retire, as Giacco did with Himont. When he was preparing to retire from Hercules, he arranged for the public sale of 20% of Himont, then Hercules' final withdrawal from the venture. As he remarked, 'A new CEO hardly wants to deal with his predecessor's pet projects.'

(4) Long before one or both CEOs depart, the partners must jointly reach an agreement on how to end the venture. As Giacco observed, 'I do not consider joint ventures as a long-term strategy. They are too difficult to manage, given the separate constraints facing partners. Ultimately, the parents' objectives and ambitions are likely to diverge. Consequently, partners need to determine to whom the venture has the greatest value and arrange for the venture's transfer to that parent. In most cases, this partner will already have emerged by taking a dominant role in managing daily operations.'

Scenario 3: False expectations about partners' capabilities

Whether intentionally so or not, many alliances collapse when one or both partners' presumed 'strengths' fail to produce tangible results. In the former AT&T–Philips NV venture to jointly manufacture and sell telecommunications equipment in Europe, AT&T learned a tough lesson on the political realities of European national champions. As Jacques Meyer, international market planning director for AT&T, acknowledged, 'Philips NV with its Netherlands headquarters and production has often been touted as a European champion. We naively believed its strength and reputation in telecommunications stretched beyond the Netherlands. Yet, we discovered the strict national limits of European telecommunications competitors in an unsuccessful bid to win a large slice of the French telecommunications market. Yes, Philips NV was a European competitor, but its clout did not go far beyond the Dutch national frontiers.'

The GM–Daewoo link also suffered from wide gaps between what its partners pledged and what they actually delivered. 'GM sought the Korean venture to tap Daewoo's low-cost labour advantage, and Daewoo was anxious to build up export sales through GM's wide marketing and distribution network in the US. Neither side was satisfied. Greater prosperity in Korea, combined with militant labour unions seeking higher wages, eroded the cost competitiveness of manufacturing in Korea. Nor had GM's Pontiac division, responsible for selling the Korean-made Le Mans, done a stellar job in selling these autos (*Business Week*, 1991b). The venture's poor results combined with GM's own internal management upheaval prompted GM to sell its 50% share in October, 1992.

Scenario 4: Same bed, different dreams

With some alliances, partners suffer from having incompatible agendas. Over time, these differences can become magnified and lead to varying levels of commitment and support for a venture from parent management.

When the alliance is unable to bridge the differences, partners often end up going their separate ways.

Analysts attribute many of the problems in US–Japanese ventures in auto parts to an incompatibility in their goals. US suppliers often have a narrow focus: to gain access to the Japanese auto transplants in the US. The Japanese firms, however, have broader ambitions: to secure a foothold in the US market. The time frame for these agendas can be quite different. Over time, differences between the short- and long-term focuses of partners' objectives become exacerbated. In particular, tensions build when the Japanese insist on offering valuable customers price reductions, at the joint venture's expense.

Take the case of a joint venture between ITT Automotive and Sanoh of Japan. Shortly after the venture was launched, the yen rose against the dollar. The costs for some of the parts the new firm was importing from Japan sky-rocketed. Yet despite the rising costs, Sanoh still insisted that the venture allow Honda, its largest customer, to set prices while the alliance footed the bill for a costly factory retooling. According to Charles Peters, senior vice-president at ITT Automotive, 'It got to the point that the only way we were going to make money was to strike oil under the plant' (*Business Week*, 1989).

Yet problems with conflicting ambitions and objectives in alliances are not exclusive to partnerships with Japanese firms. A former joint venture between Corning and Ciba-Geigy of Switzerland derailed because of growing differences in the two partners' goals and ambitions. According to Stephen Albertalli, recently retired director for investor relations at Corning, it is not uncommon for partners to have slightly divergent interests as a venture progresses. In some instances, the parties hammer out a new, mutually agreeable agenda for the alliance. In other cases, the differences prove irreconcilable and the companies part ways. When the former 50–50 Ciba–Corning Diagnostics joint venture was launching its medical services partnership, Ciba merged part of its therapeutics business with Corning's diagnostics operations. However, much to the surprise of both partners, as the venture progressed it became clearly apparent that Ciba needed to contribute substantially more of its proprietary therapeutics know-how and operations to make the venture a success. Yet the Swiss pharmaceuticals giant preferred to go it alone in many of these businesses. Hence, it had no interest in contributing additional therapeutics to the partnership. However, without the added Ciba contribution, the venture had only a meagre future. Consequently, the partners negotiated for the sale of Corning's share to Ciba.

AT&T and Italtel suffered a similar fate. While deregulation within the European telecommunications industry offers substantial opportunities, telecommunications partners often disagree on what strategy and technology to employ in order to capitalize on market opportunities. Italtel and AT&T have been linked in a variety of cooperative endeavours, most notably cross-equity shareholdings in which Stet – Italtel's parent company – owned 20% of AT&T's Dutch-based operation, NSI International, and AT&T held a 20% stake in Italtel. Stet liquidated its equity stake in NSI in 1993 and AT&T will probably sell its Italtel shares in 1994.

According to Ramesh Barasia, vice-president for marketing at AT&T Network Systems, 'We (AT&T and Italtel) basically disagreed on how the European telecommunications market would develop. It had nothing to do with a management argument on how to run the alliance. Nor was it a case of "they were right and we were wrong" and vice versa. It was a case of two partners basically having different visions on the future direction of telecommunications in Europe and what is the best technology and strategy for developing the market.' Within Italy, the Italian telecommunications market is undergoing dramatic changes because of new concessions offered for a second, competing wireless network and the need to replace existing outdated equipment with new technology. Yet, adds Barasia, 'One does not simply yank one system out and replace it with new technology.' Instead, the telecommunications industry/monopoly chooses a certain technology and migration path and incrementally adds new equipment to advance the system. AT&T obviously was pushing its digital 5ESS (5 Electronic Switch System) yet Italtel had its own Linea UT digital telephone exchanges. Based on their disagreements over what technology, products and platforms to use, Italtel then opted to form a JV with Siemens' Italian subsidiary, which also produces Linea UT exchanges. The new Italtel/Siemens venture aims to market the Linea UT switches domestically and in export markets.

Scenario 5: Inability to cope with diverse management styles and cultures

One of the greatest challenges of alliances – managing the wealth of diversity inherent in partners' cultures and strengths – can also trigger their downfall. There is no simple remedy for how to cope with this diversity. No matter how willing the partners may be to work together, the challenge of coping with cultural and management differences can be formidable. And when partners face adverse market conditions, there can be little time to devote to the task of bridging differences. (See Box 13.2 on the trials and tribulations of the Corning–Vitro venture.)

Moreover, given the sensitivity of the issue, few alliances want to attribute a venture's collapse to this cause. Nevertheless, the mere frustrations of running a venture's business, combined with cultural differences, can engulf an alliance. For instance, strains in Western–Japanese alliances from corporate, industrial and national cultural differences abound. Commonly, disputes arise over clashes in work ethics, labour practices and decision-making styles. Unless a venture's management addresses these issues immediately, misunderstandings can swell into insurmountable problems. For example, in a Komatsu–Dresser venture in the construction equipment industry, executives complained of cultural clashes in decision-making styles. As one former Dresser executive said 'Crucial decisions were often made during Friday evening bull sessions – held in Japanese. I only heard about decisions affecting my division from my Japanese subordinates on Monday morning.' (*Business Week*, 1991a). Eventually, the atmosphere became so rancorous that the venture hired an industrial consultant to teach a class to employees at all levels entitled *Taking the Mystery Out of Dealing with the Japanese*.

Cultural clashes can in fact be equally troublesome – between Western companies, whether the grouping is US–European, UK–French, US–Mexican or some other such. Many of the difficulties plaguing a partnership between Metal Box Packaging of the UK and Carnaud of France stemmed from trying to mix two very different corporate cultures. In particular, the British managers increasingly felt alienated by what they saw as the high-handed, confrontational style of the partnership's French leader. The French executive in question, who had been trained at France's most prestigious schools, was described by a former colleague as 'a beautiful example of the best and worst of French management' (*Financial Times*, 1991).

Box 13.2   Cumbersome alliance management derails Corning–Vitro

Fuelled by regional integration, Corning and Vitro forged a strategic alliance in the consumer housewares business to compete in the rapidly changing North American market. Both companies believed that they could tackle the new market challenges and opportunites more effectively together than either could achieve trying to 'go-it-alone'. However, less than two years after launching the venture in January 1992, substantial losses forced the partners to abandon their JV plans. Their woes illustrate how the challenges of venture management and cultural differences can engulf even the best-conceived alliance.

Setting the stage
Corning and Vitro sought to maximize their complementary market strengths. For Corning, the Vitro link offered a springboard to the

continues

continued

Mexican market, where the company had little presence or experience. Similarly, Vitro secured a foothold through Corning's distribution network in the US market, where it had not been successful trying to sell its consumer products alone. As key market players in the industry, the alliance also averted direct competition between them in their home markets and enabled them to compete as a team for global markets. Both companies also strengthened their product lines with new brand names, such as the addition of Corning's Visions to Vitro's product offerings. And Corning, which had considered selling off its consumer products division, garnered greater economies of scale by channelling new Vitro products through its sales outlets. Plus, both companies knew and respected each other, reinforcing their commitment to work together.

Spurred by their ambitions, New-York-based Corning and Vitro of Mexico merged their consumer housewares operations – including research, manufacturing, marketing, distribution, and so on – into two separate but linked joint venture companies. Yet stiff competition from low-cost Asian imports derailed the JV operations. Plummeting revenues – over $21 million for Corning alone – forced Corning and Vitro to abandon their ambitious JV plans and settle for a simpler, narrower cross-distribution agreement.

Manoeuvring the alliance minefield

But what went wrong? Notwithstanding complex structural and ownership issues (see Chapter 3) a poor understanding of each other's management style and culture exacerbated an already tense situation. Below are some of the problems Corning and Vitro encountered:

Remember not every culture defines and solves problems the same way While both partners agreed that they needed to boost competitiveness of their operations, cultural differences made it difficult to agree on what the key issues were and how to solve them. For example, the two partners had different ideas on how to define and provide 'service'. Corning was concerned about service to retailers, such as Wal-Mart and K-Mart. Once a manufacturer agrees to deliver merchandise on a given date, the company must honour its commitment to maintain its reputation and business. Yet, Vitro had different ideas. Having operated for years in a closed Mexican economy with little competition, service as defined by reliability and promptness was not a major issue. And although the Mexican market is becoming more demanding in service, the partners still had to bridge substantial differences in how they define service.

Have we reached a decision? According to Stephen Albertalli, recently retired director of investor relations for Corning, 'We always anticipate that decisions within an alliance take longer since every major decision is a joint decision. However, what we did not anticipate was the speed in which we needed to take decisions in order to respond

continues

continued

to market threats.' There was also confusion over how each partner's internal decision-making process worked, who had decision-making power and how far down within the joint venture companies did decison-making authority go. Corning would sometimes think that a decision had been made because its decision-making strategy granted individuals at a certain managerial level the authority to take action. Yet, within Vitro, managers at this same level would still have to take the issue to more senior executives. So there was plenty of confusion over whether and by whom decisions were taken.

Concluded Albertalli, 'Had we known each other a bit better, we could have taken decisions faster. But we did not. In sum, we always do our best to run our ventures in a democratic fashion. However, there are times for dictators and times for democracies. I am afraid the market now requires a dictator and very autocratic decisions.'

Analyse how different accounting regulations affect a venture before selecting its structure Different Mexican and US accounting regulations, combined with the complicated structure of the alliance as two separate joint venture entities, created a real accounting nightmare for Corning and Vitro. For example, once senior management agreed on a cost-cutting measure, both companies then needed to agree in which corporation's books the transaction should appear. Thereafter, the transaction often had varying implications because of differences between Mexican and US accounting regulations, often mandating further adjustments.

Consider using an acid test Finally, given the management difficulties and cultural challenges in alliances, a simple acid test on the business plan – as outlined in Chapter 6 – prior to launching a deal may save companies from entering a doomed venture. Before sealing an alliance, try making one final evaluation of the venture's ability to fend off adverse or changing conditions. Gather initial statistics on a venture's profitability and exaggerate the costs and operational bottlenecks. For example, discount prices by 20%; move revenue projections out by one year; increase marketing costs by 50%; and increase administrative costs by 50%. Now does the venture measure up to the partners' expectations? Are the partners willing to proceed or do these figures warrant a re-evaluation of the partnership?

Scenario 6: Unrealized market expectations

Westinghouse's interest in its 50–50 joint venture with Toshiba to manufacture and market colour display tubes (CDTs) for television sets and computer terminals, a partnership known as Toshiba-Westinghouse

Electronics Corp. (TWEC), fizzled out when most US computer manufacturers moved production offshore to lower their operating costs. As Yoshio Aono, president of Toshiba Display Products, sees it: 'We divided TWEC's business strategy into two phases. The first stage covered investments and operations to manufacture and sell 19- and 20-inch CDTs for small televisions. The second phase entailed additional monies to expand operations to include production of 30- and 32-inch CDTs for computer terminals and bigger televisions.' However, between the two stages, the computer industry in the US drastically changed. Unable to compete against lower-cost Asian imports, key industry players – namely IBM and Hewlett Packard – switched their production to nations with lower labour costs. In effect, the venture's US computer market dried up overnight. Since Westinghouse's main priority was the computer industry, not the television market, the US partner withdrew from the venture.

In a similar example, weak US sales for the Korea-built Pontiac Le Mans passenger car was a major impetus behind the decision by General Motors and South Korea's Daewoo Group to terminate their JV in October, 1992. US sales of this subcompact manufactured by the 50–50 venture, Daewoo Motor Co., collapsed to just 39,081 cars in 1990, down 39% from its 1988 peak, and fell a further 15% in 1991. 'Each side blames the other. Daewoo complains that the Pontiac Motor Division was not promoting the Le Mans aggressively enough, probably because GM did not want it to draw sales from other divisions. Pontiac managers argue that the car's initial poor quality and on again/off-again supplies because of labour strife soured dealers on the car' (*Business Week*, 1991b).

Likewise, Du Pont's disappointment with its 50–50 joint venture in optical media, Philips Du Pont Optical (PDO), stemmed from unrealized market expectations. When the two partners formed PDO in 1986, they estimated that sales in the global audio, video and data markets should exceed $4 billion by 1990. Yet by 1990, their hopes for billion-dollar and higher sales levels had faded. Instead, the partners concentrated on how to disband PDO. Du Pont was primarily interested in the professional market for high-density data storage disks, Philips in the consumer market for audio and video discs. However, the professional data market failed to materialize as Du Pont had expected, and the US MNC reconsidered its commitment to PDO. The consumer activities of PDO were transferred to Polygram, Philips' subsidiary in the recording industry, with the professional data activities being sold to independent firms.

Dismal market shares and sales have plagued many US–Japanese JVs in the auto parts industry. Anxious to prise open doors at such Japanese transplants in the US as Honda, Nissan, Toyota and Mazda, many US firms have sought Japanese partners. However, few of these expectations have actually materialized. Of 126 US auto suppliers that entered into joint ventures in the 1980s, almost all were losing money in mid-1989. Although Japanese auto manufacturers pledged to double their purchases of US auto parts – to $19 billion by 1994 – it is too early to say whether this change alone will be enough to reverse the tide.

Scenario 7: Cooperation sours in the market

Some executives caution alliance partners against naively believing that they can join hands in all other business functions, yet keep marketing and sales separate. Inevitably, they say, the strains of competing head-on against each other in the market are likely to trigger an early divorce. Certainly, corporate and industry characteristics can force some ventures to keep their marketing and distribution responsibilities in the parents' hands, as happens in several auto ventures. Car executives concede that this is still a very difficult relationship to manage.

The early troubles beleaguering a Komatsu–Dresser venture in the North American construction equipment industry stemmed from marketing clashes. Upon establishing the venture, the partners agreed to merge their manufacturing, engineering and finance operations for North America. But the Komatsu and Dresser product lines remained distinct and were sold through existing, separate dealerships. Unfortunately, the strategy created a marketing nightmare in which the two halves of the venture wound up competing with each other, creating deep animosity among Komatsu and Dresser dealers. Other difficulties complicated the situation. 'The Komatsu–Dresser venture began providing Dresser dealers with Komatsu excavators and wheel loaders. The move infuriated Komatsu distributors, who feared the products would cut directly into their sales. "The only thing that is different is the paint and decals,' said a Midwest Komatsu dealer." Internal rivalry between the partners within the venture also made it difficult for dealers to obtain critical product and parts information. Said one dealer, "Dresser executives would not give information to their Komatsu counterparts because they were afraid of losing sales."' (*Business Week*, 1991a).

After a weak financial performance in 1990 (Komatsu–Dresser posted a $14.4 million loss on flat sales of $1.3 billion), the two partners tried to fix their marketing problems. The venture combined its marketing and product support organizations for the two brands. In addition, with encouragement, approximately half of the Komatsu and Dresser dealers merged. None the less, the venture never fully recovered from its early problems, making joint management of the alliance difficult. Changes within Dresser also complicated the situation. When Dresser spun off all non-energy related operations, this included its 50% stake in the Komatsu venture. The JV became part of Indresco, a company owned and managed by the former Dresser executives handling non-energy businesses. Yet the venture's continued weak performance and problems then prompted Indresco to reduce its stake in the JV from 50% to 18% in September, 1993.

Besides having competing marketing and distribution networks, some alliances run aground in the marketplace because of conflicting product lines. For instance, the AT&T–Olivetti alliance encountered problems because these two MNCs had competing computer product lines. As Jacques Meyer, international market planning director for AT&T, analysed it, 'We were unsuccessful at merging [with] them because the two product lines were insufficiently different.'

Similarly, several ventures in Japan have ended bitterly because of one partner deciding to compete head-on with its partner for the same customer base. US-based Borden recently split from an alliance with Meiji Milk Products to sell dairy products in Japan after an association of some 20 years. Borden publicly declared that its joint venture partner set out to systematically destroy the relationship. The troubles first started when Meiji, the partner responsible for distribution, appeared to be slowing its promotion of Borden products. The Japanese firm then launched its own ice cream brands, which competed directly with the Borden products.

Scenario 8: The mythical convergence of telecommunications and computers

During the 1980s, corporate and academic leaders enthusiastically discussed the possibilities of marriages between telecommunications and computers. The convergence theory was based on the principle that, thanks to microchips and fibre optics, the basic technologies used in data processing and telecommunications were fast becoming identical. Hence, the two businesses appeared to be set to merge into a single information industry. To this end, various MNCs eagerly sought partners or acquisition targets to prepare for blending these two powerful technologies and industries.

For instance, the UK telecommunications giant STC wanted to capitalize on its ties to International Computers Limited (ICL), IBM sought Germany's Rolm Corp. and AT&T took an equity stake in Olivetti. Yet many of these corporate marriages ended in divorce after the much-vaunted synergy between the industries failed to materialize. Today AT&T is no closer to being a big-league player in computers than is IBM in telecommunications. STC has been acquired by Canada's Northern Telecom, and Fujitsu has acquired a majority stake in ICL. IBM sold Rolm's manufacturing and development business to Siemens and formed a joint venture with Rolm Corp. to market and service Rolm systems in the US. The Olivetti–AT&T partnership broke up.

Jacques Meyer offered his view of the debacle. 'Much has been written about the confluence of telecommunications and computers. But when you face the business reality of having a telecommunications company and a computer firm actually work together, it is an entirely different matter. In our problems with Olivetti, it was neither incompetence nor bad will. We simply did not have the capabilities and expertise to assist each other. As a computer company, Olivetti did not have the specialized technical and engineering capabilities to adapt our PBX boxes to European telecommunications standards. Nor did they have the marketing skills and know-how to sell PBXs and other AT&T telecommunications equipment. Similarly, AT&T is a telecommunications company, steeped in industry traditions of government regulation and monopolies. AT&T did not fare well trying to sell Olivetti's computers in the fiercely competitive, open US computer market.'

On a cautious note, the failure of alliances between telecommunications and computer companies in the 1980s to create a single information industry may carry lessons for the many companies forging links in the 1990s to capitalize on the 'information highway'. Certainly, technology has advanced more. Audio, visual and data information now can be transformed into the same digital format and transmitted in huge quantities via fibre-optic cables, paving the way for the creation of a new market for multimedia communications. In fact, there is considerable excitement surrounding the new 'convergence' of communications, television, computer and entertainment industries to create 'information superhighways'. However, as the failed alliances in the 1980s illustrate, it is not so easy to join companies from different sectors in order to create a new information industry. Industries shape companies and their cultures. Cultural disparities among industries can be as difficult to manage as national or regional differences. Plus, these alliances usually pool complementary technological strengths between companies. Yet which company takes the technology lead in developing and exploiting a new information industry? What is the technical role for the other partner(s)? Who handles marketing responsibilities? How will services be distributed? How do partners craft an equally important role for each other in the alliance? These and many other questions can be stumbling blocks for alliances seeking to create a new communications market.

Scenario 9: Strengthen a company's presence in Japan

Many Western MNCs have used some form of alliance, whether joint ventures, distribution links or equity participations, to prise open the Japanese market. Given the high costs and complexities of operating in Japan, developing links with an insider has been an attractive strategy. However, the growing importance of Japan and Asia to many firms' global strategies increasingly requires many Western firms to assume greater management involvement and control in their Japanese businesses.

MNCs point to a number of trends as reasons why they can ill-afford to leave critical strategic and operational issues in the hands of alliances and now prefer to run their own show in Japan. As Japan and its key corporations expand their global power and influence, many MNCs must strengthen their presence and operations in Japan. An executive at a US MNC has analysed this need: 'In the past, many Western firms believed Japanese firms would eventually adopt Western business practices as they expanded abroad. Yet the reverse is actually occurring. Increasingly, Western MNCs adopt Japanese management and operating practices to compete against globe-trotting Japanese MNCs in many worldwide markets. In effect, Westerners need to learn how to play by Japanese rules. There is no better place to learn than right in Japan.' A further trend is that of several MNCs now using Japan as a focal point for their Asian operations. This new focus further fuels interest among Western firms in buying out their Japanese partners. (See Box 13.3.)

Box 13.3   Converting a Japanese venture to sole ownership

How one MNC is managing the exit

Experienced executives caution firms to handle delicately the transformation in Japan from a joint venture, distribution link or equity tie to an acquisition. For instance, Company A, a major US MNC in health and related sciences, has carefully negotiated changes to its marketing partnerships, particularly its 70-year-old relationship with its principal distributor. An executive with Company A cites the following driving forces behind senior management's decision to expand its Japanese presence and seek control of its distribution partnerships:

- Learn how to counter unrelenting competition worldwide from Japanese firms to the US MNC's key products.
- Establish production and R&D operations in Japan rapidly to gain exposure to Japanese state-of-the-art breakthroughs in the US MNC's core technologies.
- Enhance market strategies with direct links to customers rather than rely on distributors with little or no business experience with Company A's products and markets.

continues

---

continued

In a drive to build up its Japanese presence, Company A first established its own R&D and manufacturing centres in Japan, then mapped out a strategy to change its distributor relationships. Some of its distributors were small-sized firms in weak financial positions. Hence, the US firm was able to negotiate and manage amicable acquisitions. However, its principal distributor (Company B), a trading company with annual turnover in excess of $5 billion, was financially sound and obviously not an acquisition target. (In fact, the US MNC was interested only in Company B's division responsible for marketing and distributing its products.) Also, Company B had been doing an admirable job of selling Company A's products, which accounted for 20% of Company B's sales and 40% of its earnings from operations.

Consequently, negotiating a change in this relationship posed a formidable challenge. After considering its strategy, Company A decided to employ Japanese tactics. Its management began by hinting and asking for suggestions on how it could secure closer direct links to its markets and customers in Japan. It also relied on *nemawashi* – the Japanese process of consensus building – to jointly work on a solution. And in an effort to illustrate its commitment to the Japanese market, Company A's executives pointed out how Japan had been delegated as a region in its own right, reporting directly to the CEO.

Eventually, the two MNCs agreed on a step-by-step approach. First, Company A formed a separate 50–50 joint venture company with the Company B division responsible for its markets. After a year, Company A assumed majority equity control of the joint venture. Then, over time, Company A plans to boost its equity until it achieves 100% control. According to a Company A executive, 'There is no doubt Company B was disappointed with the change.' Nevertheless, the transition was diplomatically engineered to avoid any damage to the reputation and image of Company B. Company A also made special efforts to allay any fears among Japanese employees about working for a Western firm. In summary, adds the executive, 'The Company B division already had a very strong allegiance to Company A, having sold its products for decades. Yet this closeness created a false impression and risk that Company A management could simply fold the division directly into our operations. Clearly, we had to work with great dedication to boost enthusiasm and convince the Japanese employees of the change. We emphasized how the alliance/acquisition indicated our commitment and staying power in Japan.'

Scenario 10: Exit the industry

A few MNCs have come to use joint ventures as an initial step toward total withdrawal from an industry or market. However, many executives, such as H. P. Appleby, vice-president at Himont, consider this the exception rather than the rule. Howard Hill, a Detroit-based lawyer, agrees. He believes that approximately 10 to 20% of alliances use the venture to exit an industry. There are nevertheless occasions when economic and social factors make it difficult for a company to divest itself completely of a business, at which point a joint venture strategy becomes the best alternative.

As Hill explains it, 'Exiting an industry via a joint venture permits management to withdraw with the flags flying. It can help to alleviate any negative backlash from local communities and labour unions. For instance, Chrysler and General Motors recently formed a venture to produce manual transmissions. GM had a plant in Indiana that barely reached 30% capacity. Meanwhile, capacity at Chrysler's neighbouring plant was over 150%. When Chrysler approached GM to purchase its underutilized facility, GM suggested first beginning with a joint venture, to minimize any negative repercussions in its markets and the local Indiana community.'

Kodak has also used a joint venture strategy to withdraw from the pharmaceuticals industry. Kodak's pharmaceuticals subsidiary – Sterling Drug – formed a series of ventures with Elf Sanofi of France in the late 1980s for the production, marketing and distribution worldwide of some prescription and over-the-counter drugs. Yet faced with dismal conditions within the global pharmaceutical industry – falling drug prices, competition from generic brands, rising development costs, and government pressures to reform healthcare and control prices – Kodak announced plans in mid-1994 to withdraw from the industry and concentrate on its more traditional businesses. Negotiations are under way to sell its drug operations to Elf Sanofi.

When MNCs use a partnership to exit an industry, management should be frank about its intentions. Tim Leuliette, director of ITT Automotive, says: 'Management needs to inform employees and customers. They are not stupid and will sense some uneasiness and/or indifference to the venture. Unless management responds to their uncertainty, it can be very damaging to the company. In most cases, at least the inner circle of senior management is aware of the company's intention to shed a business. This circle should not pretend or try to hide their true objectives. It is quite easy to spot a dissolution candidate. And most employees and customers can also read the tea leaves. Any negative repercussions will be much worse if management fails to address the concerns of employees, customers and local communities.'

Scenario 11: Financial crunch forces premature exit

Many alliances collapse because one or more partners fail to contribute their portion of capital toward financing alliance endeavours. No company has unlimited resources, and in many cases the financial needs of an alliance are sacrificed to advance a partner's internal investments and operations. According to Tim Leuliette, 'ITT Automotive currently has 10 ventures. As the costs of developing new technologies spiral, our partners will find it difficult to contribute their 50%. Hence, I suspect many of these alliances will end up as 100%-owned ITT Automotive entities in the future.'

In some cases, a company simply does not have the resources to continue its investments in a venture. Some executives argue that many US firms face too many short-term pressures to incur monumental financial responsibilities in a global alliance. Leuliette considers that many alliances derail because US firms are unwilling to play for such high financial stakes. Suppose, for example, he said, that 'a US–Japanese joint venture breaks up. The US executive complains, "Boy, those Japanese will get you every time. They want you to cooperate for a while until they are ready to strike out on their own." Yet if one examines the figures, US companies spend between 3 and 4% of sales on R&D, while Japanese MNCs spend a minimum of 5 to 7%. Often the Japanese firm gets tired of carrying greater financial weight in the alliance. I believe MNCs really need to scrutinize their resources before they commit to a venture.'

A financial crisis often forces one partner to sell its share in an alliance to raise valuable capital. Financial strains prompted Chrysler to sell its stake in Diamond Star Motors (DSM) to its partner, Mitsubishi Motors, at end-1991. However, as Howard Hill said, 'DSM is hardly a failure. In many respects, the venture has been a model of cooperative behaviour. The two partners jointly produced an outstanding car. The car – the four-wheel-drive Eagle Talon – is a smash hit in the market. It is a competitively low-priced sporty auto that embodies Japanese engineering and manufacturing excellence. Plus Chrysler has gained valuable exposure to Japanese management techniques and principles [See Chapter 12]. Mitsubishi secured an important foothold in the US market. I suspect former Chrysler chairman Lee Iacocca would have loved to hold on to DSM.'

Chrysler's sale of its 50% DSM stake, for approximately $100 million, did not signal the end of Chrysler–DSM cooperation. New agreements specify the conditions under which Chrysler retains important links to DSM, and Chrysler will buy approximately 50% of the DSM car output for sale through its dealers. Chrysler and Mitsubishi will also maintain important supplier links for DSM. And Chrysler employees will continue to work or train at DSM to further advance Chrysler in its goal of invigorating its operations with Japanese management techniques. Says one Chrysler spokesman, 'Chrysler initially invested $100 million as part of its 50% share in DSM. Not only has Chrysler received back its initial investment, [but it] still maintains these valuable operating links and benefits from DSM.'

Scenario 12: Having partners cash in at the right time

As the last scenario illustrated, financial pressures can force one partner to sell its share in a venture. Yet some experienced observers suggest that the other partner may actually on occasion be encouraging a financially weak partner to sell out. For instance, several analysts suspect that Mitsubishi may have nudged Chrysler along in its decision to sell its 50% ownership of DSM. As one industry executive described that situation, 'Chrysler split the costs and responsibilities of building a state-of-the-art auto-manufacturing plant, valued at over $1 billion. The Japanese car company also gained a badly needed foothold in the US market with Chrysler's assistance. Now DSM is a success, producing a fabulous car. Why not try to own 100% of the operation, particularly since you also have continued commitments from Chrysler to sell and market the output?'

Similarly, analysts say that Toshiba did not shed many tears when Westinghouse abandoned their joint venture in colour display tubes (CDTs) for televisions. According to Robert Kaemmerer, former executive at the Toshiba–Westinghouse venture, 'Toshiba initially wanted a partner to help defray the several hundred million dollar investment for CDT operations.' Moreover, Toshiba was in the mid-1980s under heavy attack in the US for its involvement in supplying proprietary technology to the former Soviet Union. Toshiba was eager to team with a reputable US MNC to boost its image and minimize any negative backlash from the Soviet affair. Now the plant is running smoothly and CDT market forecasts are improving with the arrival of HDTV. There are few reasons to hold onto a partnership.

Nor was Mitsubishi Electric at a great loss when Westinghouse withdrew from their alliance in high-voltage circuit breakers in the late 1980s. Shortly after Westinghouse left the venture, market activity picked up handsomely. As Roger Barna, president of Mitsubishi Power Products, remarked, 'Some managers wonder whether Westinghouse would have actually withdrawn had the US MNC realized how well the business would recover.' The turnaround stems from a resurgence in spending among US utility companies for power transmission and distribution (T&D) products. Many utilities cut back their T&D spending in the 1970s and 1980s in order to finance expensive nuclear energy programmes. Most nuclear programmes are now complete and the utilities have ended up with outdated, inefficient T&D products that must be replaced.

References

Business Week (1989). When US joint ventures with Japan go sour. 24 July, p. 30

Business Week (1991a). A dream marriage turns nightmarish. 24 April, p. 94

Business Week (1991b). Why GM and Daewoo wound up on the road to nowhere. 23 Sept, p. 55

Financial Times (1991). A troubled marriage. 12 Sept, p. 18

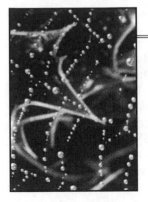

14

Conclusion

The spread of competitive alliances raises a number of questions for which there are no definitive answers. Are alliances truly a long-term strategic development or merely a short-term expedient allowing companies to adapt to the globalization of markets and technologies? Given the management challenges and difficulties within alliances, are successful ventures the exception to the rule? What effect will collaborative ventures have on the structure and management of a multinational corporation? Can a company be too heavily dependent on the alliance option for its own good? As bilateral and multilateral alliances proliferate, how will the nature of companies or of industries change? Are firms in danger of being caught in entangling alliances? How real is the threat of losing valuable technology to a partner/competitor? How will governments react to the spread of transborder business linkages?

Balancing the alliance equation

One key issue that each company must address is the degree to which it should rely on alliances. Some companies warn that too much reliance on ventures and on a partner's know-how can endanger the company's long-term ability to develop state-of-the-art technologies. Pushing the idea to the limit, there is a risk that some companies will become so dependent on outside sources to acquire technology, products or market know-how that their competitive edge will be reduced to their negotiating skills.

A second, contrasting danger is to ignore alliances. Collaboration is rapidly changing the competitive structure of a number of industries, and as companies see their competitors lock arms, it becomes increasingly difficult for them to operate alone. For instance, witness some of the linkages among corporate players in the telecommunications industry. Once British Telecommunications (BT) and US long-distance carrier MCI announced plans for a $5.3 billion alliance – including a $1 billion joint venture for corporate communications services – pressure heightened on other global players to seek allies. In particular, Deutsche Telekom, France Telecom and US long-distance operator Sprint recently reached an agreement to establish joint ventures targeted to the communications needs of multinational corporations. Both the MCI–BT alliance and the Deutsche Telekom, France Telecom and Sprint pact include arrangements for the European partners to take equity stakes in their respective US partners. Not to be left out, AT&T pushed ahead to seal a pact with Unisource, a Dutch–Swiss–Swedish consortium providing telecommunications services to companies in Europe.

Long-term challenges for alliance strategists

Some critics charge that alliances have lost their lustre. This is, in fact, irrelevant, for partnerships have never held much allure for MNCs. If possible, most MNCs would naturally prefer to operate alone, yet few of them can muster the resources to operate single-handedly in the global economy.

Certainly, many executives have been frustrated when dealing with partnerships, suggesting that living with an alliance is far from easy. Tangible proof of this is available simply from the number of alliances that disband. However, firms should not shun this strategic option simply because the divorce rate is high. The challenge for management is to find the right mix of alliances, independent subsidiaries and acquisitions for their global strategies. There are clear dangers in both underreliance and overreliance on partnerships.

Jacques Meyer of AT&T emphasized the value of alliances but cautioned against the dangers of overdependence on them. As he explained, 'After the breakup of the Bell system in the mid-1980s, AT&T went full speed ahead with an ambitious international expansion strategy. We relied almost entirely on alliances. Indeed, many executives within AT&T referred to our global strategy as the "alliance strategy". Unfortunately, many of these alliances failed. We now realize that alliances serve well in some markets, while management should employ other approaches elsewhere. In sum, we want to have a multifaceted strategy, with alliances serving as a key element.' Alexander Giacco, former CEO of Hercules and Himont, concurred. 'Alliances are certainly not a panacea for all MNCs. None the less, the strategy can serve as a very important means to an end that often cannot be achieved without a partner.'

Walking a fine line between collaboration and competition

With alliances it is always possible that today's ally will use the arrangement to become an even fiercer competitor tomorrow. Much depends on a partner's ability to gain as much in new skills and knowledge from the alliance as possible. However, learning from an alliance does not come through osmosis. Management must make a concerted effort to transfer and disseminate information. MNCs must find the right mix of flexible organizational structures, management rotations, presentations from returning alliance executives and alliance gatekeepers to maximize the learning and information benefits available from having such corporate links. At present, the learning objective is rarely written into the contract or business plan for many alliances. Managers and employees must be well briefed on why and how to keep their ears and eyes wide open.

The risks of turning an ally into an even fiercer competitor also depend on how well partners can maintain their equality of strengths. Certainly, alliances offer an opportunity to share the hardships of developing new technologies, products and markets 'but sharing should not lead to complacency'. Experienced alliance practitioners advise firms never to underestimate the importance of remaining equally strong partners. Management must use the internal resources made available from partnerships to continually improve their competitive advantages. Consequently, if and when an alliance does break apart, each party will still be able to walk away as a competent, strong global competitor.

The perils of polygamy

The sprawling complexity of alliance networks suggests that partnerships are hardly a corporate fad for the 1990s but are instead a reality of doing business in today's global markets. As more and more companies conclude alliances, the entire complexion of the global business environment is changing. In many industries, few companies can afford to have a single partner. According to some analysts, Renault and Volvo became too dependent on each other, at the expense of seeking other partners. Their divorce and misfortunes illustrate the risks of tying up a company's destiny with a single partner.

Instead, most firms form a series of alliances, each with partners that have their own web of collaborative arrangements. Companies such as Ford, Toshiba, Philips, AT&T, Toyota, Nissan, Mitsubishi and IBM are at the hub of what are often overlapping alliance networks, which frequently include a number of fierce competitors. Despite the inherent dangers of linking numerous competitors to the same company, many executives argue that the phenomenon is inevitable.

According to a Munich-based consultant, 'Companies will not be able to be so choosy any more and will have to accept the fact that they may be dealing with a firm that has close ties with their competitors. When British Aerospace agreed to sell the Rover Group to BMW, rumours suggested that Honda would retaliate by severing all ties to the UK car company after 14 years of collaboration. In the end, however, pragmatism triumphed. Both Honda and Rover could profit from ongoing collaboration. While the two companies liquidated their cross-shareholdings, they continue their cooperation on key vehicle projects. Plus, the BMW wedge driven between Rover and Honda now frees the latter to shop around for new European partners.

In fact, given the growing complexities in industries such as the automobile sector, few MNCs will be satisfied with only one relationship to meet different technological, product and market needs. Instead there will be more and more partners with concomitantly increasing possibilities of conflicts of interest. For instance, Mitsubishi and Chrysler have a long-standing relationship exemplified by Chrysler's former equity share in the Japanese company plus multiple product and component projects. Over the past few years, Mitsubishi has also ambitiously courted other partners, such as Daimler Benz, Volvo and Hyundai. Similarly, Ford, which has a solid relationship with Mazda, also has links with several other companies, including VW and Nissan. In turn, each of these auto makers also has its own roster of cooperative ties, all competing against each other in the global auto market.

The complicated relationship between Intel and IBM is another good example. Intel and IBM have been technology partners for 12 years, since the introduction of the first personal computer. IBM's personal computer business is Intel's largest customer for the latter's 486 and Pentium microprocessor chips. In fact, thanks to IBM's business, Intel has approximately 80% of the market for microprocessors. Yet, since 1991, IBM has been working closely with Motorola – a key competitor of Intel – on the development of the Power PC micro-processor chips. In early 1994, IBM also reached an agreement to manufacture clones of Intel's 486 and Pentium microprocessor chips designed by Cyrix, a Texas-based semiconductor firm. In a direct challenge to Intel, the IBM–Cyrix pact aims to reduce IBM's dependence on Intel. Yet Intel is not standing on the sidelines. Intel and Hewlett Packard also recently announced an R&D pact to develop a new gener-ation of microprocessors. Complicating matters further, Hewlett Packard recently bought a 20% equity stake in Taligent, an Apple–IBM joint venture to develop advanced software for new computing technologies, such as the Power PC chips.

Increasingly, firms must learn how to manage and balance the obligations of having such multiple links. The task of managing complex, competing relationships can indeed be daunting, yet there are a few key principles worth highlighting. Some of the tips provided in this book include the following:

- When linking up with a firm, check not only its alliance track record but also review its roster of partners for any potential conflicts of interest.

- Structure narrowly focused agreements. What will Ford's or Toshiba's or Siemens' network look like in five years from now? And what will be the implications of that in terms of your own network, now and in the future?

- Educate employees about the perils of the corporate venture game. Inadvertently passing on information can sound the death-knell to a partnership, so staff should know precisely what they can and cannot discuss with different partners. Besides the venture's own staff, it is necessary to educate all employees on the company's different networks and the potential perils involved.

- Establish a central coordinating unit. This unit is vital in managing information flows. Information should be easily assimilable into the corporation, but make sure there are no leaks in the pipeline.

The government factor

Fears of alliances serving as a Trojan Horse have not gone unnoticed by governments. The growth of alliances continues to present new public policy challenges to governments. Management therefore needs to factor in the potential impact of different nations' likely reactions to corporate alliances. Clearly, some government reaction is positive, such as an easing of antitrust rules as many nations now use a global, rather than a national, market as a benchmark. Recognizing the need for companies to pool resources to compete in today's global economy, the US and the EU have gradually relaxed antitrust restrictions on cooperation in areas such as R&D, production and marketing. Furthermore, governments in Eastern Europe and the Soviet republics are adding their own doses of extra freedom in the market by replacing outdated industry laws and practices with new creeds to encourage foreign investment, frequently through joint ventures. Government initiatives to form regional trading blocs, such as the North American Free Trade Agreement, also encourage more companies to seek partners to brace for both the opportunities and threats presented by these new expanded markets. Analysts point to a projected boom in Mexico–US joint ventures as businesses take advantage of NAFTA.

Alliances can of course raise a number of troubling issues for governments: of sovereignty, control, national defence and international trade. Sovereignty is defined as the ability to control one's borders and the entities therein, but how is the nationality of a cross-border alliance determined, and what about the products and technologies it develops?

The issue is not fanciful. Few US and European companies will forget the US government's efforts to block construction of the USSR–West European Yamal gas pipeline by embargoing the use of General Electric's technology (rotors, nozzles, and stator blades) manufactured by the US firm and its French licensee Alsthom Atlantique (AA) for turbines manufactured for the project by UK, German and Italian companies. The extraterritorial storm was extremely hard on the companies involved. Firms were caught between the demands of the sponsoring European governments and the US administration, which claimed sovereignity over the technology and its inventor. The French government basically ordered AA (a subsidiary of the state-owned CGE) to furnish the parts.

Without arguing the pros and cons, the US was able to act in what the administration felt was in the national interest. But suppose instead of being a licensee relationship, AA and GE co-developed the rotors in a jointly owned R&D facility in Belgium: under what country's export control laws would that technology fall?

Another critical area is national defence, where governments look to their ability to control strategic industries and companies. But corporate alliances with no nationality – or multiple nationalities – erode that control.

Several alliances have been stalled or even derailed in the name of national security. General Dynamics' link with Mitsubishi Heavy Industries to collaborate on the FSX jet certainly caused turmoil. In the late 1980s, the US government opposed the transfer of General Dynamics' proprietary technology for the FSX fighter jet, on grounds of national security. Among other things, the debate raised the level of anti-Japanese sentiment in Washington, because of US trade deficits with Japan. The $7-billion-dollar project finally went through, after months of acrimonious wrangling and hefty Japanese concessions to source 45% of the FSX work from the US.

Or what happens to alliance partners when governments feud? A row between the UK and Malaysian governments left many UK companies with Malaysian partners in limbo. Following a UK newspaper article alleging the Malaysian prime minister had accepted payments from UK companies, the Malaysian government announced no government contracts would be awarded to British companies. Yet many UK companies – in links with local Malaysian partners – were in the process of bidding on multimillion dollar public works projects when the controversy erupted.

Ultimately, whether for antitrust or national policy priorities, companies will have to contend with government involvement in alliances and the dangers that it can present. Currently, it is a mixed blessing: on the positive side, some regulatory changes in antitrust and trade liberalization are paving the way for smoother alliances; on the negative side, however, increasing government opposition and intervention in the corporate venturing arena add an extra twist to the already complicated alliance phenomenon.

Index